Offsite Architecture

Architects have been intrigued by prefabricated construction since the early twentieth century. Recent advances in design, engineering and manufacturing processes have led to a significant expansion in the use of pre-assembled components, which are fitted to finished structures on site. Collectively, such processes are becoming known as "offsite construction."

A ground-breaking text, *Offsite Architecture* establishes the current – and future – state of thinking in this field. A range of the most highly regarded thinkers and practitioners from around the globe share their ideas and practical findings on offsite prefabrication, examining theory and practice, opportunities and challenges, successes and failures.

A timely response to the growing interest in this method, the book provides *the* fundamental basis for a critical, reflective approach to offsite architecture. Contributions from both academics and professionals make *Offsite Architecture* required reading for practitioners as well as students taking courses in architecture, prefabrication, construction and engineering.

Ryan E. Smith is an Associate Professor of Architecture at the University of Utah, USA. He has investigated offsite design and construction for nearly a decade through industry-applied research. He is author of *Prefab Architecture* (Wiley, 2010) and *Building Systems* (Routledge, 2012). He is past Chair of the Board of Directors of the National Institute of Building Sciences Off-Site Construction Council. He is a Senior Research Fellow at the Centre for Offsite Construction at Edinburgh Napier University in the UK.

John D. Quale is Director and Professor of Architecture at the University of New Mexico School of Architecture + Planning, USA. His expertise is in sustainable design, affordable housing, prefabrication, the environmental impact of construction, and collaborative and integrated design processes. He is the author of *Sustainable, Affordable, Prefab: The ecoMOD Project* (UVA Press, 2012) and *Trojan Goat: A Self-Sufficient House* (UVA Press, 2002), about his leadership of the 2002 UVA Solar Decathlon Team in a national design/build house competition sponsored by the US Department of Energy.

"Quale and Smith have brokered for us a glimpse into the proverbial fray of practicing prefabrication. They've assembled a multi-national group of current thinkers, designers, and researchers who offer individual testaments on its constitution. The result is a productive frisson between theory, history, and case studies, each tailored to regimes of philosophy, policy, and place."

– **Billie Faircloth**, *Partner, Kieran Timberlake Architects*

"Offsite construction may also be the best, most efficient response to rapidly rebuilding our cities for long-term sustainability. . . There's a human, even a humanist, angle here, as well; empowered to be part of the process, the vast knowledge now sequestered in the trades can emerge fully into the process to help us all achieve better, smarter results. The result could be a more open architecture, one that promotes and reinforces the constant optimization of both design and manufacturing as a single process."

– **Chris Sharples**, *Principal, SHoP Architects*

Offsite Architecture

Constructing the future

EDITED BY RYAN E. SMITH AND JOHN D. QUALE

Routledge
Taylor & Francis Group

LONDON AND NEW YORK

First published 2017
by Routledge
2 Park Square, Milton Park, Abingdon, Oxon OX14 4RN

and by Routledge
711 Third Avenue, New York, NY 10017

Routledge is an imprint of the Taylor & Francis Group, an informa business

British Library Cataloguing-in-Publication Data
A catalogue record for this book is available from the British Library

Library of Congress Cataloging-in-Publication Data
Names: Smith, Ryan E., editor. | Quale, John D., editor.
Title: Offsite architecture : constructing the future / Ryan E. Smith and John D. Quale.
Description: New York : Routledge, 2016. | Includes bibliographical references and index.
Identifiers: LCCN 2016027389| ISBN 9781138821378 (hb : alk. paper) | ISBN 9781138821392 (pb : alk. paper) | ISBN 9781315743332 (ebook)
Subjects: LCSH: Buildings, Prefabricated.
Classification: LCC NA8480 .O35 2016 | DDC 720/.4—dc23
LC record available at https://lccn.loc.gov/2016027389

ISBN: 978-1-138-82137-8 (hbk)
ISBN: 978-1-138-82139-2 (pbk)
ISBN: 978-1-315-74333-2 (ebk)

Typeset in Univers
by Keystroke, Neville Lodge, Tettenhall, Wolverhampton

Contents

Figures

Tables

Contributors

Mathew Aitchison, PhD, is Associate Professor in Architecture at the University of Sydney, Australia, where he directs the Innovation in Applied Design Lab. He is currently performing funded research on prefabrication and advanced manufacturing. His book publications include *Visual Planning and the Picturesque* (Getty, 2010), the first publication of Nikolaus Pevsner's treatise on urban design and architecture, and, more recently, *The Architecture of Industry: Changing Paradigms in Industrial Building and Planning* (Ashgate, 2014), of which he is editor and contributing author.

Paul Broadstone is an Assistant Virtual Design and Construction Manager at Whiting-Turner. Whiting-Turner has been pioneering offsite construction, multi-trade prefabrication, and near-site prefabrication applications. He works to integrate digital and physical prefabrication outcomes in construction delivery.

Charlotte Bundgaard, PhD, is an Associate Professor at the Aarhus School of Architecture, Denmark. She is the author of many publications including *Montage Revisited* (Arkitektskolens Forlag, 2013). She has contributed to a large multi-institutional research project on tectonics, sustainability, and industrialization, disseminated in the publication *Towards an Ecology of Tectonics: The Need for Rethinking Construction in Architecture*.

Dana Buntrock is a Professor at UC Berkeley Department of Architecture, USA. She has spent seven years living and working in Japan. Her research focuses on material and construction products and methods in Japan. She is author of *Japanese Architecture as a Collaborative Process* (Spon, 2002) and *Materials and Meaning in Contemporary Japanese Architecture* (Routledge, 2010).

Jonathan W. Elliott, PhD, is an Assistant Professor of Construction Management at Colorado State University, USA. He performs quantitative and qualitative research on socio-technical aspects of construction delivery. Specifically, he investigates construction employment skills training, training for underrepresented populations and developing nations, renewable energy and pedagogy, and interdisciplinary construction education.

Kevin Grosskopf, PhD, is Professor of Civil Engineering at the University of Nebraska, USA. His research expertise is in building safety and sustainability with extensive funding from the US Department of Labor. More recently, he has been studying offsite construction delivery and labor. He is widely published in top journals in civil engineering including the *ASCE*, *ASTM*, and *ASHRAE*.

Robert Hairstans, PhD, is an Associate Professor and Head of the Centre for Offsite Construction + Innovative Structures (COCIS) at Edinburgh Napier University, UK. He leads market feasibility, supply chain integration, and technical compatibility research on new construction and forest product innovations. His work includes communicating offsite construction knowledge internationally between industry and universities. He is author of *Offsite and Modern Methods of Timber Construction: A Sustainable Approach* (TRADA, 2010) and *Building Offsite: An Introduction* (Forestry Scotland, 2016).

Kihong Ku, DDes, is an Assistant Professor of Architecture at Philadelphia University, USA. He researches collaborative design technologies, processes, and innovations. This involves investigation of digital fabrication utilizing parametric modeling, prototyping and fabrication tools for construction and building simulation tools, and architectural robotics. His research has been funded by various public and private funding agencies including NIOSH, Skanska USA Building, the Research Affiliates Program at Virginia Tech, and Philadelphia University.

Helena Lidelöw, PhD, is an Associate Professor in Civil Engineering and Industrialized and Sustainable Construction at Lulea University of Technology, Sweden. She is also the Engineering Manager at Lindbacks, the largest offsite manufacturer of light-frame panelized and modular construction in Sweden. She is the author of more than 50 scientific publications and some textbooks on the subject. She also teaches and gives lectures on the industrialization of construction globally.

John Macarthur is Director of the Research Centre for Architecture, Theory, Criticism and History (ATCH) at the University of Queensland, Australia, where he also teaches architectural design. His research focuses on the intellectual history of architecture. He has edited four books and published over 120 papers including contributions to the journals *Assemblage, Transition, Architecture Research Quarterly, OASE,* and the *Journal of Architecture*. His major work, *The Picturesque: Architecture, Disgust and Other Irregularities*, was published by Routledge in 2007. Two books edited with colleagues were published in 2015: *The Baroque in Architectural Culture, 1880–1980* (Ashgate) and *Hot Modernism: Queensland Architecture 1945–1975* (Artifice).

John D. Quale is Director and Professor of Architecture at the University of New Mexico School of Architecture + Planning, USA. His expertise is in sustainable design, affordable housing, prefabrication, the environmental impact of construction, and collaborative and integrated design processes. He is the author of *Sustainable, Affordable, Prefab: The ecoMOD Project* (UVA Press, 2012) and *Trojan Goat: A Self-Sufficient House* (UVA Press, 2002), about his leadership of the 2002 UVA Solar Decathlon Team, a national design/build house competition sponsored by the US Department of Energy.

Talbot Rice is an Emeritus Research Associate in the School of Architecture at the University of Utah, USA. His research expertise is in offsite design and construction and the business of offsite construction manufacturing, working with government and private companies to answer questions relating to prefabrication markets, products, business operations, design for manufacture, and factory development and layout.

Roger-Bruno Richard is a Professor of Architecture at the University of Montreal, Canada. He directs the Groupe de recherche architecturale en systèmes constructifs industrialisés (GRASCI), which focuses on industrialized building systems. He specializes in strategies and technologies of industrialization. He is author of three building systems and numerous articles and book chapters on the topic and is internationally recognized in the field. He was a Research Fellow at the University of Tokyo in 2007 and a Visiting Researcher at the University of Hong Kong in 2015–2016.

Ivan Rupnik, PhD, is an Associate Professor in Architecture at Northeastern University, USA. He is co-author of *Project Zagreb: Transition as Condition, Strategy, Practice* (Actar, 2007) and author of *A Peripheral Moment: Experiments in Architectural Agency* (Actar, 2010). He is actively publishing and curating on the subject of contemporary housing delivery systems. He is Reviews Editor and Board Member for the *Journal of Architectural Education*.

Fausto Sanna qualified as an architect in Italy, after graduating, *summa cum laude*, from the University of Genoa. In 2015, he was appointed Senior Lecturer in Architecture at the Arts University Bournemouth, UK. His main research interests revolve around timber construction.

Chris Sharples is a Principal at SHoP Architects in New York City. SHoP is an internationally acclaimed design firm specializing in the integration of technology. SHoP has completed many offsite construction projects and is currently working on the design and construction of Atlantic Yards, which is slated to be the tallest offsite-fabricated modular building in the world when completed.

Ryan E. Smith is an Associate Professor of Architecture at the University of Utah, USA. He has investigated offsite design and construction for nearly a decade through industry-applied research. He is author of *Prefab Architecture* (Wiley, 2010) and *Building Systems* (Routledge, 2012). He is past Chair of the Board of Directors of the National Institute of Building Sciences Off-Site Construction Council. He is a Senior Research Fellow at the Centre for Offsite Construction at Edinburgh Napier University in the UK.

Kasper Sánchez Vibæk holds a PhD from the Centre of Industrialised Architecture at the Royal Danish Academy of Fine Arts, where he served as an Associate Professor from 2011 to 2013. He was a Visiting Scholar at the University of Pennsylvania. He is author of *Architectural System Structures: Integrating Design Complexity in Industrialised Construction* (Routledge, 2014). Presently, he is working in the field of system architecture, quality, and sustainability in developing Soft Cells for Kvadrat, a textile company that develops, produces, and sells acoustic solutions with high design content for construction projects worldwide.

Foreword

Every successful method of building evolves and is sustained as a direct expression of the forces that bear on a society at a given point in time. The invention and proliferation of balloon framing in North America came about only as a result of an abundance of raw materials (our forests), the available energy to process them (our rivers), labor in short supply relative to demand (our patterns of immigration), and the enormous generative pressure of an entire continent's worth of buildings to build. Those and other factors combined to inspire and give purpose to breakthroughs in the mass production of standardized timber elements and inexpensive fasteners that led to a new way of building in nineteenth-century North America. Other times and places found other solutions that served them best – a history of making that is most often collapsed into the history of style. Craft traditions fostered by the guild system in concert with the extra-economic inspirations of religion and centralized political control gave us Europe's great gothic cathedrals. Only with a surfeit of disempowered labor, the availability of monumental stone, and unchecked despotic leadership can architects ever have their pyramids.

Construction methods – those that succeed in reaching mainstream acceptance and use – are always a response, then, to exogenous forces. A built solution can endure only if and when it is positioned just right at the intersection of pressing social, cultural, material, technological, and – perhaps most critically in contemporary society – economic need. The test for any new construction method, the basis for its success, is how well it can serve to channel, leverage, or alleviate those immutable real-world conditions. In addition, like the ubiquitous balloon frame or its under-appreciated descendant the C stud, a robust solution will elegantly address many challenges at once. A failed solution may beautifully solve a few problems and relieve a few pressures, but not enough to achieve inevitability in use. Architects and engineers are duty-bound to innovate in the service of our clients' needs, and society's. But in the end, it is the "invisible hand" that determines which innovations will survive to become a new standard.

The idea of streamlining the efficiency of the building process through the prefabrication of components is nothing new. Modular did not just "fall off the truck." We have a long and noble history now, stretching back to Thomas Edison's experiments in concrete home construction and reaching the present with contributions from architectural eminences as grand as Frank Lloyd Wright and Walter Gropius. When the shipping industry containerized in the middle of the last century, young, avant-garde architects such as Paul Rudolph, Moshe Safdie, and the Metabolists in Japan took it as a license to explore – in provocative form, if not always in method – the implications of a similar modularity in the construction of housing. But each in turn failed to achieve mass acceptance, in part due to their propositions originating in *style*, in their distance from elegantly *solving*, in their failure to adapt their proposed architectures to the full complexity of forces that influenced the act of building in their day.

As useful as they were in keeping interest alive and developing a record of research for subsequent generations to use, the spikes of interest in offsite construction we find in previous eras were, in the end, merely cries in the wilderness. The collision of societal pressures and available methods and technologies that might have sustained them were simply not present yet in the required intensity. Today, for better and for worse, that is all very rapidly changing.

The principal new force bearing on construction (and the reason I added that bittersweet "for worse" above) is the climate crisis. The imperative to build in such a way that we do not contribute to the continued destabilization of our shared natural environment – an imperative increasingly accepted by clients as well as technicians – prioritizes a host of new problems for which offsite construction has always had the right solutions. As a measure of its potential robustness as a response, these solutions present themselves simultaneously in several areas. First, there is the simple, up-front reduction in embodied energy that is possible with this manner of construction. For instance, compared to traditional concrete and steel, SHoP's modular residential tower adjacent to the Barclays Center in Brooklyn (known as B2 after its original site designation in the development) represents a roughly 25 percent reduction in material use and associated carbon emissions. This is due to the nature of modular itself: buildings based on a structural grid that, like bamboo scaffolding, finds its strength through the intelligent arrangement of light members, not energy-hungry brute force.

Beyond the simple mitigation of atmospheric carbon, offsite construction may also be the best, most efficient response to rapidly rebuilding our cities for long-term sustainability. Here, encouraging density is the answer, relieving as much land as possible from the burdens of human development while creating intensively-used population centers that can be effectively served by low- and zero-carbon means of transportation as an alternative to means powered by internal combustion engines. Modular is poised to be the answer, uniquely capable of providing the required number of new housing units efficiently and affordably.

But increased population density brings with it, too, by necessity, an increased need to ensure quality of life in urban environments. Here, too, offsite offers another potential best practice that can become a positive incentive for its widespread adoption. By consolidating up to 80 percent of construction activity within the factory, modular buildings are very good neighbors, even during the often contentious process of being built in congested areas. Polluting truck trips are minimized. Onsite waste – everything from sheetrock offcuts to appliance boxes – is substantially reduced. Noise, compared to traditional means of construction, is kept very low. What strikes you at B2, as you stand and watch modules being lifted and fitted into place on the corner of Flatbush Avenue and Pacific Street, is how quiet it all is, how tiny (and tidy) the staging area can be as compared to a "normal" job site, and how little the erection of this very large tower disrupts the day-to-day rhythms of life in the thriving and famously eco-conscious neighborhood all around. At any given moment, the majority of the build team is off site, in the factory, working in a controlled environment.

Those palpable, "people-friendly" features of offsite construction are not a side-benefit; together with increased material efficiencies – and, in time, as the supporting industry matures, ever-greater efficiencies in schedule and cost – they are prime factors in convincing more and more public and private clients to act in their own social and economic best interest, to discover once and for all that what may appear newfangled is in fact common sense.

So today we may be seeing offsite construction better situated than ever to provide a suite of meaningful innovations in response to a confluence of societal challenges, providing a greater portfolio of solutions to a number of broadly recognized societal needs. We also, today, find ourselves better served than at any time previously with the technological tools that can make offsite construction an enduring success. There is a real synergy between the broad and well-established move toward digital processes of modeling and fabrication in the AEC industry and the specific demands of modular. The combination of parametric, real-time visualization and data management technologies known as building information modeling (BIM) provides the shared platform for the coordination of work across trades that is essential for the success of offsite construction. This technology-driven process not only enables a high level of coordination across building trades, it also supports a direct-to-fabrication approach to building component manufacture and assembly. In short, it promotes process innovation in addition to product innovation.

In that sense, contemporary technologies can provide a means to encourage the essential transition from a building to a manufacturing mentality in offsite construction. Where traditional construction is characterized by waves of trades passing over the site in alternating sequence, offsite demands – and virtual design and construction provides the means for – the close collaboration between trades throughout the process. In the new model, the electrician, the plumber, the cabinet maker, the wall finisher, the iron worker, and, crucially, the architects and engineers assisting in overseeing them are all collaborating side-by-side, sharing information on a single digital model, learning from each other in real time. The possibilities for beneficial feedback loops occurring with this method are so much greater than when trades work in isolation that, once widely established, we can expect progress in offsite construction to resemble the same "hockey stick" graphs that currently describe the climate crisis that this manner of building can do so much to mitigate. There is a human, even a humanist, angle here, as well; empowered to be part of the process, the vast knowledge now sequestered in the trades can emerge fully into the process to help us all achieve better, smarter results. The result could be a more open architecture, one that promotes and reinforces the constant optimization of both design and manufacturing as a single process.

In our own efforts as architects and engineers, whether they be in research, applied technology, or both, we all approach offsite construction with a great sense of hope and a passion for its enormous promise, tempered by the knowledge that, as in any area of invention, the challenges and the number of potential pitfalls are substantial. Taking a look back, the legacy of frustration in the field – the on-again, off-again efforts to transform the building industry in this way over nearly a century – do little to give us comfort. But, as I have outlined above, today may truly be a new day for offsite construction. The grand forces that always govern the act of building are for the first time truly aligning in its favor. There is a great deal yet to be done to consolidate the significant gains of recent years, to leverage all the capabilities of our technology, to spread the message, and to truly establish offsite as a viable alternative within the famously inertial mainstream. Whole economies will have to be rebuilt, whole cultures of education reversed, and whole systems of labor overturned and replaced. But, working together, now more than ever before, I believe we can get there.

Chris Sharples, Principal, SHoP Architects

Preface

Offsite construction – planning, design, fabrication and assembly of building elements at a location other than their final installed location to support the rapid and efficient construction of a permanent structure.[1]

Synonyms: prefabrication, industrialized construction, modular, manufactured construction, pre-assembly, systems building, modern methods of construction

The idea of the systems-built tower, the factory-built house, and the pre-assembled bathroom pod has been discussed, researched, prototyped, and developed by designers and industrialists since the nineteenth century. Small prefabricated buildings and sophisticated components systems were developed in some parts of the Western world and East Asia as early at the seventeenth century. Since the early twentieth century and continuing into today, the architectural discipline has been fascinated with prefabricated construction. This fascination, combined with more sophisticated design, engineering, and manufacturing processes, has positioned the building industry on the cusp of a radical transformation from methods of conventional construction that are often dysfunctional and inefficient, to a significant expansion in the use of pre-assembled components, panels, and modules to be fitted on site into a finished structure. Increasingly, these processes are collectively becoming known as "offsite construction."

Parallel with the interest in offsite construction is recognition of the many challenges in deploying these methods. The first challenge is that offsite construction is progressing rapidly without respect to the failures and successes of the past. Opportunistic investors, developers, and entrepreneurs tend to idealize offsite construction without understanding the process by which it unfolds. As with all new/old ideas, success is often found when implementation is informed by the many theoretical and practical challenges. Episodic failures on projects using prefabricated construction perpetuate the assumption that these failures are inherent to offsite construction, as opposed to problems with the people, assumptions, or processes. This undermines progress in the construction industry, limits the potential for increased human and environmental productivity, and ultimately reinforces the negative reputation in the conventional construction industry of a systems approach to building.

Another important challenge is the hype associated with several high-profile offsite projects, which some in the media have presented as the wave of the future, and the only logical construction solution. The touted benefits of offsite prefabrication have been exaggerated not only by those looking for a story to tell the media, but also by those in the construction sector looking to capitalize on society's fascination with seemingly Lego-like construction that is promoted as an inherently faster, greener, smarter delivery method. The disconnection of offsite architecture today from its deep and somewhat conflicted history of failed projects is problematic for current practice. In addition, offsite professionals have likewise segregated offsite practices and products from the social, technological, and theoretical context in which offsite architecture has emerged. Although it may outperform traditional construction in some key indicators today, offsite architecture represents a sliding scale of opportunities rather than a definitive "catch-all" answer to construction's many inefficiencies and risks.

In the last two decades, many contemporary architectural, engineering, and construction industry researchers have become focused on the dysfunctional processes used in conventional fabrication and construction. These researchers, as well as innovation-minded practitioners, believe that the solution for much of this dysfunction may be found in far greater dependency on offsite construction. As such, the third challenge is that many of these researchers and practitioners are virtually unknown outside their immediate environment. Not surprisingly, they are unknown to the general public, but more disturbingly they are unknown to many of the architectural, engineering, and construction professionals they intend to serve. The developed world nations of North America, Europe, East Asia, and Australia each have a unique context in which offsite means and methods have developed, creating a varied "library" of strategies that can be adapted throughout the world. In addition, researchers from industry and academia investigating the connection between design and fabrication in the construction supply chain publish their findings in narrow academic journals or have their ideas tied up in the proprietary intellectual property of the companies where they work. This global voice of critically minded innovators and researchers needs a forum in which to communicate with a broad range of those who are able to financially advance the offsite construction agenda.

This book, *Offsite Architecture: Constructing the Future*, is a reader to present the current thinking and research on offsite practices. It serves as both a sample and a thoughtful collection of essays. The purpose is to gather the most sophisticated thinkers as well as their findings and speculations on offsite prefabrication: theory and practice, opportunities and challenges, successes and failures. The book serves to establish the fundamental theory for a more critical and reflective practice of offsite architecture that is increasingly gaining momentum in the design and construction market. Our intention is to reach academics, students, and practitioners alike.

This book is not a catalogue of building systems, products, companies, or case study projects. There are many books, blogs, and websites that track these developments. The book is also not a practice implementation guide. Rather, it is an academic text, seeking to investigate the relationship between offsite prefabrication as a technical solution and the socio-economic-environmental context in which it emerges. To date, prefabrication has been a topic treated as technologically deterministic, but as with any technology, offsite stems from the historical, systemic substrate of its social underpinnings. The book's editors and contributors work to reveals these contingencies. The reader is sectioned into two parts: offsite theory and offsite practice.

Part A: Offsite theory introduces fundamental theory on offsite prefabrication that has emerged from the Industrial Revolution forward to today. Authors discuss ways in which to view prefabrication through unique lenses – design, manufacturing, construction, and public opinion – and trace developments through history and contemporary practice.

Part B: Offsite practice contains chapters that uncover the relationship between offsite prefabrication technology and the contextual conditions in which it is used. Topics include economic, political, social, and environmental concerns in relation to offsite construction. Specific contemporary offsite methods being practiced today are discussed in detail.

Ryan E. Smith and John D. Quale

Note
1   See Glossary.

Acknowledgments

The editors would like to thank all of the contributing authors for their time and energy in putting together the chapters. A special thanks goes to Talbot Rice, Emeritus Research Associate at the University of Utah, for his work in formatting and preparing the contents for submission and publication.

Part A
Offsite theory

Chapter 1

Industrialized building system categorization

Roger-Bruno Richard

Introduction

The strategies and technologies of industrialization have demonstrated a capacity to offer to the vast majority of people, at an affordable price, almost all the products available on the market today (automobiles, computers, etc.). Whereas some construction materials and components are already industrialized (trusses, pre-stressed slabs, curtain walls, etc.), it is not the case for the building as a whole. Conventional construction is still a service-oriented, client-initiated, labor-intensive approach; a different architect–engineer team, a new set of working drawings and a different team of general contractor/sub-contractors are set up each time a building or a group of buildings is projected, as if it was a prototype.

A fully industrialized building industry will be product-oriented. Due to the size of a building and to its relation with a site, the product will generally not be a completed building but an industrialized building system: a set of coordinated parts and rules where the same details are applicable to many different buildings located on various sites.

Yet, there is no single best universal industrialized building system in the world, but different categories and types to meet different specificities; some strategies and technologies will be more appropriate than others in a specific context for reasons of resources, program, local conditions, etc.

Three basic building system categories can be extrapolated from the fact that buildings are connected to a site whereas sophisticated technology is usually centralized in a factory (Figure 1.1).

The first two categories represent the two extremes:

- As a building is bound to be tied to its foundations, the *site-intensive kit-of-parts* concentrates at the site the final assembly of components or sub-systems delivered from different manufacturers.
- As maximizing factory production is the normal path to industrialization, the *factory-made 3D module* divides a building into volumetric modules completely finished at the plant and easily connected to the infrastructure once at the site.

Figure 1.1
The three
categories of
industrialized
building
systems

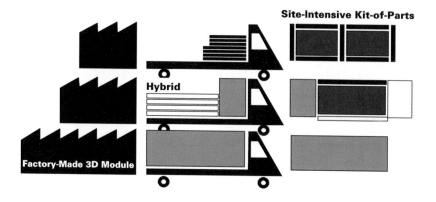

The third category is reaching for the best of both worlds:

- The *hybrid* involves manufacturing the complex parts at the plant and leaving the heavy or large-scale tasks to the site.

Industrialization

Whatever the product, industrialization involves *a generic organization based on quantity and offering an individualized finished product*:

- A "generic organization" will set up a *continuous interaction between all the participants* (manufacturers, assemblers, designers, managers, distributors, installers, etc.) in order to maintain an effective delivery of the products.
- "Based on quantity" means *aggregating a market large enough to amortize a process capable of simplifying the production*. Simplifying the production is the fundamental goal of industrialization, as it is the way to reduce the costs and thereby make the products available to the vast majority of people (Richard 2005a). Simplifying the production means obtaining a complex result from a single or a few operation(s), avoiding the repetitive linear sequences related to handicraft methods like nailing studs one by one or installing a series of formwork supports to cast a slab on location.
- "Offering a finished product" means giving clients the opportunity to see what they will get before being financially committed and even to participate in the design process, as the product can be highly individualized through the "mass-customization" strategies already applied by most industries.

A generic organization does not imply that all the participants are working for the same large corporation or company. Quite the contrary! Organizational structures are becoming more "horizontal," concentrating on the management and relying on consultants and sub-contractors for the design, the manufacturing, the assembly, the marketing, the distribution, etc.; the initial capital investment can then be as low as 10 percent to 20 percent of the total funds involved. The horizontal approach is particularly relevant in the case of buildings since a large number of manufacturers are already involved at the component level and many of them could easily move up to the sub-system level.

Industrialized building systems

Buildings are quite different from most other industrialized products: they can never be entirely completed at the factory since they are by definition related to a site. For that reason and in order to meet diversified programs with the same approach, the products are not finished buildings but systems generating buildings.

A building system is a set of coordinated parts and rules where the details are resolved before actual buildings are planned. The same standardized parts and their details are designed to be re-used in multiple ways for a large number of buildings, therefore aggregating a large quantity while allowing for diversity and even individualization. Within an industrialized building system, the construction details are proven and not re-invented each time a building is planned, as is often the case with the traditional "professional service" approach still applied today.

The main parts of a building system are its sub-systems, which correspond to the main functions of the building. *A building system is usually composed of five major sub-systems: structure, envelope, partitions, services and equipment.* However, the structural sub-system will normally play a transcendental role.

Each sub-system groups together a series of components that are composed of parts. For instance, a beam is a component of the structural sub-system and its connector one of the parts; a window is a component of the envelope sub-system and its glazing one of the parts; a door is a component of the partition sub-system and its frame one of the parts; the mechanical shaft is one of the components of the services sub-system and the drainage conduit one of the parts; the kitchen counter is one of the components of the equipment sub-system and its sink one of the parts.

Building systems can either be "open" or "closed". An open system can exchange parts, components and even sub-systems outside its original production environment. The parts, components and sub-systems are then considered as "interchangeable". By definition, an open system can offer more choices to the user and a larger market to any manufacturer that abides by the rules in terms of efficiency (performance criteria), dimensions (modular coordination) and interfaces (compatibility).

Sometimes, a system will not include all the sub-systems, either because a sub-system is outside the technological scope of the manufacturer or in order to leave it to diversified local contexts. Then, an open sub-system can be introduced, either extracted from another system or chosen from the offerings of independent manufacturers.

Many systems integrate two (sometimes three) sub-systems in order to further simplify the process while reducing the operations as well as the costs. For instance, a load-bearing sandwich panel can meet both the structural and envelope criteria, a load-bearing precast concrete wall panel can also act as a party

5

wall assuring fireproofing and soundproofing between two different apartments, a modular closet can provide a partition between two rooms of the same apartment by incorporating the appropriate soundproofing measures, etc.

The ten types of building system

So far, the three basic building system categories have generated nine building system types, from "A" to "I", whereas a series of more specific geometries is offered within each type:

1. The site-intensive kit-of-parts, i.e. the site becomes the final assembly line: *post & beam ("A"), slab & column ("B"), panels ("C")* and *integrated joint ("D")*.
2. The factory-made 3D module, i.e. the building is made up of 3D modules completely finished at the plant: *sectional module ("E")* and *box ("F")*.

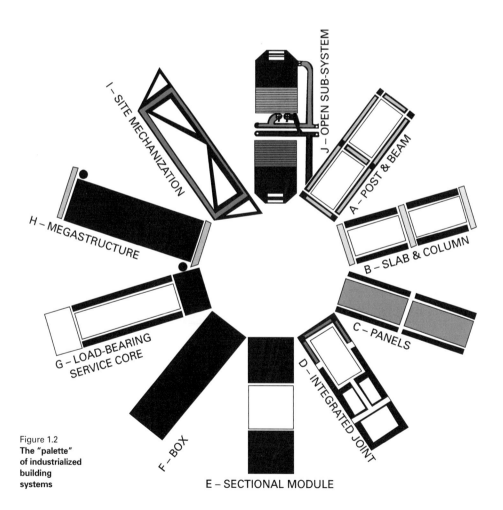

Figure 1.2
**The "palette"
of industrialized
building
systems**

3. The hybrid, i.e. optimal sharing of the work between the plant and the site: *load-bearing service core ("G"), megastructure ("H")* and *site mechanization ("I")*.

Since some systems do not provide all the sub-systems, the range of complementary and compatible sub-systems can be considered as a tenth type, the *open sub-system (J)*.

By analogy with painting, the three building system categories can be seen as the basic three colors (i.e. blue/red/yellow) from which the initial "palette" of nine building system types is generated, from "A" to "I", with the addition of the open sub-system as a tenth element whenever a system is not complete.

The site-intensive kit-of-parts

The site-intensive kit-of-parts involves a few simple components produced in large quantity at specialized plants and delivered separately to the site, thereby implying a series of jointing operations once at the site. It is similar to the Meccano or Erector Set systems used by youngsters.

The four types of system within the site-intensive kit-of-parts category are distinguished by the geometry of the structural sub-system: post & beam ("A"), slab & column ("B"), panels ("C") and integrated joint ("D").

Due to the great precision offered at the factory, the components/sub-systems are detailed to be easily and rapidly assembled at the site. As one moves from "A" to "D", the site work is further simplified: a post & beam system needs more connections and infill than a slab & column one, panels imply linear sequences

I – SITE-INTENSIVE KIT-OF-PARTS	Description	Sub-divisions
A – POST & BEAM	Skeleton requiring horizontal and vertical infill	• Segments • Continuous post • Continuous beam
B – SLAB & COLUMN	Simplification through the introduction of a single horizontal element	• Solid slab • Ribbed slab • Slab incorporating a perimeter beam
C – PANELS	Load-bearing flat components distributing loads and contributing to soundproofing	• Lightweight framed • Lightweight solid • Reinforced concrete • Prestressed concrete • Mixed
D – INTEGRATED JOINT	Monolithic component simplifying connections by locating the joint outside the geometrical meeting point	• Point to point • Skeleton • Planar

Table 1.1 **The site-intensive kit-of-parts**

of connections and integrated joint allows for one-to-one connections as the geometrical meeting point of axes becomes a monolithic element.

A – Post & beam: skeleton open to horizontal and vertical infill at the site

Advantages
- Loads concentrated on points, thereby allowing for maximal planning freedom.
- "Skeleton" serving as connector to a variety of interchangeable slabs and vertical panels.
- Adaptability on the three axes.
- Possibility of offering continuous columns to reduce the number of joints and cantilevered beams to provide additional spans.

Limitations
- Higher structural costs due to the concentration of loads on the beams and the columns.
- Major site connection and infill operations.

The continuous post is the optimal option in terms of reducing the number and complexity of connections at the site. It is notably the feature of the Shawood and the Muji Infill + laminated wood systems in Japan, both of which use easy-to-fit steel connectors. In Canada, the Bone system is based on a modular punched-steel tube similar to those used for heavy-duty storage structures.

The Munich Genter Strasse low-rise project designed by Otto Steidle enhances the versatility of continuous precast concrete columns by offering corbels at every half-story, thereby allowing for split-levels, one-and-a-half-story rooms, etc. A similar approach is applicable to high-rise structures by using column-to-column connectors, as is the case with the Ergon system in Europe.

The twin continuous post system developed by Vittorio Gregotti for the Scientific University of Palermo, notably for the purpose of integrating plumbing and ventilation conduits, is an eloquent testimony to the rich architectural expressions possible with inventive component design.

B – Slab & column: continuous horizontal elements open to vertical infill

Advantages
- Horizontal integration of the structure and sometimes the services to cover a large area with a single slab element.
- Adaptability in the two horizontal directions.

Limitation

- Need to solve the conflict between the uniform distribution of loads expected for a slab and the concentration required when interfacing with a column.

The precast concrete "ribbed slab" and the "slab incorporating a perimeter beam" are the prevailing sub-divisions.

The Broad Group (China) demonstrates the most spectacular application of the slab & column type: high-rise buildings are built at a rate of two stories per day. The slabs are open-web steel frames with short protruding column bases and tops; they are transported flat together with the tubular columns and all the interior components between them in a sandwich fashion. At the site, once the slab is hoisted and the columns inserted, the crew can immediately complete the inside, while the façade panels are installed separately afterwards.

C – Panels: load-bearing flat horizontal and vertical components providing a linear distribution of loads

Advantages

- Direct economical distribution of loads from the vertical to the horizontal axis without any transfer.
- Uniform response to the required levels of soundproofing and fireproofing.

Limitations

- The vertical axis dictates a series of continuous walls, which restricts the planning – a manageable situation in housing when they are integrated to the large number of partitions required.
- Adaptability limited to the structural bay.

Cross-laminated timber (CLT) panels are now up to eight stories high, but higher levels are presently being built; they can meet both the required soundproofing and fireproofing levels on their own whenever the proper number of plies is supplied. Glued stressed-skin wood panel systems have the advantage of reducing the dimensions of the parts compared with the traditional nailed panels; the Misawa Techno system has been applying that technology for many decades in Japan.

Lightweight steel panels offer fast and easy installation in the case of large single-story industrial or commercial buildings. In Japan, the low-rise steel panel systems are produced either by automation (e.g. Daiwa House) or robotics (e.g. Sekisui House).

Precast concrete panels are still used around the world, notably for the affordable residential high-rise towers (40+ stories) built by the Hong Kong Housing Authority. Reinforced concrete is cast in situ over a precast under-slab to reach precast load-bearing façade panels and precast party walls as well as the central vertical circulation core in order to end up with the equivalent of a monolithic structure.

Prestressed concrete slabs combined with precast walls offer large adaptable spans to medium- and high-rise multi-family housing projects; the most efficient applications use the post-tensioned connections developed in the USA by Sepp Firnkas for hollow-core slabs or the bolted oval-holed steel-angle ones initially developed in Canada for the Descon open system.

D – Integrated joint: monolithic component simplifying the connections by locating the joints outside the geometrical meeting point

Advantages
- Simple jointing operations through a series of one-to-one connections rather than dealing with four to six components (sometimes heavy) converging at the same geometrical meeting point.
- Accelerated site assembly.
- Reduction of the structural requirements by meeting both positive and negative moments.

Limitations
- Some components can be quite bulky.
- Adaptability conditioned by the geometry of the structural sub-system.

The integrated joint can take a point-to-point, skeleton or multi-plane configuration.

Multidirectional steel connectors as well as interlocking blocks can be considered as point-to-point integrated joints. Based in Thailand, Habitech International provides site-intensive low-tech packages for the production of dry (no mortar) interlocking bricks or/and blocks, in compressed soil-cement or in concrete. To fix a large wall or an opening, specific interlocking "U"-shaped units are set up around it, steel bars are inserted and concrete is cast in the voids. The system also includes complementary components such as concrete door/window frames, inverted "T" beams and vaulted infills to cast the floors and flat roofs, stairs and roofing tiles. So far, the system has been used to build low-cost housing in 36 countries around the world.

Componoform (USA) is a straightforward example of the skeleton approach: it is literally a large joint-to-joint system generating a post & beam-like structure. The planar approach applied by the Triedro units in Italy is a monolithic integration of three panels taking different directions.

The factory-made 3D module

The factory-made 3D module category implies that all spaces and all components of the building are entirely made, assembled and finished at the plant as structural 3D modules, requiring only simple connections to the infrastructure (foundations and main service conduits) and between themselves once at the site.

II – FACTORY-MADE 3D MODULE	Description	Sub-divisions
E – SECTIONAL MODULE	Small and easy-to-transport modules but incomplete, as they need a complementary component or process once they reach the site	• By addition • Checker board • By compaction
F – BOX	Autonomous unit entirely completed at the plant	• Framed at the edges • Panelized • Monolithic

Table 1.2
The factory-made 3D module

Strategically, significant capital investment is obviously required to initiate and operate a 3D module plant. Functionally, the dimensions are limited by the local transportation regulations. Of course, carrying the 3D module from the factory to the site implies paying to transport "air", since most of the volume is occupied by empty space and since transportation is usually calculated in terms of volume.

The two types of system within the factory-made 3D module category are distinguished by the ratio of factory-made content in the completed building: partial for sectional module ("E") and almost total for box ("F").

E – Sectional module: small and easy-to-transport module but incomplete, as it needs a complementary process once at the site

Advantage
• Compact transportation, as only part of the space is factory-made, the rest being built at the site.

Limitation
• Need for a significant site team to complete and finish the building, which is by definition more costly.

Three sectional module strategies have been developed: by addition, checker board and by compaction.

The classical example of the "by addition" module is the Nakagin building in Tokyo designed by Kisho Kurokawa. The twin cast-in-situ circulation towers incorporate a steel frame from which factory-made "capsules" are suspended mechanically, thereby allowing for disassembly in a progressive fashion (from top down).

Assembling modules in a "checker board" fashion may appear like getting 50 percent of the space for "free", but that is not true since the amount of work needed to finish and equip the space generated at the site will inevitably surpass any transportation economy, as demonstrated by the financial difficulties of the Shelly system in the USA.

Folding out "by compaction" modules is normally cost efficient only in the case of multiple temporary occupation or for remote areas where transportation is restrictive; that is the market served notably by the Habitaflex system in Canada.

F – Box: autonomous unit entirely completed at the plant

Advantages
- Maximal factory production (up to 85 percent of the total construction costs) i.e. freedom from the weather; precision due to sophisticated tooling; high quality control; rationalized assembly line, semi-skilled labor or automation/robotics and bulk purchasing of components.
- Simple connections to the infrastructure and between the boxes once at the site.
- Variable grouping geometries.

Limitations
- High initial capital investment and continuity of the demand to amortize it.
- Strict planning discipline.
- Significant (but not prohibitive) transportation costs, notably due to the fact that costs are related first to volume and second to weight, which means that empty boxes (living areas, bedrooms, etc.) are as expensive to transport as those filled with value-added content (kitchen, bathroom, services, etc.).
- Vertical restrictions, since a box strong enough to meet the transportation stresses is normally not capable of supporting more than two or three similar boxes.

The box can be structured in three different ways: framed at the edges, panelized or monolithic.

The framed-at-the-edge steel skeleton structure leaves all six of the faces of a box completely open, notably in order to generate larger spaces by connecting them: wide spaces are possible by jointing two or more boxes. Some European manufacturers, including Yorkon in the UK and Alho in Germany, use the approach for various types of building. In Japan, due to very restrictive road limits, the 3D framed-at-the-edge "units" are smaller, ± 2.4m in width × ± 5.5m in length (± 8'-0" × 18'-0"), and a total of 12 to 16 "units" is required to generate a single-family house; Sekisui Heim, Misawa Ceramics and Toyota Home are producing their units on assembly lines much like those in the automobile industry and no one completed house is identical to another.

Different variations of panelized steel boxes are available. In the UK, to attain high-rise status, Vision Modular Structures used a 60mm × 60mm (2½" × 2½") tubular steel column at every 60cm (2'-0") together with concrete flooring to build a 25-story student residence in Wolverhampton. In Brooklyn's Pacific Park (461 Dean Street), SHoP Architects and Forest City Ratner have built a 32-story residential tower with different variations of 3D modules produced at a nearby plant; each module is steel framed, incorporates a cementitious floor and is connected to a lateral-load-resisting steel structure.

Most North American wood-framed boxes are panelized. They are usually very large, with a width between 3.6m and 4.8m (12'-0" and 16'-0") and a length between 12m and 16m (40'-0" and 52'-0"), so only two to four boxes are required to generate an affordable and comfortable single-family house. Several wood-framed panelized boxes are also available in Europe; for instance, IKEA has joined forces with Skanska to produce the Boklok system serving the Scandinavian and UK markets.

Many applications of the ISO steel containers have been proposed: it is of course a fast and easy way to build, but rigorous standards must be met to attain the status of a full-fledged building: mainly functional efficiency (notably in terms of comfortable dimensions) and thermal insulation (as a metal box exposed to solar radiation can rapidly overheat).

Precast concrete monolithic boxes would have to be lightweight to be considered for multi-story buildings, as was achieved several decades ago in Russia for the 40mm (1⅝") thick walls and ceiling of the Koslov 3D modules. In the USA, Oldcastle and Tindall are currently producing concrete boxes featuring ± 90mm (3½") thick walls, but those dimensions could be reduced by using new high-strength concrete technologies (e.g. Ductal). Another way to pile up with precast concrete boxes, and avoid overdesigning the lower units, is to provide lightweight ones with lateral ribs in order to pour concrete columns and capitals between them; the Hab system developed by F.D. Rich (USA) took that approach, close to the "permanent formwork" described hereafter as an option of site mechanization.

The hybrid

The hybrid is intended to secure the advantages of the site-intensive kit-of-parts while avoiding the inconveniences of the factory-made 3D module: manufacturing at the plant the complex parts of the building and entrusting the site with the heavy or large-scale operations. To complete a building, a hybrid system needs to borrow some non-structural components and sub-systems from the other two categories.

The three types of system within the hybrid category are mainly distinguished by the nature of the technology allocated to the site: load-bearing service core ("G"), megastructure ("H") and site mechanization ("I").

Table 1.3 The hybrid	III – HYBRID	Description	Sub-divisions
	G – LOAD-BEARING SERVICE CORE	The "service" area is built at the plant within a module with structural capacity in order to support slabs and envelope panels generating the "served" area between them	• Point to point • Linear
	H – MEGASTRUCTURE	Framework to stack boxes in order to attain a high-rise status without piling them up	• One story • Two stories • Three stories • Four stories
	I – SITE MECHANIZATION	Bringing the factory and its tooling to the site as far as the structural sub-system is concerned	• Mobile factory • In situ factory • Tunnel formwork • Sliding formwork • Permanent formwork

G – Load-bearing service core: the "service" area is built at the plant within 3D modules with structural capacity

The factory-made structural 3D modules called "service cores" contain all the components required in the "serving" areas of a building: kitchen/WC/laundry/mechanical-electrical shaft/stairs/elevator shaft in the case of housing. Once at the site, those cores are set to support slabs, partitions and envelope panels between them in order to generate large flexible "served" areas: living room, dining room and bedrooms in the case of housing (Richard 2005b).

Advantages
- Factory production optimized by the concentration of complex high-tech services and equipment.
- Transportation costs justified by the value-added content (the cores are ± not "transporting air").
- Simplified site work since the cores act as connectors to the other sub-systems.
- Completely flexible "served" areas.
- Natural cross-ventilation of the "served" areas when linear cores are perpendicular to the façades.

Limitations
- Imposition of a strict planning discipline.
- Additional façade width in the case of perpendicular cores, compared with conventional planning where the services are usually positioned longitudinally in the middle of the building.

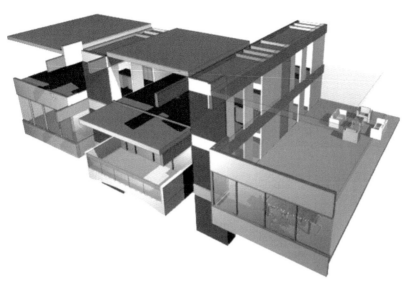

Figure 1.3
**Linear
load-bearing
service cores
perpendicular
to the façades**

The core itself is a closed sub-system but the served areas can be offered to the open sub-system market. Therefore, various floor/roof slab, exterior envelope panel and partition options can be supplied by various manufacturers, notably by local ones when the cores are exported abroad. In theory, the load-bearing service core can be to housing what the engine is to the body of an automobile or the fuselage of an airplane: the same engine can be used on different car platforms, and the same engine can be applied to different aircraft configurations.

Load-bearing service cores are either point to point like the MAH-LeMessurier system or linear like the Richardesign system (Figure 1.3).

H – Megastructure: framework to stack lightweight boxes or panels in order to attain a high-rise status without piling them up

Advantage
- Allowing lightweight boxes or panels to attain higher densities.

Limitations
- Expensive structural redundancies as the boxes or panels become live loads to the structural framework.
- The jointing between the framework and the boxes or panels could be complex, mainly due to dilatation and capillarity factors.

The megastructure is a kind of shelving frame. It may appear as an ingenious solution to go vertical without overloading the units underneath, notably since a regular lightweight box is capable of supporting only two or three similar ones. But there is a high price to pay: carrying another structure as a live load is redundant and will greatly increase the cost of the overall structural sub-system. All past tentative multi-story applications of the megastructure have never reached a real feasibility status.

I – Site mechanization: transforming the site into a factory producing monolithic concrete structures

The idea is to bring the structural concrete precasting tools directly to the site rather than transporting heavy and large-scale components one by one from a faraway plant. The other sub-systems, being both complex and compact, would be better served by factory-made "plug-in" or "clip-on" components brought to the site as bundles or in containers.

Advantage
- The logic of producing heavy components at an in situ plant in order to avoid numerous and cumbersome delivery trips.

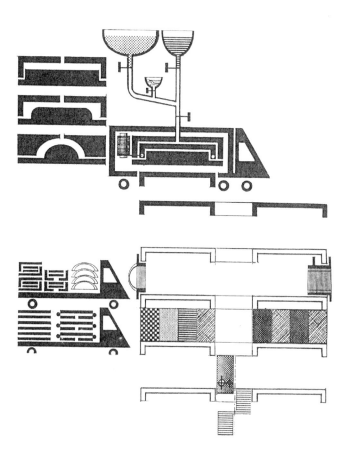

Figure 1.4
Transforming the site into a factory producing the concrete structure

Limitations

- Elaborate site-assembly operations for the non-structural sub-systems.
- Only the non-structural sub-systems would be flexible and demountable as the structure becomes monolithic most of the time.

Different technological options are offered:

- mobile factory: literally transporting the prefabrication tools to the site;
- in situ factory: using processes like sprayed concrete, tilt-up casting, etc.;
- tunnel formwork: casting an egg-crate structure within the building, as done all over the world by Outinord (France);
- sliding formwork: extruding a vertical structure;
- permanent formwork: using factory-made components (like rigid insulation blocks) or lightweight 3D modules.

Adaptability and sustainability

The need for change is universal and more and more demanding: society and technology are in perpetual evolution, while individuals are different from their neighbors and different from themselves over time. Very often, a building program becomes obsolete even before the building is completed.

Although building systems involve standardized details, they can offer a high level of adaptability, allowing for individualization and accommodating change without demolition as per the sustainability agenda.

Four strategies are used independently or together by most industries to achieve individualization (Figure 1.5): flexibility of the product, flexibility of the tool, multi-purpose framework and combinability (Richard 2010).

Figure 1.5
Four mass-customization strategies

1. *Flexibility of the product* implies a product capable of geometrical variations while in use in order to respond to different needs over space and time. For instance, many housing projects leave the dwelling unit space completely open and offer a kit of "infills" to the occupant: raised floor components (to modify the wiring or plumbing network), relocatable partitions, kitchen/bathroom/closet modules and even façade panels.
2. With *flexibility of the tool*, the process itself becomes the generator of diversified products, notably by feeding a digital model to a CNC (computer numerical control) machine, by transforming a master mold with "reservations" (e.g. inserting blockers or spacers) or by changing the form-giving apparatus governing the output of a complex machine (e.g. the die of an extruder or the mold of an injector).
3. *Multi-purpose framework* (called "platform" in the automobile industry) is a situation where the same basic product acts as a framework to accommodate different options through the addition of specialized components; that framework is designated as the "support" in the "open building" approach (Habraken 1976) and includes the structure, the collective distribution of services and the circulations. In housing, the "support" is generic and the occupants have access to "infill" components (flexibility of the product) to plan their unit according to their needs; this is the case in Japan with the NEXT21 prototype in Osaka (Osaka Gas 2013) as well as with the many high-rise condominiums following the KSI (Kikou Support and Infill) approach promoted by the Urban Renaissance Research Institute.
4. *Combinability* means generating a multitude of combinations from a set of basic components produced in large quantity. The most obvious analogy to explain combinability is music: the same seven notes modulated on a stave have been used billions of times by thousands of composers and interpreters for many centuries and yet we are still amazed by new melodies that come up almost every day. The Meccano or Erector Set kit is the iconic model of this approach: numerous types of variation can be obtained using the same basic parts, the prerequisites being the same spacing between the holes (modular coordination) and the same type of nuts and bolts (interfacing rules).

Accommodating change is a major side benefit of factory production. Taking advantage of the precision offered at the factory, most components or sub-systems are designed to be fast and easy to install at the site. When mechanical i.e. "dry" joints are used (bolting, coupling, insertion, post-tension, etc.), they can be fast and easy to dismantle and reinstall, thereby allowing for partial or total reconfiguration or even relocation in order to accommodate change without any demolition, which means longer-lasting buildings in full conformity with the sustainability agenda (Richard 2013).

Selecting a building system

Which system would be the most relevant for a specific project? As "there is no single best universal system in the world", the answer should be governed

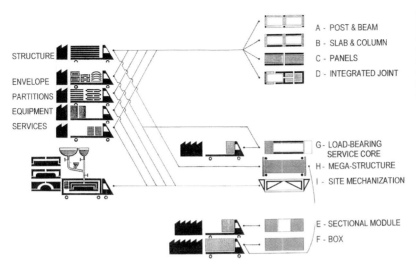

STRUCTURE

ENVELOPE
PARTITIONS
EQUIPMENT
SERVICES

A - POST & BEAM
B - SLAB & COLUMN
C - PANELS
D - INTEGRATED JOINT

G - LOAD-BEARING
     SERVICE CORE
H - MEGA-STRUCTURE
I - SITE MECHANIZATION

E - SECTIONAL MODULE
F - BOX

Figure 1.6
Industrialized building systems: allocation of the work between the factory and the site

by the given context: needs (program) and resources (the four "Ms": materials, machinery, manpower and money).

Most decisions relate to the sub-system level because the sub-systems represent specific expertise areas within the "generic organization" managing an industrialized building system. For this reason, the "palette" of options can be articulated into a diagram showing the various paths offered to the sub-systems between the factory and the site (Figure 1.6).

Selecting or developing the relevant building system is an optimization operation that should take four major factors into account:

1. the performance criteria set forward to meet the objectives of the project;
2. a comparative analysis of the context against the advantages and limitations of the various types of industrialised building system currently or prospectively available (cf. the "palette" of options);
3. the presence or the set-up of an organizational structure maintaining the continuity required to amortize the operations;
4. the presence or the development of technologies capable of simplifying the production at the factory and the installation at the site.

Conclusion

Altogether, industrialized building systems are actually much more sustainable than conventional construction, notably due to higher quality (thereby fewer deficiencies), adaptability to change without demolition, reduction of waste (up to 50 percent compared with conventional construction), minimised disturbance to the vicinity of the site and reduction of the embedded energy brought about by using simpler processes.

Industrialized building systems are introducing a new architectural language that architects and builders need to study and understand in order to really benefit from their specific advantages. As with any language, there are rules to follow in order to be coherent and achieve a meaningful and successful result.

Building systems do not pretend to meet all architectural programs, but they can be used to provide solutions for the large majority of needs and people, through space and time – becoming to architecture what "ready to wear" is to fashion. And, as we can see every day, ready-to-wear products are becoming more and more individualized.

References

Habraken, N.J. (1976). *Variations: The Systematic Design of Supports*, Laboratory of Architecture and Planning, MIT, Cambridge, MA.

Osaka Gas (2013). *Osaka Gas Experimental Housing NEXT21*, Osaka Gas, Osaka.

Richard, R.-B. (2005a). Industrialized Building Systems: Reproduction Before Automation and Robotics, *Automation in Construction*, 14(663): 442–451.

Richard, R.-B. (2005b). Looking for an Optimal Urban Residential System? *International Journal of Construction Management*, 5(2): 93–104.

Richard, R.-B. (2010). Four Strategies to Generate Individualized Building within Mass Customization (pp. 79–89), in *New Perspective in Industrialisation in Construction: A State-of-the-Art Report*, eds. Gerhard Girmscheid and Frits Scheublin, CIB and ETH, Zurich (http://cibworld.xs4all.nl/dl/publications/tg57_pub329.pdf).

Richard, R.-B. (2013). Demountable & Reconfigurable Support Structure, *Architectural Journal (China)*, 533: 44–49 (trans. Xiaoran Du).

Chapter 2

System structures

A theory of industrialised architecture

Kasper Sánchez Vibæk

Introduction

This chapter does not deal directly with architecture in the sense of an artistic or a poetic practice. Rather, it is preoccupied with the means of facilitating such architectural creation in a contemporary industrialised context. Terms like 'prefab-ricated', 'modular', 'industrialised', 'off-site' or 'factory-produced' have been used to designate this movement towards a supposedly more contemporary way of constructing our built environment. Industrialisation within the field of architecture and construction today seems to be a necessary condition – not just an option. However, it should also be stressed that, architecturally speaking, industrialisation is a *means* and not a goal in itself.

The author suggests the introduction of the notion of system structures in architectural design is a way to conceptualise a systemic level in architecture and construction that lies between general construction techniques and specific archi-tectural results. In order to make such a system structure operational, a system structure model is elaborated that seeks on the one hand to analytically grasp and on the other hand to make it possible to actively work with system structures as part of the architectural design process.

Such an endeavour has its roots in the apparent and continuously increasing gap between architectural ideation and the way that these ideas are brought to life as real, physical manifestations of our built environment. Architectural design and construction have – not least through increased industrialisation and a pronounced division of labour – become hugely complex, involving a considerable number of different fields of expertise. The resulting fragmentation of the knowledge needed to complete the task produces the risk of incoherent results.

In line with the so-called systems sciences, the author rejects the prevalent scientific view that the degree of detail 'automatically' enhances understanding, explanative power and control. The notion and the model of system structure seek to establish the idea of a systems view of buildings and architectural design that through the use of flexible constituent elements with varying degrees of integrated complexity – another central concept – facilitates discussion about how architectural wholes are appropriately put together as assemblages of what the current and future building industry is capable of producing.

This is not about reinventing architecture and architectural creation but does represent a new way to look at what is already there: an industrially produced architecture. The chapter argues that this new view can help facilitate a more active and strategic use of the present and the future building industry in order to create architecture – not just construction – specifically attached to time, place and cultural context – not just an expression of smooth processes or cost-efficient solutions.

Initially, the point of departure concerning the apparent gap between architectural ideation and execution is introduced and substantiated, thus clarifying the aim and goal of the research behind the present work. Subsequently, the central notion of system structure and its application through a model that can visualise such structure is introduced and explained. This leads to the introduction of integrated product deliveries as new emerging elements in construction with the potential of integrating (design) complexity, thus contributing to a better-controlled overall design process and end result. Drawing on examples from a case study, the specific application of system structures is then further illustrated, while a concluding paragraph sums up and points towards future research and development needs.

The gap between ideation and execution

The main aim of the research behind this work has been to examine how systems thinking can help in bridging the apparent gap between architectural ideation and its subsequent realisation as process and result in the context of contemporary industrialised construction, while simultaneously handling the increased complexity of specialisation and technical development.

That this division of the classical Greek *techne* – the art of making as one single entity – historically appears from the Renaissance onwards and that the latter part – the realisation – later becomes consolidated in the separate discipline of engineering has been pointed out by Gevork Hartoonian and Kenneth Frampton, among others. The classical conception of technology was encompassed in one single concept, *techne*, including on the one hand the architectural meaning or idea and on the other hand the work or construction needed to realise it as a physical form. The idea of an architectural form in Antiquity intrinsically implied the tools, techniques and materials to bring it to life as a unity of thinking and doing or of theory and practice (Hartoonian 1994). This unity contained in *techne* was theoretically broken up in the early Renaissance by, for example, Leon Battista Alberti, who distinguished between 'lineaments' and matter/structure (ibid). 'Lineaments' are the abstract lines and angles that define and enclose the form and that are derived from thought, whereas the physical result is realised in materials retrieved from nature (Alberti 1992). Alberti expressly stated that 'lineaments remain independent of structure and have nothing to do with materials' and that 'they also remain indifferent to purpose and form' (Hartoonian 1994: 7). The act of (architectural) design became exclusively to produce the correct configuration of lines and angles. The architect was here dissociated from the workman. This conceptual split was clearly visible in Renaissance architecture, where architectural elements in (for example) façade composition often became merely ornamental and detached from the structural logic of the building. Inspired by Hannah Arendt, Frampton described this as the separation of the 'what' and the 'how' (Frampton in Hays 2000). The 'what' is concerned with representation – or meaning – whereas the 'how' is about utility and process.

Both Frampton and Hartoonian located the next step as the formal separation of design from construction activity at the end of the seventeenth century, when the traditional guilds in Paris were replaced by the academies and the institution of the Corps des Ponts et Chaussées, later called the Ecole des Ponts et Chaussées (School of Bridges and Pavements). This marked the establishment of the two thereafter clearly separated disciplines of architecture and engineering with roots respectively in the liberal and mechanical arts. 'A sharp differentiation thus came about between ideative techniques – activities of thinking and translation into precise projects – and the work of execution, whose sole task was to put such plans into effect' (Hartoonian 1994: 5). For Frampton, architecture (and the 'what') was led into ideological distraction, removing it from the task of realisation. This was evident either in a reformulation of Antiquity as in the Beaux-Arts tradition or through utopian ideas as in the conceptual and dematerialised works of Boullée or Ledoux. Architectural ideals separated from construction could only wither in their specific physical manifestation. Engineering, on the other hand, continued to develop its mechanical understanding of nature and its superior technical performance based on the scientific 'how' and produced a formal language of its own as expressed in 'the viaducts, bridges, and dams of a universal system of distribution' (Frampton in Hays 2000: 369).

Dissolution of crafts as main building modules

However, it is not only the detachment of idea and execution that is problematic in contemporary construction. Although many partial attempts were introduced earlier, until the first mass industrialisation of building processes and products in the 1960s, the division between the crafts and professions on the one hand and the modularisation of architectural construction on the other was always identical. The building crafts could be seen as independent modules – or systems of coherent expert knowledge – with clearly defined interfaces to adjacent modules.[1] Construction specifications (i.e. drawings), had a substantial set of conventions, allowing a few instructions (such as lines and signs) to be clearly comprehended due to a large amount of tacit – or embedded – knowledge. The dimensions of the windows on the plan of a masonry building, for instance, were known to refer to the window sills, not to the sides of the actual carpentry. The carpenter knew that he had to subtract the size of the joint (for which he was responsible). It was thus not necessary for the architect as a 'specifier' to design this specific interface, only to define where it was. If the architect wanted to control the appearance of the detail, he could supply a drawing. If he did not, the craftsman's default solution would be used, still with a high-quality result, as this detail would seem coherent in the particular building. The complexity of the design task was reduced by making use of this tacit embedded knowledge of the building tradition applied by the craftsman. Local vernacular architectures are physical expressions of such traditionally coherent knowledge systems, with the different crafts as sub-systems.

Today, the crafts and construction skills have almost disappeared from the construction industry in their traditional form due to increased technical and economic demands. Large standardised material quantities, extreme precision on the technical side and a need for increased productivity with less manpower on the economic side dissolve the essentials of the traditional manually based workshop production and on-site adaptation. At the same time, the explosion in the number of choices within the building material industry has made it impossible for anyone to cope with all possible combinations in a traditional non-explicit (tacit) manner.

Although the old crafts still exist to some extent, they no longer cover construction as a whole. In contemporary architecture and construction, there is no self-evident and coherent product structure as was provided earlier by the crafts. More and new areas of specialisation have emerged as crystallisations or fusions of earlier trades such as foundation work, flooring, ventilation, alarm and BMS systems, and so on.[2] As a consequence, the task of controlling these sub-systems of trades and crafts and their interactions in a specific building project on a trade-by-trade basis has become increasingly difficult.

The challenge of architectural integration

In the fragmented sector of architectural design and construction, as found today, syntheses can no longer be grasped intuitively by one or few and are no longer embedded in any coherent building tradition. Although sophisticated IT tools have been developed to handle the complexity, these tools support a further specialisation rather than the integration of the design process. This solidifies a linear stage-based progression of construction and enhances the gap(s) between the different stages of the process from idea to result, thus preventing loops and feedback where, for example, a more product-based building industry could inform initial conceptual design.

The aim of the research behind this chapter has been 'to propose an analytical structure (interpreted as a tool or a model) for clarifying the potential of industrialised construction as positively enabling rather than limiting the architectural solution space' (Vibæk 2012: 18). The primary outcome is a so-called system structure model that, as an analytical structure supported by a conceptual framework, has been tested, reiterated and substantiated through its application on a number of case studies. The system structure model represents a systemic level in architecture and construction that lies between general construction techniques and specific architectural results – a general level of/in specific projects.

System structures

So, what *are* these so-called system structures in architecture and why are they needed or useful? System structures should be understood as abstract (system) representations of buildings focusing on the way that these are put together as combinations of thought (ideas), process and matter (materials/products). A pivotal point with reference to the classical conception of *techne* is exactly that the elements of architectural creation are (or should be?) *combinations* of thought, process and matter, rather than discrete categories or stages of creation, as in the post-Renaissance conception.

System structures are meant as a supplementary view on buildings and architectural constructions that are particularly – but not exclusively – suited for industrially produced architecture with varying degrees of off-site processes or prefabrication involved. This has to do with the fact that such solutions often 'outsource' considerable parts of both design and construction work and thus further problematize the post-Renaissance division and bilateral relation between a designer and a builder. A system structural view on any building – industrialised or not – is concerned with the constituent elements and how they come together – off site, on site or both – to form a complete whole.

The basic system entity or element in a system structure is the delivery, which closely relates to, while simultaneously seeking to merge, the two concepts from the product industry of product architecture and supply chain. While product architecture indicates a static (actual or theoretical) physical structure (or organisation) of the constituent elements of a product, a supply chain is concerned with the structure of the flow of processes, materials and operators in order to reach this final physical structure. The system structure is meant specifically for architectural construction, providing a structural and organisational view that combines an idea (of a whole) with the process and matter of its realisation.

By focusing strictly on structural/organisational aspects while intentionally omitting the specific formal, material, contextual and other qualities of a project, the system structure potentially introduces a systemic level in specific projects that lies between general construction techniques and the specific architectural results. This provides for the possibility of working with what in general systems theory is termed isomorphism and equifinality. The former, isomorphism, refers to situations where identical system structures lead to different buildings (for example, with different functionality, architectural expression or style, and so on, based on identical constituent elements). Isomorphism in system structures occurs when similar ways of conception/production are used to achieve different architectural results. The latter, equifinality, refers to situations where different system structures lead to essentially identical buildings (for example, identical formal expression and/or functional scheme based on different structural organisation of the constituent elements). Equifinality in system structures occurs when different ways of conception/production lead to similar results (see Figure 2.1).[3]

Isomorphism and equifinality point towards systemic strategies for handling some of the present complexity of architectural construction in individual projects, moving focus to a more general level looking at wholes (structures) of constituent elements without getting lost in detail, and thus counteracting the fragmentation

Figure 2.1
**System
structural
isomorphism
(left) and
equifinality
(right)**

produced by the widespread specialisation. Both isomorphism and equifinality can conceptually be used either within projects to generate different project scenarios or for identifying common denominators across individual projects.

System structure model and integrated product deliveries

But what does the system structure model look like and what does it show at the present stage of development? The model visualises system structures as chains of several deliveries as the basic system entity or element with different degrees of integrated complexity. This concept can at first perhaps be understood intuitively through the denomination of a number of delivery tiers spanning from raw materials (Tier 5), over building materials and standard components (Tier 4), to sub-assemblies and system components (Tier 3), assemblies (Tier 2) and building chunks (Tier 1), ending in the building (Tier 0). A lower tier number means higher integration and complex deliveries, while a higher tier number means lower integration and more simple deliveries (see Figure 2.2).

Simpler deliveries such as raw materials or building materials and standard components can be nested into more integrated (and complex) deliveries such as sub-assemblies and system components, assemblies or even entire building chunks before reaching the final building. A building thus becomes (or essentially always is) a combination of more or less integrated deliveries ultimately nested on site in the final building. Integrated and discretely produced sub-deliveries that form part of a larger, more complex product are widely known in the product industry, which is often considered more industrialised than construction. Drawing on such (existing) industrialised deliveries represents an efficient means of reducing complexity in focus for a given design task. As pointed out by several sources, similar deliveries are beginning to emerge as new more or less industrialised systems in construction and architecture (see for example Kieran & Timberlake 2004 and Mikkelsen et al. 2005). Following the latter, an integrated product (in construction) can be defined as 'a multi-technological complex part of a building' that can 'be configured and customised' to a specific construction project. It is furthermore 'developed in a separate product development process based on the principles in integrated product development'. In its actually produced and specifically customised state and when delivered to a customer, this building assembly becomes an integrated product delivery (IPD) that – as a kind of supra level – also can include 'marketing, shipment and servicing' (Ibid: 3).[4] IPDs in this definition should not be mistaken for the concept of integrated *project* delivery as used elsewhere. Here they introduce a more nuanced picture of the system structure of a building. Just as a building can be conceptually decomposed into its spaces

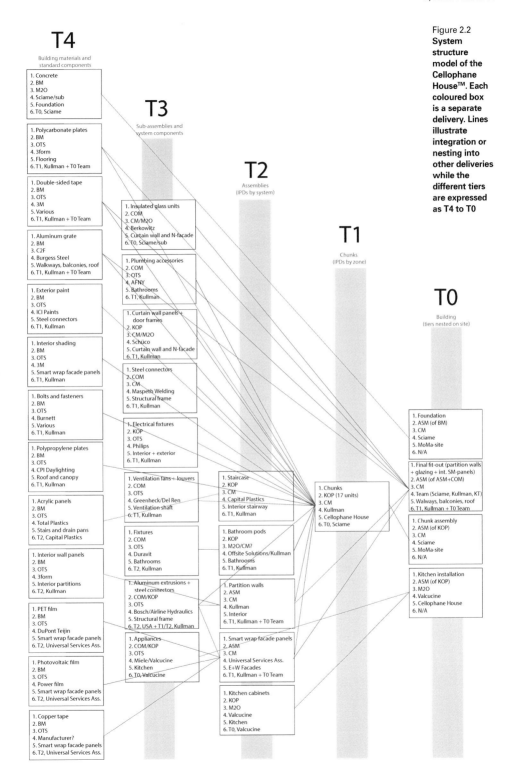

Figure 2.2
System structure model of the Cellophane House™. Each coloured box is a separate delivery. Lines illustrate integration or nesting into other deliveries while the different tiers are expressed as T4 to T0

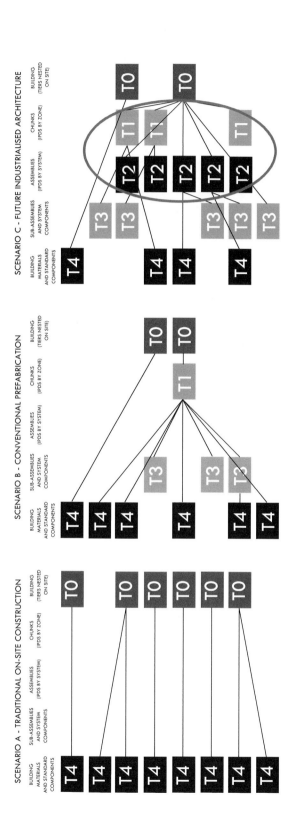

SCENARIO A - TRADITIONAL ON-SITE CONSTRUCTION

SCENARIO B - CONVENTIONAL PREFABRICATION

SCENARIO C - FUTURE INDUSTRIALISED ARCHITECTURE

(i.e. living space, kitchen, entrance) or its architectural elements (wall, opening, roof, floor), it can also be decomposed into its (more or less integrated) systems as they are actually produced and delivered. Industrialisation of architecture and construction is not just a question of off-site production or prefabrication versus on-site construction. The theoretical as well as practical graduation of different deliveries and their different degrees of integration as expressed in the system structure model gives a more nuanced view, and the model provides a means to visualise and discuss this view – a view of (potential) construction scenarios.

Through deduction, a number of theoretical construction scenarios can be created from the model i.e. traditional on-site construction, conventional prefabrication and the vision for a future industrialised architecture – the latter based widely on the use of IPDs. The IPDs (expressed as Tiers 1 and 2 in the model) have, it is asserted, particular potentials for introducing the mentioned system level between project-specific and general by enhancing the overall integrated complexity of a building project (see Figure 2.3).

Figure 2.3
opposite
Theoretical construction scenarios expressed as simplified system structures

Integrated complexity

Although it is perhaps intuitively possible to understand integration as some kind of enhanced complexity of a product or a process, it is harder to put into words what exactly contributes to this complexity. Is it, for example, the size, the number of components, the trades involved or the price of a given delivery? An integration taxonomy elaborated through research seeks to grasp *some* of the important dimensions in this sense. The taxonomy works with three dimensions and should be seen as non-exclusive, meaning that other dimensions could be added. The dimensions are preparation, standardisation and service, and each one is expressed through four different levels or degrees (see Figure 2.4). Although essentially a qualitative assessment, this (semi-numerical) multi-dimensional approach can, when the dimensions are put together combined with their different levels, to a certain extent be said to express how much the use of a certain delivery in a building project could potentially reduce the complexity of a given design task. This 'measure' is termed the total integrated complexity value for a given delivery and should be seen as local (delivery specific). It can as such *not* be summed up for an entire building and even less be used for comparing values between buildings. It does however give an idea of the different possible levers in existing and (future) potential building products (deliveries) that can be used to reduce the complexity of the overall design task by outsourcing – and thus integrating – preparation processes, standardisation decisions and/or service elements to project-external parties.

Parallel and serially nested deliveries

In some cases or for some parts of a building, the different integration levels of deliveries (expressed in the tiers of the model) cannot be distinguished in any meaningful way or are not in focus – for example, traditional trade-based site work delivery such as carpentry work or joinery. This can in the model be expressed as

Figure 2.4
**Three
dimensions
of integrated
complexity –
each with four
different levels
from low to
high**

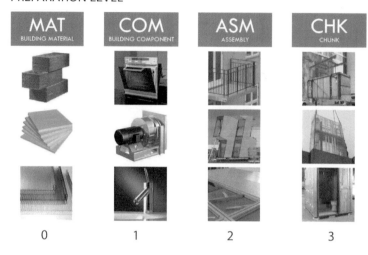

PREPARATION LEVEL

MAT — BUILDING MATERIAL
COM — BUILDING COMPONENT
ASM — ASSEMBLY
CHK — CHUNK

0   1   2   3

STANDARDISATION LEVEL

BSP — BESPOKE
M2O — MADE-TO-ORDER
C2F — CUT-TO-FIT
OTS — OFF-THE-SHELF

0   1   2   3

SERVICE LEVEL

SAL — SALE
SPL — SUPPLY
INS — INSTALLATION
MNT — MAINTENANCE

0   1   2   3

an opaque parallel delivery spanning from material delivery to site installation (Tier 4 to Tier 0). More industrialised deliveries are often serially nested, thus integrating various clearly distinguishable sub-deliveries on various tiers (for example, glass in IGUs inserted into a window frame or hinges on a door inserted into a wall assembly). However, the particular coding and detail of a system structure is always a question of focus and relevance. Different viewpoints can result in different relevance of detail of a chain of deliveries in the system structure. This quality of levelled complexity and flexible structuration inherent in the model is inspired by the so-called 'soft systems' approach as introduced by Checkland: '[A] system is in itself always an abstraction chosen with the emphasis on either structural or functional aspects. This abstraction may be associated with, but must not be identified with, a physical embodiment' (Checkland 1981: 57). The system structures and their codings are epistemological rather than ontological and serve as intermediate conceptual models or tools for human understanding.

Case study: the Cellophane House™

In the following section, some points from a case study will be used to further illustrate the application of system structures.

The limited extent of the present chapter does not allow for an exhaustive presentation of the results and the examples do not go into detail architecturally and project-wise but instead focus strictly on system structural aspects.[5] It should also be mentioned that the case represents an after-the-fact analysis of a recently built project. Although the system structure is potentially meant to work as a proactive design-supportive tool, it has still mainly been applied as an analytical and educational tool for enhanced understanding of modern building production and construction scenarios.

One of the several case studies forming part of the research was the Cellophane House™, designed and erected as a five-storey prototype building for the MoMA exhibition *Home Delivery* in 2008 by the Philadelphia-based architectural office KieranTimberlake. The office has both built and published several works with a special focus on off-site and industrialised construction and the use of integrated products in architectural creation (Kieran & Timberlake 2004, 2008). They explicitly state their '[belief] in process as the first art', which alludes to their interest in bridging the gap between the architectural ideation and the way that things are actually produced.[6]

In a system structural view, the Cellophane House™ represents a serially nested system structure where several sub-chains of off-site-produced deliveries express a gradual integration (or nesting) from the more simple building materials, standard components or sub-assemblies into assemblies and building chunks that are ultimately integrated (or nested) into the final building on site (see Figure 2.5). Not all sub-chains have equal length, meaning that in some cases building materials (Tier 4) go directly to chunk assembly (Tier 1) or to the building site (Tier 0), whereas in other cases there are several intermediate tier steps. Equally, some deliveries have destinations on various tiers, meaning that, for example, they are both integrated (nested) into more complex deliveries and are installed directly

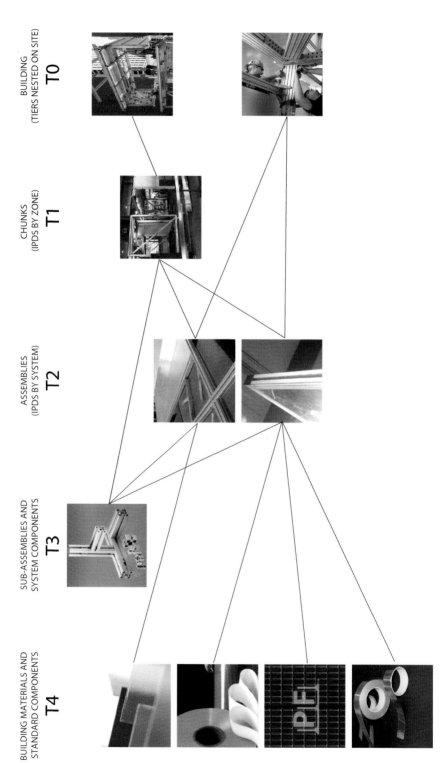

Figure 2.5 **Detail of serially nested sub-chains of the Cellophane House™ system structure**

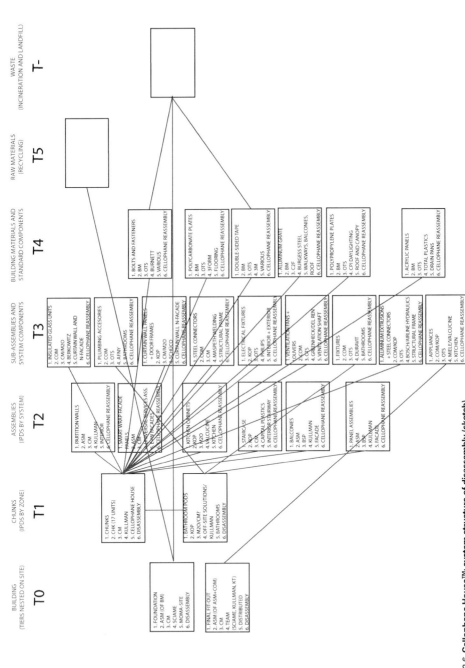

Figure 2.6 **Cellophane House™: system structure of disassembly (sketch)**

The following labels appear across the diagram:

Column headers (left to right):
- BUILDING (TIERS NESTED ON SITE) — T0
- CHUNKS (IPDS BY ZONE) — T1
- ASSEMBLIES (IPDS BY SYSTEM) — T2
- SUB-ASSEMBLIES AND SYSTEM COMPONENTS — T3
- BUILDING MATERIALS AND STANDARD COMPONENTS — T4
- RAW MATERIALS (RECYCLING) — T5
- WASTE (INCINERATION AND LANDFILL) — T-

T0

1. FOUNDATION
2. ASM (OF BM)
3. CM
4. SCIAME
5. MOMA-SITE
6. DISASSEMBLY

1. FINAL FIT-OUT
2. ASM (OF ASM+COM)
3. CM
4. TEAM (SCIAME, KULLMAN, KT)
5. DISTRIBUTED
6. DISASSEMBLY

T1

1. CHUNKS
2. CHK (17 UNITS)
3. CM
4. KULLMAN
5. CELLOPHANE HOUSE
6. DISASSEMBLY

1. BATHROOM PODS
2. KOP
3. M2O/CM?
4. OFF-SITE SOLUTIONS/ KULLMAN
5. BATHROOMS
6. DISASSEMBLY

T2

1. PARTITION WALLS
2. ASM
3. CM
4. KULLMAN
5. INTERIOR
6. CELLOPHANE REASSEMBLY

1. SMART WRAP FACADE + PANELS
2. ASM
3. CM
4. EXTERIOR + REDUCS ASS.
5. FACADES
6. CELLOPHANE REASSEMBLY

1. KITCHEN CABINETS
2. KOP
3. M2O
4. VALCUCINE
5. KITCHEN
6. CELLOPHANE REASSEMBLY

1. STAIRCASE
2. KOP
3. CM
4. CAPITAL PLASTICS
5. INTERIOR STAIRWAY
6. CELLOPHANE REASSEMBLY

1. BALCONIES
2. ASM
3. BSP
4. KULLMAN
5. FACADE
6. CELLOPHANE REASSEMBLY

1. PANEL ASSEMBLIES
2. ASM
3. BM
4. KULLMAN
5. FACADE
6. CELLOPHANE REASSEMBLY

T3

1. INSULATED GLASS UNITS
2. COM
3. CM/M2O
4. BERKOWITZ
5. CURTAIN WALL AND N-FACADE
6. CELLOPHANE REASSEMBLY

1. PLUMBING ACCESORIES
2. COM
3. OTS
4. AFNY
5. BATHROOMS
6. CELLOPHANE REASSEMBLY

1. CURTAIN WALL PANELS + DOOR FRAMES
2. KOP
3. CM/M2O
4. SCHÜCO
5. CURTAIN WALL N-FACADE
6. CELLOPHANE REASSEMBLY

1. STEEL CONNECTORS
2. CM
3. CM
4. MASPETH WELDING
5. STRUCTURAL FRAME
6. CELLOPHANE REASSEMBLY

1. ELECTRICAL FIXTURES
2. KOP
3. OTS
4. PHILIPS
5. INTERIOR + EXTERIOR
6. CELLOPHANE REASSEMBLY

1. VENTILATION FANS + LOUVERS
2. COM
3. OTS
4. GREEN/HECK/DEL REN
5. VENTILATION SHAFT
6. CELLOPHANE REASSEMBLY

1. FIXTURES
2. COM
3. OTS
4. DURAVIT
5. BATHROOMS
6. CELLOPHANE REASSEMBLY

1. ALUMINUM EXTRUSIONS + STEEL CONNECTORS
2. COM/KOP
3. OTS
4. BOSCH/AIRLINE HYDRAULICS
5. STRUCTURAL FRAME
6. CELLOPHANE REASSEMBLY

1. APPLIANCES
2. COM/KOP
3. OTS
4. MIELE/VALCUCINE
5. KITCHEN
6. CELLOPHANE REASSEMBLY

T4

1. BOLTS AND FASTENERS
2. BM
3. OTS
4. BURNETT
5. VARIOUS
6. CELLOPHANE REASSEMBLY

1. POLYCARBONATE PLATES
2. BM
3. OTS
4. 3FORM
5. FLOORING
6. CELLOPHANE REASSEMBLY

1. DOUBLE-SIDED TAPE
2. BM
3. OTS
4. 3M
5. VARIOUS
6. CELLOPHANE REASSEMBLY

1. ALUMINUM GRATE
2. BM
3. CJF
4. BURGESS STEEL
5. WALKWAYS, BALCONIES, ROOF
6. CELLOPHANE REASSEMBLY

1. POLYPROPYLENE PLATES
2. BM
3. OTS
4. CPI DAYLIGHTING
5. ROOF AND CANOPY
6. CELLOPHANE REASSEMBLY

1. ACRYLIC PANELS
2. BM
3. OTS
4. TOTAL PLASTICS
5. DRAIN PANS
6. CELLOPHANE REASSEMBLY

on site. The analysis is made from the perspective of the architectural office but even then, and due to their specific focus on and interest in using industrialised and integrated solutions, the sub-chains of the system structure reveal considerable detail. However, when choosing already existing industrialised products – such as the applied bathpod system – some of the design complexity has already been integrated further upstream (read: has been defined by others into a product) and is subsequently not a specific project concern in focus for the architect, thus remaining opaque in the particular coding of the system structure. Such integrated complexity (see above) could, for example, be the definition of and consequently also the restriction to one or few materials, a specific construction method and detailing, or predefined component choices and colour schemes. In the extreme, it results in a completely standardised product.

Another interesting feature of the Cellophane House™ seen from a system structural view is that the project explicitly addressed the issue of design for disassembly as part of the original design concept. As the prototype had to come down by the end of the MoMA exhibition, KieranTimberlake used the occasion to focus not only on how it was put together but equally how it could come apart and potentially also be reused; in that sense, it even became an exercise in design for reuse or design for reassembly. This fact served in the present research to illustrate how system structures can be equally used for showing and/or planning the afterlife of a building and its constituent elements (see Figure 2.6). A building need not necessarily be turned into scrap nor reduced back to its constituent raw materials at the end of its useful life. If they are thoroughly designed, elements on various integration levels (read: tiers) can be reused such as by relocating the entire building in another setting, using building chunks in a reconfigured retrofitted version, reapplying assemblies in other buildings or simply by reusing building components such as structural members, flooring or windows. This is perhaps the most powerful single argument for deliberately introducing system structural analysis as an integrated part of the architectural design process, which in the future will increasingly need to include the later disassembly design and recycling scenarios. The system structure provides a means of visualising and articulating such aspects.

Key conclusions and further research

The notion of system structure and the system structure model represent the author's proposal for an analytical structure – or tool – that can help to clarify the potential of industrialised construction as positively enabling for architecture, thus bringing architectural ideation in closer contact with the way that buildings are constructed. The aim is to contribute to bridging the apparent gap between architectural wholes (of thought/idea) and subsequent realisations (in terms of process and matter) in order to counteract fragmentation and incoherent architectural results. The model proposal is substantiated by the meaningful results of applying the model in its present state to different case studies; examples from one of the cases have been presented above.

The system structure model draws on several sources of systems thinking and introduces an epistemological system level that lies between general construction techniques and specific architectural results. The analytical use of flexible constituent elements (termed deliveries) of varying degrees of integrated complexity in several dimensions introduces a new, more nuanced way of looking at the issue of on-site/off-site construction and industrialised architecture. Although prefabrication has often been promoted as *the* solution for a better-controlled construction process and for better quality in the end result, maximised prefabrication does not always equal optimisation either from an architectural or from an economic point of view. The best possible balance between off-site and on-site processes and the best combination of existing construction products (thus integrating complexity) and project-specific solutions is always project specific in itself. Architecture – even when industrialised – will never result in completely standardised solutions.

The current sustainability agenda and the demand for environmentally sustainable solutions make it of utmost importance to control resource use and material cycles. This is perhaps, as pointed out above, the most powerful single argument for introducing the use of system structures or similar conceptual tools as a proactive and integrated part of the architectural design process, which in the future will need to include the later disassembly design and recycling scenarios of buildings and their constituent elements. Both architectural practice and research need, it is here argued, systems thinking and related tools to handle this complexity, and preferably used as an integrated part – a system of thought – already from the early design phases of architectural design.

However, there is still a need for a considerable amount of future research, development and refinement concerning the model as an analytical tool for general understanding, as well as its practical applicability as a proactive design tool. One path could be to also include entirely non-physical deliveries into the model, such as design and technical consultancy services. This might be done in order to further enhance a holistic and systemic design view where thought, process and matter merge, thus equally embracing the concept of integrated project delivery and other organisational issues of the construction sector. The model presently mainly focuses on the physical dimensions and remains analytical, although here it does introduce a new way of thinking about – or looking at – architecture and construction. It is the author's hope that the introduction of the system structure model and its related concepts can inspire both theoreticians and practitioners to work towards a more adequate use of industrialised techniques for the provision of our future built environment.

Notes

1   The British sociologist Anthony Giddens uses the notion of expert systems to explain how people in their everyday life draw on large amounts of embedded knowledge when, for example, taking the bus or using the telephone (Kaspersen 2005: 439 and Giddens 1990).
2   BMS (Building Management System) is a computer-based control system that controls and monitors the building's mechanical and electrical equipment (http://en.wikipedia.org/wiki/Building_management_system, accessed on August 8, 2011).
3   For a detailed introduction to the concepts of isomorphism and equifinality, see for instance Bertalanffy (1968).

4   Author's translation from Danish.
5   For a more elaborated presentation including several other case studies, please refer to Vibæk (2012, 2014).
6   See www.kierantimberlake.com/profile/ profile_1.html, accessed on July 10, 2012.

References

Alberti, Leon Battista (1992) *On the Art of Building in Ten Books*. Trans. Joseph Rykwert, Neil Leach & Robert Tavernor. MIT Press, Cambridge, MA/London.

Bertalanffy, Ludwig von (1968) *General System Theory: Foundations, Development and Applications* (revised edition). George Braziller, New York.

Checkland, Peter (1981) *Systems Thinking, Systems Practice*. John Wiley & Sons, New York.

Giddens, Anthony (1990) *The Consequences of Modernity*. Polity Press, Cambridge.

Hartoonian, Gevork (1994) *Ontology of Construction: On Nihilism of Technology in Theories of Modern Architecture*. Cambridge University Press, Cambridge.

Hays, K. Michael (ed.) (2000) *Architecture Theory Since 1968*. MIT Press, Cambridge, MA/London.

Kaspersen, Lars Bo (2005) Anthony Giddens. In: Andersen, Heine & Lars Bo Kaspersen (eds) *Klassisk og moderne samfundsteori* (*Classical and Modern Social Studies*), pp. 430–463, Hans Reitzels Forlag, Copenhagen.

Kieran, Stephen & James Timberlake (2004) *Refabricating Architecture*, McGraw-Hill, New York.

Kieran, Stephen & James Timberlake (2008) *Loblolly House: Elements of a New Architecture*, Princeton Architectural Press, New York.

Mikkelsen, Hans, Anne Beim, Lars Hvam & Martin Tølle (2005) *SELIA – Systemleverancer i byggeriet: en udredning til arbejdsbrug (Integrated Product Deliveries in Construction: A Preliminary Account)*, Institut for Produktion og Ledelse, DTU, Kgs Lyngby.

Vibæk, Kasper Sánchez (2012) *System Structures in Architecture: Constituent Elements of a Contemporary Industrialised Architecture*. PhD dissertation, Royal Danish Academy of Fine Arts, School of Architecture, Copenhagen.

Vibæk, Kasper Sánchez (2014) *Architectural System Structures: Integrating Design Complexity in Industrialised Construction*. Routledge, London.

Chapter 3

Constructing dialogues

On architectural potentials of montage

Charlotte Bundgaard

The changing landscape of industrial production contains the seeds of a radically different architecture than the one known from previous waves of industrialization. Unlike the production machinery of the 1960s, which was dependent on large quantities, the new information-controlled, change-friendly technology of our times makes it possible to produce products for many varied and small batches. As building components, by virtue of advanced IT-based production methods, become still more unique and individualized, the opportunity arises to develop industrialized architecture that is not based merely on a rational repetition of identical building components. This leaves the field open for creating a heterogeneous, expressive and characterful industrial architecture that is open to the desires of users and to changing demands over the course of time.

In this chapter, I propose the concept of *montage* as a driver for establishing a new perspective on industrially based construction. Montage is already embedded in and an indispensable part of the entire complex of industrialization, but here it is additionally conceived as an active architectural strategy. Montage holds the potential to unleash and introduce dynamics and tension in industrial architecture. The aim of introducing montage is to engender a new industrial conception of architecture. Such a conception would place industrial architecture in a contemporary perspective with the potential to seize the new possibilities for individualized mass production; a perspective that presents a clear alternative to repetitive architecture; a perspective that is based on the changed conception of the architect's role and the architectural work. Moreover, montage is presented as a means of creating active architectural dialogues, not only within the realm of industrialization, but also when industrial building methods meet on-site-oriented, craft-based construction fields. Instead of working, thinking and developing solely within fully industrialized production environments, there seems to be a need for creating intelligent new ways of bringing together advanced industrial solutions and more traditional building methods.

Figure 3.1
Building activities at Aarhus Harbour in 2015; still based on prefabrication and repetition

The dual nature of montage

Montage is about prefabrication and assembly. Almost every building project uses montage to a greater or lesser extent. Buildings are assembled from building elements – some factory-made, others made on site. Nevertheless, since the 1960s, there has been a certain reluctance to use this concept because of its negative connotations of monotony. If we take a look at other art forms, montage is, however, alive and well as an entirely natural and contemporary way of creating art. Within the field of architecture, there is a need to reassess and revitalize the concept of montage. We must stop thinking of montage solely as a production-related aspect, and instead develop it equally as an active architectural strategy. In order to rethink the concept of montage within architecture, it is necessary to make forays into the other visual arts, where montage as a principle of composition is supported by a rather well-established tradition and aesthetic theory.

Montage has a dual nature, which can be identified by the dichotomy between *montage as a constructional strategy* and *montage as an aesthetic strategy*.

The dual nature of montage, as both an artistic strategy of the avant-garde movement and a technical procedure related to mass production, makes it a central concept of the twentieth century. The term "montage" is more commonly used in the arts than in architecture, but one can detect both aspects of the term in architecture. Most noticeable is the technical, processual aspect connected with industrialization and prefabrication, in which prefabricated building elements are assembled at the construction site by means of a montage process. In this case, montage should be considered as *assembly*. Building elements are

physically assembled using a procedure that focuses on the interfaces of elements
and the space of the joint. This definition of montage as assembly contains a number
of technical implications, and it zooms in on the space of assembly between components, rather than approaching the entire work. This focus on the act of montage
as a focal point for prefabrication has resulted in a situation in which many issues are
decided according to the possibilities offered by the montage technique: the size
of building elements, modular coordination, principles of measurement, methods
of assembly, tolerances, and so on. The problem of accuracy becomes urgent, and
standardization becomes the new mantra.

Figure 3.2
**Montage as a
constructional
strategy**

The other dimension of montage, montage as an aesthetic strategy, is based
on the concept of *juxtaposition*, which involves ways of composing entire works
from different elements. Here it is not the actual physical act of joining, but rather
the concept, the strategy, that is at stake. We might think about formally complex
works such as early buildings by Frank Gehry, which are dynamic compositions
made from different materials that meet and overlap, creating contrasts. Or Rem
Koolhaas' approach to programmatic issues including programmatically indeter-
minate aspects, which are filled in and changed over time. So while Gehry is an
exponent of dynamic compositions, Koolhaas centres around the open, the unfin-
ished and the processual. But they still operate without the fundamental challenge
that is introduced when an industrial approach is the premise. What would happen
if we demanded that the montage-based work of architecture should provide both
the technical procedure and the aesthetic approach?

Montage is all about juxtapositions, about bringing together elements from
different contexts to form a new whole, but not necessarily a harmonious whole,
nor a finished or "closed" whole. If we take the concept of montage at face value,

there are a lot of "cracks", many possibilities for wedging in new meanings, for making changes along the way and for adding new layers over time.

The first wave of industrialization in the Danish context

Before elaborating further on the strategy of montage, it might be useful to shed light on the mechanisms that drove the first wave of intense industrialization as it developed in Denmark in the 1960s–1970s. Repetition of prefabricated building components and a systematized building process were the means for solving the massive housing shortage that characterized the years after World War II. What drove developments in the 1960s towards an intensive industrialization of residential construction was the desire to create rational processes of production that would increase pace as well as quantity. Most of the housing projects were built according to industrial principles, using prefabricated elements, most often in concrete, for both the structural system and façades. Huge cranes handled these elements, which gave birth to the nickname "crane track construction" for this kind of construction. Because of logistics in the building processes, these building projects were often shaped as long housing blocks with repetitive façades, and today they are often criticized as dull and monotonous.[1]

The building sector was bound by a specific task: to build a huge amount of housing in a very short time, while developing new building methods and using new building materials that could be handled by unskilled workers. The task was pinpointed in the "Montagecirkulæret", a regulation that was formulated in 1960 as a concretization of the ambitious governmental strategy for efficient industrialization of the building sector. The Montagecirkulæret stated as follows:

Figure 3.3
The Gladsaxe
Plan (1962)
was built at
an incredible
tempo, but
without
any new
architectural
thinking

The programme furthermore requires that the planning of individual building projects should be organized in such a way that it will be possible to use, to the greatest extent possible, mass-produced multiple-use building elements resulting from continuous production.

This, among other things, requires: that the building programme be straightforward; that projecting be carried out based on modular coordination; that, to as great an extent as possible, repetition be employed, including the use of uniform (standardized and typified) building elements; that plan solutions be generally clear and applicable; and that buildings be given a simple design.[2]

Reading this Danish regulation on montage building, it is evident that the aim was to establish continuous serial production, based on modular coordination;

Figure 3.4
Brøndby Strand (1969–74) is one of the period's most consistent examples of a varied site plan with several floors of large flats and traffic separation

Figure 3.5
Brøndby Strand: horizontal and vertical repetition

that repetition was to be used; and that buildings were intended to be uncomplicated. Whereas residential building had previously been an isolated event, the aim was now to establish continuous production with repetition as the central element. This governmental montage regulation undoubtedly had an enormous impact on developments in the Danish building sector. Never before or after have we faced a period with such a comprehensive building development and productivity increase. In terms of the objective of rapid growth and of producing a large number of new homes with high technical standards, the Danish industrialization policy was a success. It was a dynamic period, characterized by a desire for change, in which the entire building industry joined efforts and created significant productivity gains, doubled the production of housing in less than ten years and established component industries, and so on. Yet, at the same time, we must also view this period with scepticism, since it was a period of Danish architectural history that saw a significant drop in architectural quality. Repetition may have given rise to architectural experimentation, but it remained rigid and monotonous and thus demonstrated the limitations of the industrial production machinery rather than its potential.

However, one could raise the question of whether the impoverishment of the built environment was an inevitable consequence of the limited possibilities of the production machinery, or whether it resulted from the inability of the architectural profession to use the technical and aesthetic possibilities that the principle of montage opened up. There can hardly be any doubt that, in that period, the production machinery, together with social demands for speed and efficiency, imposed restrictions on the development of the building sector. There was little room left for architectural variety. Nevertheless, still one wonders why architects did not oppose but actually agreed to the construction of one monotonous building after another. Perhaps the answer is that they welcomed this development, which they saw as the materialization of the modern dream of good housing for everybody – the embodiment of the democratic principle of equal rights to all citizens built in 1:1. They were probably also fascinated by the efficiency and pace, being able to build many square metres in very little time. Repetition as a principle was, therefore, not solely dictated by the dependence of the young industrial production machinery on large batches of identical elements. Repetition was also a way of achieving rapid growth and of creating a universal framework for people's lives.

As an architectural vision, repetition was never redeemed. It remained rigid and monotonous and thus provided proof of the limitations of the industrial production machinery, rather than of its potential. Innumerable examples from the history of architecture – dating as far back as the architectural orders of Antiquity – prove the potential of repetition as a concept. Throughout the twentieth century, the potential of the repetition principle was discussed as a direct consequence of industrialized mass production. James Strike describes how repetition as a design parameter was regarded in the Bauhaus period:

It was recognized that there would be a new relationship between the designer and the object and that the phenomena of anonymity could be realized as an exciting design concept. The issue of repetition, inherent in mass-production systems, led to other interesting design explorations. The relationship between identical units was explored through the geometry of transformation, translation, rotation and reflection, together with the notions of stacking, nesting and fitting. The issue of linear repetition was considered as something which would modify the historical idea of rhythm in architecture.[3]

But it never came to such experimentation and exploration of the potentials of repetition in the 1960s. Peter Smithson addresses this problem in his article "Simple Thoughts on Repetition":

We have the sort of number of like-parts that were common in the past, it is only that we have the miracle of making them so easily. Looked at this way, we have incredible means available to us. With these numbers we can use repetition as Bernini did, turn it off and on, change gear with it so to speak – it is not something to be fought against.[4]

This article was published in the early 1970s and can be seen as a conclusion to a couple of decades of intense industrialization of the building sector. The architectural challenge was never taken up in earnest. The constraints of the industrial

Figure 3.6 **Æblelunden north of Copenhagen by Vandkunsten (2007–09): the façade is articulated into a characteristic jigsaw-puzzle-like pattern through simple variation. Windows and doors are placed alternately in the façade elements and the space between them, and also the balconies form a shifting pattern creating an overall rhythmic syncopation. The solutions both at the structural level and at the façade component level show an urge to limit the number of different types of elements in order to reduce costs, but, at the same time, the actual range of building elements is brought into a subtle play, creating architectural variation and identity**

Figure 3.7 **Tietgen Dormitory in Copenhagen by Lundgaard & Tranberg Architects (2003–06): delicate repetition. A combination of innovative and known building technology with a high degree of prefabrication and repeatability has been used in order to realize the complexly shaped building**

production machinery triumphed over the architectural vision of freedom. Endless repetition, poor quality of execution and lack of vision in handling the concept of repetition were to be the stigma of the 1960s.

In the early 1970s, at the same time as Smithson criticized the lack of vision regarding the principle of repetition, a counter reaction became a reality in Denmark. Increasing competition from single-family houses and the desire to create diversity required ever-greater variation of the production machinery, a variation that proved to be problematic in terms of the production machinery's demand for large batches. Many different types of elements were created, resulting in rising costs, and when the crisis began in 1972, it brought developments to a definitive stop.

But the crisis was not only about production and growth. It was equally a strong reaction against the architecture of large systems, against monotony and uniformity. When a competition focusing on low-rise, high-density housing was held in 1972, the aim to create architecture characterized by variety had a great impact, but only for a short period of time. The production machinery was not geared to the new shorter, smaller batches with many variations. Craft-based building practices once again began to gain ground, and the development of building systems and principles of assembly slowed down, leaving behind an unexplored field concerned with the structural and architectural potential of montage construction.

Montage and the second wave of industrialization

Whereas this first wave of industrialization was dominated by a logic based on the repetition of a small number of different elements produced through mass production, we are now experiencing a second wave of industrialization that is characterized by advanced IT technology and high-tech manufacturing processes. This development is often named "new industrialization" and both as a concept and as a production process it derives from the product industry and builds on new computer technology and new business models. This new industrialization is not only concerned with efficient production but also with establishing new organizational patterns and structures of collaboration between the many different actors engaged in construction. Radically changed conditions have developed and this has been referred to as an actual paradigm shift for the building sector. However, these changes are primarily based on technological, organizational and collaborative dimensions, not on architectural visions. Nevertheless, they do have a decisive impact on the way architecture is conceived. The expanded use of computers means that the design phases are now more closely linked to industrialized production and the construction phases of building. Data are easily processed and design attempts can be informed and tested right away. This situation changes the role of the architect:

As a result of this evolutionary track work, the contents and procedures of architectural practice have shifted the weight from "design" to "management" and architects now have the role of "technocrats" who spend their time processing flows of information that guide the assembly of complex technical building constructions and the needs of the management system. One could even go so far as to describe architects as "captive supporters" of the very technologies they are subject to – as these technologies may happen to obstruct visionary improvements of architectural construction.[5]

The development is moving towards complete and integrated solutions, such as integrated product deliveries, complete building units, turnkey projects, and so on. By introducing montage as a strategy, I want to stimulate a debate about alternative ways of dealing with a new industrial reality. Whereas one might claim that the architect's role has been weakened during periods characterized by intense industrialization of the building sector, the architectural aim of montage might reinstate the architect in a central role. The role of classic creator is relinquished, but the new role is an equally demanding one, in terms of the ability to deal with complexity and dynamics, to initiate open processes and to create a characterful, strong architecture on industry's terms. It takes a strong design process to manage and articulate the complexity and composite nature of architecture.

Montage as an architectural strategy

Industrialization implies that buildings are made from readymades, from prefabricated building components that are supplied and assembled quickly and efficiently. This form of production provides the basis for the development of an industrialized architecture that utilizes and exposes the juxtaposition of building components and thereby naturally cultivates montage as an architectural strategy. A new montage architecture is identified as a "juxtaposing architecture", which relates to terms such as "dynamic", "changeability" and "flexibility", an architecture that can be modified over time and that can adapt to changing demands.

In my book *Montage Revisited: Rethinking Industrialised Architecture,*[6] I have developed the concept of montage within industrialized architecture and extended it to include not only the act of assembling prefabricated building components on site, but also dynamic, creative thinking about the design work of the architect. In the process of writing the book, it was necessary and also indeed fruitful to turn to sources beyond the fields of architecture and industrialization in order to obtain knowledge and gain inspiration. Concerning the concept of montage, I turned to the arts, where montage is present and significant, not least in Modernist visual arts in the period around the 1920s. In this period, montage and the related concept of collage were not only manufacturing techniques, but also active artistic strategies. The deliberate juxtaposition of elements taken from different contexts, the way they are connected and assume positions of reciprocal tension, the materialities they bring into play: these are all elements of a strategy aimed at the creation of significant works that are not only to be experienced and enjoyed, but are also intended to confront and provoke.

Likewise, a number of case studies on non-industrial architectural works provided new perspectives. It proved fruitful to look into a variety of projects that touched upon relevant issues, but without being linked or tied to an industrial agenda.

Four narratives of montage

As to the field of arts, a number of categories were extracted in order to draw attention to crucial elements in a possible strategy. Presented as four narratives of montage,[7] these four components play a major role in constituting artistic works of montage: the fragment, the surface, the interspace and the joint. The four concepts refer to: the elements you work with (the fragments); that which joins them together (the surface); the exposure of the juxtaposition (the interspace); and the link that connects the elements physically (the joint). In relation to industrial architecture, the four elements can be translated as: *the building component, the structural skeleton, the interspace* and *the architectural joint.*

These four elements are elaborated in narratives that draw parallels between the arts and architecture. They reveal some of the fields that will be central to the development of a modern, dynamically based design strategy. As a short overview of some main points, the following conclusions are drawn. The building component is the basic element of a work of montage, and its importance is emphasized by developing, at manufacturing level, building components that possess individually and materially expressive qualities. The production machinery is geared for creating, through a standardized process of production, components that are not just one of many identical components, but that are given individual form. Making use of these opportunities is seen as a prerequisite for creating expressive and dynamic montage architecture. The next step is to choose a method of positioning these components in relation to each other. This is where the structural skeleton, which is partly a physical construction and partly a conceptual approach, would seem to provide the answer. As building components become increasingly loaded with technology, they come to be seen more as independent units that can simultaneously provide content to and support a structure. It is no longer enough to think in terms of the supporting and the supported. Other factors have to be taken into consideration in order to state the principles behind the juxtaposition of components. The interspace is introduced as a buffer zone, as a field or sphere of additional energy, which allows for offsets and irregularities among juxtaposed elements. If the interspace was approached as an element in itself, as a building block that can be manipulated, it could become a vital component in creating a work of montage. The joint and the space around the joints represent a crucial element, since the joint is the physical lock that connects components. Furthermore, the joint assumes the role of the narrator, communicating the architectural approach to the work. Lastly, the joint is a demanding element that has to accommodate and combine very different components.

Layers and interspaces

Through the investigation of a number of non-industrial case studies, relevant architectural positions materialize.[8] Carlo Scarpa's thinking in layers in his Castelvecchio project (1958–65) is especially promising as a suitable means of articulating the montage dimension. Layering as a method can create and manage multi-dimensional unities where different, perhaps opposing, themes are at play.

Stratification, or layering, is a designation for working with layers, and describes a method of separating and organizing material. It is a method that both restricts and liberates. The defining of layers creates delimitations, but at the same time opens the opportunity for freedom within the individual layer. The layer forms a framework for the material, but does not necessarily define how the material should be treated and formed. The layer constitutes a kind of common denominator or heading, to which the parts relate.[9] Layering, as a principle, provides space for the individuality of the parts without introducing fixed hierarchies, while the definition of a layer is variable and opens up ways of constituting specific themes, such as the organization of a building.

Figure 3.8
Castelvecchio in Verona by Carlo Scarpa (1958–65): light plays an important role in the articulation of the meeting between materials and surfaces

Figure 3.9
**Castelvecchio
in Verona by
Carlo Scarpa
(1958–65):
horizontal
and vertical
surfaces,
dark and
light tones,
and rough
and smooth
materials meet
each other
in precisely
treated
connections**

The reasoning behind layering could establish a new perspective on the organization of the individual parts and systems in the industrial universe, with a special emphasis on discussing the integrated product delivery system. The integrated product delivery system divides the building up into logical subcontracts, but does not ensure architectural cohesion. In this case, the idea of the layer can contribute new perspectives on concepts such as relations and neighbourships, and create alternative architectural hierarchies and relationships.

Scarpa's articulation of the interspaces is also inspirational to an industrial universe. Scarpa clearly exposes the juxtaposition of new and old. In the meeting between the new, orthogonal, precise elements and the existing, organic building mass, he establishes an interspace or gap that creates an interval, at the same time accentuating both the existing substance and the new addition. The interspace is defined by precise edges, so that it appears clean-cut on one side and coarser on the other. The interspace can be nothing, just air even, but it can also be an element in itself, creating a connecting link that is the intermediary between two situations.

Moreover, when Scarpa chooses to base his design on the parts, to accentuate the individual aspect and provide it with a narrative dimension, his approach is well suited to the industrial universe, in which the part is equivalent to the building component and the textural and narrative articulation deals with creating building components with individuality and narrative qualities. When he also allows individual elements to meet across the exposed interspaces and perceives the work's context as a layer, then the contours of a design strategy in which the architect explicitly articulates the montage dimension materialize. The way he draws attention to and accentuates the individual element and lets it find room to speak points towards a corresponding attention to the individual building component in an industrially produced building. The possibility of creating unique components in industrial production processes opens up a world of individual, characterful and diversified building components that take on different roles and locations in the building. Whereas repetition and uniformity characterized the industrialized architecture of the 1960s, there now exists the possibility of deliberately cultivating and emphasizing differences and shifts. The building components do not necessarily have to be neutral and general, but they should preferably be developed into sensuous and meaningful components that can contribute individual features and thereby play a more active role as architectural markers. This is an enormous and exciting challenge for both architects and the entire production segment of the building sector.

Between manual practices and industrial production

Off-site versus on-site, industry versus craft, system versus individual, speed versus accuracy: developments in the realm of building construction are frequently explained through dichotomies. In particular, the even more powerful position of industrial production at the expense of craft in contemporary construction has significant consequences for the way we conceive and construct architecture. Rapid developments and sophisticated technologies render the industrial field still more advanced and complex, while a rethinking of craft as a discipline is to a much lesser extent a subject of investigation. The reason for this is not that traditional building methods have been erased by industrial means; on the contrary, they often run side-by-side or are even mixed within building projects. David Leatherbarrow points out that there are two different types of procedure that both exist in contemporary building: manual practices and industrial production. He also underlines that we as architects do not have to choose either one or the other:

> In the terrain called technology, no fork in the road demands a choice between craft and industrial methods; instead of assuming or mapping out a divergence, we must discover and describe a convergence; we need to see how manual and conceptual technologies intersect with one another along the lines of a unified understanding of building production.[10]

According to Leatherbarrow, the difference between contemporary architectural construction and the building practices of the past can be revealed through the distinction between construction as the putting together of materials and construction as the joining together of elements. The craft of building is characterized by extracting materials from nature, bringing them to the building site, assembling and finishing them on site: the putting together of materials. In the industrial off-site method, the architectural elements are produced and assembled in a factory and then, as readymade building elements, transported to the building site and joined together with other elements. As Leatherbarrow points out, builders as well as architects have to know about both manual practices and industrial production.

Figure 3.10 **Gyldenrisparken in Copenhagen by WVW – Witraz, Vandkunsten, Wissenberg (2005–13): renovation, transformation and refurbishment of public housing in Denmark is an important contemporary task. Gyldenrisparken shows a way through elegant façade solutions with precisely articulated building elements**

Encountering the non-industrial

Introducing montage as an architectural strategy opens up the conception of industrialization and points out potentials for new and more dynamic kinds of industrialized architecture. This openness manifests itself within the realm of industrialization, but potentially also in the meeting between the industrial field and more traditional construction practices.

Contemporary building practices are to an increasing extent affected by the fact that we cannot continue primarily building new buildings. We have a huge existing building stock that has to be involved when considering a future strategy. The existing building stock will require renovation or transformation in years to come, and an extensive part of future architectural assignments will involve existing buildings. This task does not necessarily mean that we will experience an even sharper distinction between purely craft-oriented and purely industrial building projects. On the contrary, there are interesting potentials in implementing industrialized building methods in strategies concerning renovation or transformation. Encounters between the industrial and the non-industrial could provide interesting answers that combine the advantages of industrial production with solutions from manual practices.

Instead of concentrating on the developments of industrialization exclusively within the industrial realm, it might be fruitful to initiate investigations that address the meeting between industrial and traditional building practices and how we manage to collaborate across the different fields. Developing advanced industrialized systems that embrace every aspect of a building project, both regarding the physical building solutions from structure to detail and the organizational collaboration and delivery pattern, is one way of moving the industrial field forward. Another challenge could be to address the active integration of the industrial into existing buildings. Here the strategy of montage might provide a starting point. Montage is about juxtaposition, about bringing together elements from different contexts to form new wholes. By introducing the building component as an individual and characterful architectural element, by selecting the interspace and the joint as important points of attention, by pointing at layering as a way of both uniting and separating material substance, and by indicating openness and changeability as active properties, the way is cleared for expanding the strategy of montage beyond the limits of the purely industrial realm.

How do we build on top of, next to and into existing buildings using industrial solutions? How do we push the limits and introduce solutions that activate the most compelling, daring and visionary aspects of industrialization? Precision, optimization and rationality are all industrial virtues that could create a strong impact when meeting more traditional building methods. Precision might be one of the strongest virtues of the industrial – precision regarding both technical properties and solutions, and design and form. Through IT-based production methods, industrial solutions can obtain a maximum precision both when it comes to technical aspects, such as energy performance and resource optimization, and when it comes to experiential identity, due to specific use of materials, detailing, texture, and so on.

Figure 3.11 **Elbphilharmonie in Hamburg by Herzog & de Meuron (2007–17): transformation projects allow for interesting encounters between advanced technological solutions and craft-based existing buildings**

Creating architectural dialogues between new and old, industrial and traditional, could provide possible answers to the latent industrial-oriented problems of monotonous repetition, weak architectural significance, neutrality and all-too-smooth surfaces. Deliberate encounters between the industrial and the non-industrial might contribute to accentuating and sharpening the virtues of the industrial and introduce new fields of investigation and development. The inherent differences between industrial and craft-based approaches to building could be regarded as a source of strength and wealth in which one approach accentuates the other. Instead of creating isolated domains, we might gain new insights by creating stronger and richer dialogues between the multiple construction fields.

It is my strong conviction that we have to collaborate, widen the perspective and be open-minded and courageous if we want to provide viable answers to contemporary challenges and prepare for a post-industrial future.

Notes

1   Madsen, Ulrik Stylsvig, Beim, Anne and Beck, Tenna. (2012). *At bygge med øje for fremtiden*. Copenhagen: CINARK og Kunstakademiets Arkitektskolens Forlag, p. 10.

2   Excerpts from *Montagecirkulæret*. (1960). Quoted in Bertelsen, Sven. (1997). *Bellahøj, Ballerup, Brøndby Strand: 25 År der Industrialiserede Byggeriet*. Hørsholm: Statens Byggeforskningsinstitut, p. 61.

3   Strike, James. (1991). *Construction into Design: The Influence and New Methods of Construction on Architectural Design 1690–1990*. Oxford: Butterworth-Heinemann, pp. 141–2.

4   Smithson, Peter. (1971). "Simple thoughts on repetition". *Architectural Design, 41*, p. 479.

5   Beim, Anne and Madsen, Ulrik Stylsvig (Eds.). (2014). *Towards an Ecology of Tectonics: The Need for Rethinking Construction in Architecture*. Stuttgart/London: Edition Axel Menges, p. 21.

6   Bundgaard, Charlotte. (2013). *Montage Revisited: Rethinking Industrialised Architecture*. Aarhus: Arkitektskolens Forlag.

7   Ibid, pp. 38–52.

8   In my book *Montage Revisited: Rethinking Industrialised Architecture* (see above), I analyse the following architectural projects: Alison & Peter Smithson's Hunstanton Secondary Modern School (1949–54), Carlo Scarpa's Castelvecchio (1958–65), Candilis-Josic-Woods-Schiedhelm's Freie Universität Berlin (1964–73) and MVRDV's Silodam (1995–2002).

9   Schultz, Anne-Catrin. (2010). *Carlo Scarpa: Layers*. Stuttgart/London: Edition Axel Menges, p. 6.

10 Leatherbarrow, David. (2001). "Architecture is its own discipline". In Piotrowski, Andrzej and Robinson, Julia Williams (Eds.). (2001). *The Discipline of Architecture*. Minneapolis: University of Minnesota Press, p. 88.

Chapter 4

Mapping the modular industry

Ivan Rupnik

Over the past three decades, one of the most dreamed dreams of the factory-made home, that of an open system of volumetric components, has become a reality in North America, albeit with relatively little acknowledgement or involvement from the architectural discipline.[1] In the 1920s, Walter Gropius had dreamed of a modular system of volumetric components. By the 1960s, Moshe Safdie, in Montreal, and Kisho Kurokawa, in Tokyo, had provided built examples, but these examples imparted minimal impact on the contemporary building vernacular. (See Figures 4.1 and 4.2.) Now, an open and highly flexible system of light wood-frame "boxes", "bricks" or "modules" ranging in width from 12' to 16', with a depth of up to 72' and a height of 11', is being utilized, with some variation, in as many as 200 facilities across the United States.[2] (See Figures 4.3–4.6.) In 2015, the Modular Building Institute (MBI) reported that permanent modular construction accounted for 2.9 percent of all construction that year, with a projected goal of 5 percent share of the construction market by 2020.[3] While this new industry was hit as hard by the recession as conventional construction, it has recovered more rapidly, particularly in the Northeast.[4]

In this chapter, I will map out the contours of this new industrialized housing delivery system: first, through its distribution across the United States and particularly in the Northeast, where it is currently most concentrated; second, through its relationship to manufactured housing, the single largest industrialized housing delivery system in the United States; and third, through an examination of some of the more fruitful, if not always entirely successful, interactions between the architectural discipline and the modular industry. Since this chapter can by no means suffice as a complete mapping of this new industrial ecology, I will conclude with a proposal about how a more thorough understanding of the modular industry, within a broader context, could proceed.

A comparable scale to the North American modular industry was achieved in the Soviet Union during the 1960s, with a number of systems consisting of volumetric components of reinforced concrete, but this modular system has never achieved the gargantuan scale of application of Soviet panelized systems.[5] Recently declassified reports suggest that the sheer numerical superiority of industrialized housing delivery on the other side of the Iron Curtain, along with weapons production, led the Central Intelligence Agency (CIA) to expend its resources in verifying these systems.[6] By 1968, more readily available data on

Figure 4.1
overleaf above
On-site prefabrication of Habitat 67 module (Moshe Safdie, Montreal, 1967)

Source:
J. Mossman, Home Work Graduate Research Studio, 2010–11, advised by author

Figure 4.2
overleaf below
On-site montage of Capsule Tower modules, prefabricated off site (Kisho Kurokawa, Tokyo, 1972)

Source:
J. Mossman, Home Work Graduate Research Studio, 2010–11, advised by author

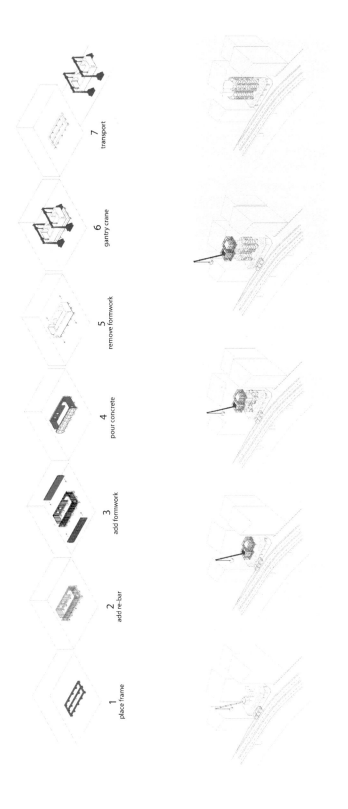

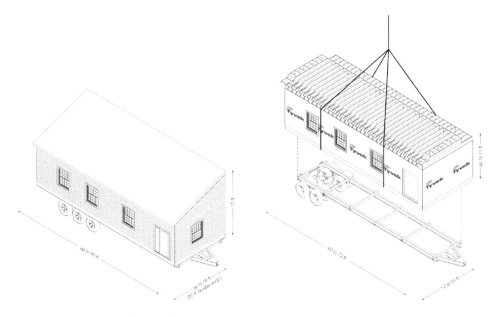

Figure 4.3 **Manufactured (left) and modular (right) units**

Source: J. Jalbert, Industrialized Housing Delivery Ecologies Research Studio, 2014–15, advised by author

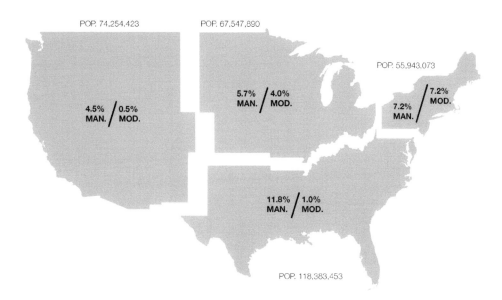

Figure 4.4 **Manufactured and modular housing as a percentage of total new construction in 2013**

Source: J. Jalbert, Industrialized Housing Delivery Ecologies Research Studio, 2014–15, advised by author

Figure 4.5
Map of 34 modular facilities located in the Northeast region

Source: J. Jalbert and H. Maddahi, Industrialized Housing Delivery Ecologies Research Studio, 2014–15, advised by author

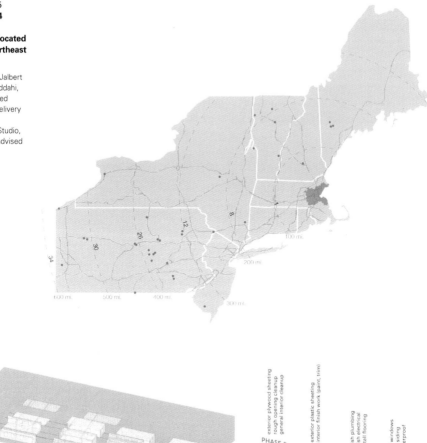

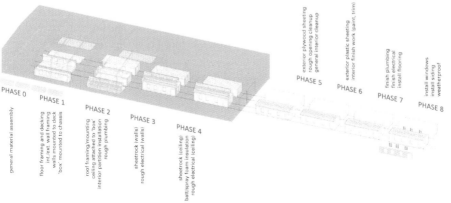

Figure 4.6
Epoch Homes, Pembroke, NH, a mid-sized modular housing fabricator

Source: J. Jalbert, Industrialized Housing Delivery Ecologies Research Studio, 2014–15, advised by author

Soviet and other European industrialized housing delivery systems was compiled into a report by the Department of Housing and Urban Development (HUD), titled "Industrialized Building: A Comparative Analysis of European Experience".[7] This report concluded that at that time, the "most advanced development [of indus-trialized building] is found in Eastern European countries".[8] It was acknowledged that "sufficient economic data" was not available to conclude whether industrial-ized building, particularly systems consisting of volumetric reinforced concrete modules, was actually economical in Eastern Europe, or whether it would be in North America. However, the report still looked favorably upon the establishment of a similar program in the United States, the hope being that "automation and computer control" could provide more cost control, as well as consumer input, in future applications.[9]

A year after the publication of the report, HUD, working in tandem with the Department of Defense, initiated a program to "improve the process of providing housing for lower income families by demonstrating the value of industrialized (factory built) housing construction methods", "by eliminating or reducing barriers to industrialized housing construction".[10] Coined "Operation Breakthrough", this initiative was conceived as a "demonstration program" targeted towards the private building industry and consumers. By supporting the "development and testing of 22 selected housing systems", HUD hoped to "help in developing new technology by moving it out of the research laboratory" and therefore "convince industry".[11] While the relatively scant literature on this project has often pointed to the low number of constructed units compared to those initially planned, the real lack of breakthrough is clearly outlined in a 1976 report to Congress titled *Operation Breakthrough: Lessons Learned about Demonstrating New Technology*. The failure of this endeavor was not the lack of constructed units, despite the $72 million ($304 million today) spent on the project between 1970 and 1974, but rather the lack of constituencies successfully swayed by the initiative. Overall, the manufacturers, builders and consumers targeted for the project did not "create sufficient housing markets to support the high production level required for efficient industrialized housing".[12]

The report did credit Operation Breakthrough with supporting "some useful changes in the housing industry", specifically by "encouraging changes in building code requirements and supporting statewide building codes" more attuned to the logics of industrialized building.[13] It was local building code that most often increased the cost of this federal program, with "code inspections at the construction site (limiting) the work that could (have been) completed at the factory."[14] A second limitation identified in the report was the "prejudice . . . against prebuilt housing" exhibited by both the homebuyer and by financial institutions, who were "reluctant to support experimentation with innovative construction methods".[15] While the complete history of this process has yet to be researched, one of the most direct changes in the building code brought on by Operation Breakthrough was certainly the passage of *Manufactured Home Construction and Safety Standards*, or the *HUD Code*, in June 1976. Overnight, a building system that had already evolved to deliver the mobile home, a recreational vehicle, was now transformed and adapted by HUD into delivering a manufactured home or HUD Code Home, a regulated form of permanent housing delivery. Technologically speaking, the change was not significant, with the primary building system remaining light wood-frame construction assembled in factory conditions. Legislatively, however, the process was now more clearly regulated and streamlined, occurring primarily off site, which helps explain why one in every ten housing units constructed each year are manufactured homes. In 1979, the formation of the Federal Emergency Management Agency (FEMA) created what would become the single largest consumer of manufactured homes, or, as FEMA calls them, Temporary Housing Units (THUs), further supporting the growth of this industry.[16]

While the recent history of the modular housing industry is much more difficult to ascertain, since it lacks the clear regulatory framework of the manufactured industry, it is nevertheless closely linked to the development of its larger sibling. A number of modular housing fabricators first began their operations as manufactured housing fabricators, often utilizing the same facilities and many of the same methods following their transition.[17] The most significant tectonic differences between manufactured and modular housing is that the former is constructed on a permanent chassis, leaving the factory entirely constructed, while the latter is constructed without a chassis, leaving the factory only partially constructed and with significant work, such as the façade, left to be completed on site. The more significant difference is a legislative one, with manufactured housing having its own building code while modular housing is still regulated by the local building code, causing some of the same problems faced by Operation Breakthrough.[18] While these differences help explain the large market share of manufactured housing in the West, Midwest and especially the South, where one in every eight housing units is a trailer home, it does not explain the shift to and steady growth of modular housing fabricators in the Northeast. The explanation for the growth in this region is likely attributable to a number of architectural practices who have become increasingly involved with the modular industry, expanding not only its consumer base into the higher-end market but also its potential to deliver multi-unit housing.

As a housing delivery system, the modular industry usually works directly with small and medium-sized builders, particularly in the Northeast, offering conventional light wood framing and sheet rock hanging, as well as fully prefabricated assemblies, such as windows and doors, in a factory environment, customized to each order. Modular fabricators also offer delivery services that complement these fabrication services, with builders completing the remaining phases of each project by engaging more traditional trades on site. In some cases, modular fabricators have formed long-term relationships with certain builders, which has allowed them to offer customizable model homes. In other cases, homebuyers work directly with the builders, who in turn work with the fabricators.[19] However, in most cases, the interaction between fabricator and architect is limited, as the builder is often positioned in between. In contrast, one architectural practice in the Northeast, Resolution: 4 Architecture (Res: 4), has developed a close relationship with a number of modular fabricators over the last decade, and provides a unique case study into the potential synergies of the modular industry and the architectural discipline.

Res: 4 first became involved with modular through the *Dwell* Design Invitational design competition, which they won in 2003 and completed in 2004, thereby initiating a decade of investigation of the modular industry through at least 28 completed projects. As Karrie Jacobs, *Dwell* magazine's first Editor-in-Chief, explained at a symposium in 2010, "the mission of *Dwell* . . . and the mission of prefab", the "ultimate modernist fantasy", were "inextricably linked" since *Dwell*'s founding in 2000.[20] In the 2003 competition, which consisted of 16 invited submissions, Res: 4 stood out for their reversal of a long-standing tendency in the architectural discipline, namely that of designing a prototype for industry to then mass produce. Instead, they attempted to comprehend the particular norms, conventions and limitations of a particular delivery system, modular. Jacobs would later lament that *Dwell* should have given all of the competitors a "kit of parts" to "design a home . . . a better home" than what was currently on the market, leaving the particular prefabricated system up to the competitors.[21] Jacobs' hypothetical variant of the 2003 competition, one that privileges the established conventions of an existing housing delivery system over the kind of "one-off" designs that she felt "architects traditionally are trained to do", provides an interesting counterpoint to the Museum of Modern Art's *Home Delivery* exhibition of 2008. While this exhibition commissioned a number of prototypes that the institution hoped could serve as the models for some future industry to mass produce, the 2003 competition and the Res: 4 response provide a third, more pragmatic ontological model.[22] Res: 4's evolving approach to modular, more than their theoretical explanation of that process, parallels earlier theories regarding the role of the architect in industrialized housing delivery.

Jacobs' hypothetical competition, rooted in the established conventions of industrialized housing delivery, and MoMA's curation of new prototypes for future industry bear an uncanny resemblance to the controversial exchange that occurred a century earlier at the *Deutscher Werkbund* Congress in 1914. This contemporary discussion echoes that which occurred between Hermann Muthesius, who advocated for a closer study of the logics of mass-production and mass-consumption trends as a basis for a new design methodology, and Henry van de Velde, who defended the privileged position that he and a number of architects had achieved as the authors of prototypes for mass production.[23] In the context of this historical parallel, Res: 4's approach reprises some of the critiques of both of these positions leveled by Adolf Loos, who encouraged architects to seek out "our culture, our ways of life and the commodities which enable us to live this life" instead of seeking "to replace our present day culture".[24] Loos prided himself on his ability to identify those artifacts of mass production and mass consumption, from fine Viennese veneers to imported "bathtubs and American washstands", through whose engagement an architect could participate in broader cultural trends; as one of his collaborators, Karl Kraus, eloquently explained, giving "culture . . . a space to play itself out".[25] Stanford Anderson has appropriately titled this sensibility "critical conventionalism", an attitude he and others have also discovered in the formative work of Le Corbusier.

In the 1921 *L'Esprit Nouveau* article "Eyes That Do Not See III: Automobiles", Le Corbusier sought to formulate a role for the architect in industrial society that combined two broad activities. First, architects needed to learn to "see" contemporary industrial culture in order to then develop new discipline-specific methods for engaging such culture. These new "eyes" would be informed by natural "selection", coming from evolutionary theory, as well as an understanding of mass "competition between innumerable firms" in order to identify already "established standards".[26] To help his colleagues, particularly those lacking his basic German proficiency and familiarity with the theories of the Werkbund, Le Corbusier applied this lens to the prime archetype of the architectural discipline, the Parthenon. While achieving an individual "perfection", the Parthenon was itself only "a product of selection applied to an established standard", a standard that in social, spatial and tectonic terms had "already for a century . . . had all of its elements organized" simultaneously by numerous competing Greek city states.[27] Academicist training had taught architects to see the synchronic virtuosity of the part-to-whole or, to use Le Corbusier's terms, "detail"-to-"ensemble", relations of the Parthenon, but by adding an image of an earlier temple at Paestum, located on what was then the periphery of the Greek world, Sicily, Le Corbusier hoped to teach French architects to see the diachronic evolution and adaptation of a stand-ard or type through this historical example. Similarly, he hoped to demonstrate this evolution through their own auto industry, using a pair of photos showing an organized standard, a car from 1907, and a more established standard, a car from 1921.[28]

Scholars have often overemphasized Le Corbusier's use of the car to explain his theories of standardization, largely at the expense of the more nuanced argu-ment he was making in the 1921 article. It has similarly overshadowed his more careful and prosaic selection of already organized and partially established stand-ards for mass housing from American technical journals and advertisements included in his 1922 article "Maisons en Série".[29] Writing two decades later, Le Corbusier would point to his 1921 article as a demonstration of his early abil-ity to identify "the type and distinguish it from its variants", to see diachronic time, before engaging in his own process of developing a particularly architectonic approach to standardization.[30] Although it was primarily the role of "big industry" to establish the standards of mass housing, the chaotic nature of late free-market capitalism necessitated that the architect be able to critically select from these standard methods and products. For this reason, Le Corbusier included a variety of building systems in the 1922 article on the "serial house", including Thomas Edison's costly and complicated "single-pour system". Nevertheless, he chose to focus most of his efforts on a much simpler concrete system, one that relied on the potentials of mass-produced formwork, windows and doors, as well as block for the walls and slabs, to generate a high degree of flexibility, for the builder, the architect and potentially the dweller.[31] In 1922, this mélange of reinforced concrete frame and block infill was only one of a number of competing systems existing in the United States being offered to Europeans after the Great War, and yet, almost certainly due to its simplicity and flexibility, this system has become a kind of global vernacular.[32] Le Corbusier never claimed to be the author of this building system, with his own theoretical background suggesting that it was possible to participate in but not direct cultural production, but it simply served to affirm that he was more attuned to the shape of diachronic time and industrial capitalism than many of his colleagues. He did clearly hope to be competing with "innumerable" other architects in a competition to respond to these established standards in architectonic terms and he did posit that mass-production techniques, like mass culture, should be studied by architects, but he believed it was in four other areas that the discipline should focus and in which he hoped to excel. First, architects needed to understand how a "series is founded upon a process of analysis and experimentation", potentially participating in the process, but with big industry taking the leading role in "establishing a series (of standards) for all of the ele-ments of a house".[33] It was then up to architects, competing like Greek city states or car companies but relying on common standards, to "create a serial state of mind": to "create a state of mind for constructing serial houses" by considering how to manage the assembly of prefabricated parts, to "create a state of mind of dwelling in serial houses" by considering the social implications of mass housing, and, most importantly, to "create a state of mind for conceiving serial houses", or "houses in series", by evaluating current conventions of architectural design and inventing new ones, when necessary.[34] With these tasks in mind, Le Corbusier established a "series of experiments" in a "laboratory" in the south of France, starting with a single villa, moving to a group of housing units and ending, somewhat prematurely, with the approximately 50 units at the *Quartiers Moderne Fruges*. While the physical product of this endeavor disappointed Le Corbusier himself, it was precisely this experimentation that helped him refine his own highly influential mode of architectural conception.[35]

Like Le Corbusier, Joseph Tanney, Robert Luntz and their collaborators at Res: 4 made a conscious decision to critically engage a novel but increasingly conventional housing delivery system that was somewhere between an organized and established standard, namely the North American modular industry. Res: 4 began the process with a more generalizing idea of the industry, discovering through the process of constructing their 28 projects four fabricators with whom they work most optimally.[36] (See Figures 4.7–4.9.) In the case of Simplex Homes, the fabricator who has produced the largest number of Res: 4 projects, the architects' greater comprehension of Simplex's standards enabled them to introduce new standard details and methods, all of which could coexist within the current production flow of the factory and some of which have been incorporated into standard practice. Through this extended engagement with Simplex and other fabricators, Res: 4 have also refined their own project, emphasizing that they are developing "a system of design rather than a system of fabrication", which they call the "modern modular", another contribution to the evolution and adaptation of architectural conception.[37] Informed by a pedagogy that, directly or indirectly,

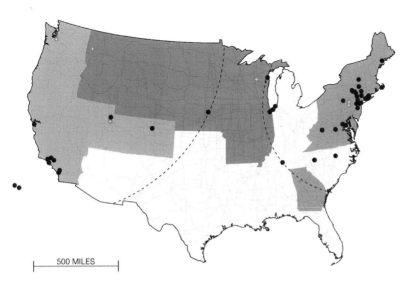

Figure 4.7
Modular fabricators (white plusses in grey circles) with areas of delivery and Res: 4 built projects (black circles)

Source:
A. Lockwood, Industrialized Housing Delivery Ecologies Research Studio, 2014–15, advised by author

500 MILES

Ivan Rupnik

Figure 4.8
**Typical
assembly of
modular units
(left) and one
of Res: 4's
assemblies, the
Fischer Island
House (right)**

Source: J. Jalbert
and A. Lockwood,
Industrialized
Housing Delivery
Ecologies
Research Studio,
2014–15, advised
by author

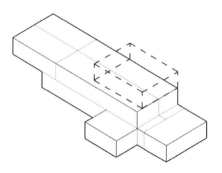

drew upon the theories, methods and forms of Le Corbusier, the design approach
of Res: 4 actually provides useful insight in comprehending and challenging the
Swiss-French architect's earlier theories. This dialogue points to a simultaneous
deficiency in the dissemination and analysis of the dense empirical evidence generated by both experiments and an absence of theoretical tools to establish new
experiments and assess those that have run their course.

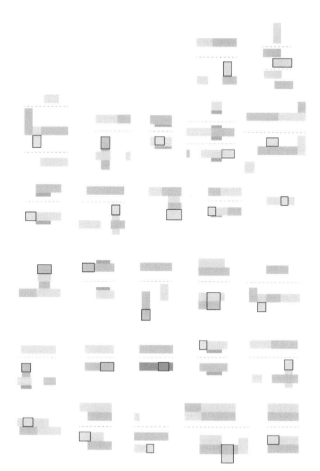

Figure 4.9
**Configurations
of Res: 4's
modular
assemblies,
2004–14**

Source:
A. Lockwood,
Industrialized
Housing Delivery
Ecologies
Research Studio,
2014–15, advised
by author

Res: 4 is not the only architectural practice directly engaging with the modular industry over the last decade. The vertically integrated develop–design–build firm Onion Flats has begun to systematically explore the potential for multi-unit modular housing delivery in Philadelphia. In 2012, Onion Flats designed and constructed Belfield Homes, three row-house units of subsidized housing assembled from standard light wood-frame boxes similar to those utilized by Res: 4. Through the course of this project, Onion Flats expanded into fabrication through their own modular factory, located near Philadelphia's western edge. Following this experience, the expanded consortium delivered 27 units of market-rate housing, Stable Homes, completed in 2014. Their third multi-unit modular housing project, Ridge Flats, consisting of 147 apartments, has run into problems due to "limited capabilities and limited finish options from the wood frame modular manufacturers," which has in turn led to a complete redesign.[38] Multi-unit modular housing delivery has also been deployed in at least two projects in New York City, Peter Gluck's completed seven-story Stack building and nARCHITECTS nearly completed ten-story My Micro building. (See Figure 4.10.) In both projects, a steel frame, infilled

Figure 4.10
Typical modular unit used in nARCHITECTS' My Micro, 2015

Source: Photo by author

with light steel framing, replaces the more typical light wood framing used in more conventional modular housing construction. One of the most notable challenges in both cases has been the staging and assembly of the modules in a tightly constrained urban site. An even more ambitious modification of more typical modular construction, the B2 Tower, was attempted in the planned thirty-two story residential towers at the Atlantic Yards complex in Brooklyn, designed by SHoP architects. Whereas the Gluck and nARCHITECTS projects presented relatively incremental adjustments to modular housing delivery, here the project contractor, Skanska USA, hoped to develop an "innovative building system" of significantly larger and more complex steel modules, fabricated much closer to the site, at a facility in the Brooklyn Navy Yards.[39] After significant delays and concerns about the stability of the structure, the project halted at a height of ten stories on August 27, 2014, at which point the developer of the project, Forest City Ratner Construction (FCRC), filed a lawsuit against Skanska. (See Figure 4.11.) Despite this high-profile fiasco, a number of modular fabricators in the Northeast, including larger facilities, like Simplex, as well as smaller ones, like Epoch Homes in New Hampshire, still

Figure 4.11
Halted on-site assembly on SHoP's Atlantic Yards project, 2014

Source: Author

Figure 4.12
Fabrication of a module for a multi-unit housing project in Philadelphia, Simplex Homes, Scranton, PA

Source: Author

see low- to mid-rise multi-unit housing as their primary area of future growth. (See Figure 4.12.) For both of these fabricators, private universities in the region have been the primary clients. In Boston, the first of that city's most emblematic low-cost multi-unit housing typologies, the triple-decker, was constructed using modular "bricks" fabricated in upstate New York in 2011. Like the organized but not yet established or perfected automobiles at the turn of the last century, the plan of this project haphazardly negotiates between the logics of fabrication and assembly, and those of building code and occupation, which is most clearly visible in its treatment of fire egress.

When examined through Le Corbusier's theories regarding the relationship of individual architects to big industry, the current situation in modular housing delivery suggests that standards have certainly been established for the delivery of light wood-frame housing of three stories in height, whether it is single family or multi-unit, and that ten-story steel systems are potentially organized but have yet to be established. In the case of the B2 Tower, it also seems suspect that greater efficiency should be achieved using a number of modular units equivalent to the typical yearly output of a modular facility than using the highly established standards of steel-frame construction, where the efficiencies of offsite construction are achieved on site. The Gluck and nARCHITECTS projects do point to the potential of steel frames, something that is also visible in a unique, architect-driven modular housing delivery system, Connect Homes.

Connect Homes, a modular housing delivery system developed by two architects, Gordon Stott and Jared Levy, is deeply informed by the earlier experiences of the system's authors' work at Marmol Radziner, as well as a critical examination of the current logics of the modular industry and the intermodal shipping container. This led them to move away from the more typical module width of 14' used by the modular industry in their own light wood-frame units and at Marmol Radziner in their steel units to their 8'-wide steel module.[40] (See Figures 4.13 and 4.14.) This dimension enabled the system to be shipped without the special permits required for oversized loads, while the steel frame allowed for a much higher degree of precision in the alignment of units on site. This in turn resulted in a much higher degree of completion of interior finishes off site, moving from the typical completion of 60 percent in conventional modular to that of 90 percent or more. Like Le Corbusier's own investigations into the architecture of the serial house, these architects also strived for and achieved a freedom in the construction, dwelling and, most importantly, conception of the individual iterations of this system, with the steel frame allowing a free plan and a free section for each individual commission. This investigation is still largely in the early phases of standardization, with only a relatively small number of units delivered, and current challenges related to height limitations and thermal bridging. Nevertheless, the Connect Homes system provides an important example of an architect-driven delivery system, one that is deeply informed by an analysis of various industrial ecologies and is able to evolve and adapt through each commission. The seeds for the new standards of a modular multi-unit housing project are more likely to be found in this line of architectural research than in the one-off attempts and commissioned prototypes that have been generated so far in the Northeast.

In her lecture on the early evolution of *Dwell* in 2010, Karrie Jacobs argued that "culturally a very big thing happened in the last ten years" to "prefab", both in terms of mass production and mass consumption.[41] The maturity of the modular industry's systems of delivery for single-family housing, on the one hand, and the

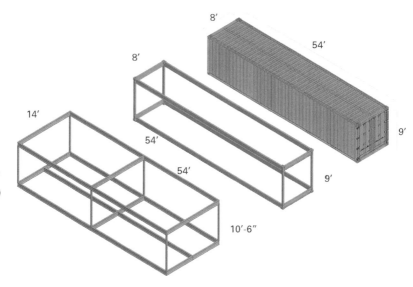

Figure 4.13
Comparison of module sizes: Marmol Radziner Architects (left), Connect Homes (center), and shipping container (right)

Source: R. Burns, Industrialized Housing Delivery Ecologies Research Studio, 2014–15, advised by author

US 20110162293A1

(19) **United States**

(12) **Patent Application Publication** (10) Pub. No.: **US 2011/0162293 A1**

LEVY et al. (43) **Pub. Date:** **Jul. 7, 2011**

(54) **MODULAR HOUSING**

(76) Inventors: **Jared LEVY**, Los Angeles, CA (US); **Gordon STOTT**, Los Angeles, CA (US)

(21) Appl. No.: **12/985,514**

(22) Filed: **Jan. 6, 2011**

Related U.S. Application Data

(60) Provisional application No. 61/292,630, filed on Jan. 6, 2010.

Publication Classification

(51) **Int. Cl.**
  E04H 1/02 (2006.01)
  E04B 1/343 (2006.01)
  E04G 21/14 (2006.01)

(52) **U.S. Cl.** **52/79.9**; 52/143; 52/122.1

(57) **ABSTRACT**

A volumetric module that can have all of its exterior claddings, windows, doors, interior finishes, cabinetry, plumbing, electrical, mechanical, and roofing installed and completed in the factory minimizing work to be completed in the field, and a method to protect the fully finished building module during transport with a series of demountable transport panels. The finished and protected building module is transported to a site utilizing the intermodal shipping network or by different modes of shipping and transportation. At the building site, the finished building module is placed on a foundation or other form of support, the transport panels are removed from the module revealing a fully finished building module suitable for use as a habitable building both in it singular use as well as the creation of a larger habitable building by joining finished building modules at the building site.

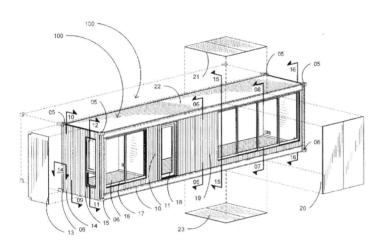

maturity of practices like Res: 4 to work within the industry, and Connect Homes to work in tandem with it, on the other, validate this assessment to a degree. The developments of the last five years in the modular industry and the architectural discipline suggest that mid-rise multi-unit housing may constitute the primary area of growth, in terms of market and innovation, for the next decade. Historically speaking, this would parallel the development of two other industrial housing delivery systems. First, it would parallel precast concrete multi-unit housing, which first appeared in the United States during the 1910s, achieved a technological maturity in the 1940s in Western Europe, and industrialization in the 1960s in Eastern Europe, before declining in the 1970s. Second, it would parallel modular housing in Japan, which appeared in the mid-1950s, achieved a technological maturity driven by strict seismic codes in the late 1980s and mass industrialization around the turn of the millennium, and is now beginning to decline due in part to its own sophistication, which makes it difficult to export, and in part to population decline.[42] Modular housing in North America first grew out of manufactured housing during the late 1970s and early 1980s so its technological maturity, 30 years later, follows the patterns of the earlier industrialized delivery systems closely. The energy crisis of the 1970s combined with the decline of population in Western and Eastern Europe proved decisive for the energy-guzzling precast concrete systems of the postwar period. The current (or ongoing) energy crisis could actually benefit the modular industry, which already utilizes a renewable resource, lumber, and which offers a higher degree of efficiency for fabrication and energy performance for occupation due to off-site construction. This seems, therefore, like a key moment to afford the secret lifecycle of the module, along with the actual current distribution of fabrication facilities and suppliers, and a better understanding of the changing mass-consumption trends, the same attention by the architectural discipline that has been given to commissioning prototypes and playing with automotive robots.

Representatives of the modular housing industry are often the first to acknowledge the relatively small percentage of market share they hold nationally – currently only 2 to 4 percent, with the exception of the Northeast at 10 to 12 percent – and they are also aware that their system is in many ways nearly identical to the predominant mode of housing construction, light wood frame. Nevertheless, this industry has been able to do something that neither HUD nor MoMA have been able to do, which is to change the standard practice of conventional builders, just as *Dwell* magazine has been able to change the tastes of a relatively broad sector of consumers. Res: 4 has shown that the disruptive impact of architectural practice can push modular fabricators to evolve economically and that while the system in and of itself is not cheap, it can be used to make custom design more economical for a larger segment of the market. Like Le Corbusier, they too have identified the delivery system with the greatest potential to become a new established standard, precisely because it is so close to conventional construction and because it aligns with current market demands for single-family and low- to mid-rise multi-unit housing.[43] The work of Onion Flats has also shown the relative ease with which this system can be adapted to low- and mid-rise housing typologies, although here a number of new issues have arisen for which standard practices have yet to be developed.

In the Northeast, the modular industry has acknowledged the fact that growth will occur primarily in the delivery of multi-unit housing. Based on the two completed projects in New York City, by Peter Gluck and nARCHITECTS, these typologies may require a gradual shift to steel frames and light steel-frame infill. Connect Homes has also shown that a hybrid system of steel-frame and light wood-frame infill is also viable, and offers a much higher percentage of off-site completion to the current standard. Just how difficult it would be for current modular fabricators to shift from light wood frame to steel is a question worthy of further research, but many of the current standard practices and facilities would certainly remain viable. Another step in the evolution of modular from single family to multi-unit could entail the introduction of a more renewable structural system, like laminated timber, but the immediate success of such a transformation would be predicated on understanding the current ecology of this industry. There is also little evidence that modular would replace current mid- to high-rise housing delivery systems, but in the North American context, there is significant demand for the typologies that modular seems well suited for.

Lacking a good understanding of the current modular industry makes any forecast difficult to prepare. Nevertheless, the kind of support for design speculation afforded by MoMA in the *Home Delivery* show or by FCRC and Skanska at the Brooklyn Navy Yards has certainly had a significant impact on this industry. The kind of federal support given to the promotion of reinforced concrete systems through Operation Breakthrough, half a century ago, would be difficult to imagine in the current political and economic climate, but changes in the legislative context, similar to those that streamlined the delivery of manufactured housing in the late 1970s, might be feasible and would certainly have an impact. The kind of modification to building permitting currently being considered in the inter-mountain west for commercial modular structures could also serve as a model for the Northeast, where modular housing is already much more common.[44] Significant change in the current modular industry could also come from the introduction of new fabrication technologies. Here, the transformation of conventional heavy timber construction in Japan, whose market share is comparable to conventional light wood-frame construction in the United States, through the introduction of cheap CAD-CAM technology may be a more appropriate model than that country's highly sophisticated steel modular systems, whose market share is comparable to that of modular in the Northeast.[45] There is also some indication of political will in Massachusetts, the only state in the Northeast with no modular fabrication facilities to date, to explore the potential of supporting the establishment of a modular facility in the Boston area.

The modular housing industry has been in a state of crisis since companies began to shift from the more secure delivery of manufactured housing and to compete with traditional homebuilders. The recession across the United States and the general lack of recovery of single-family construction, as opposed to multi-family, in the Northeast have only perpetuated this feeling of insecurity. For

Figure 4.15
A mapping of the territorial logics of conventional (left) and off-site (right) construction

Source: Author, after a series of diagrams drawn by Zdenko Strizic (1902–1990)

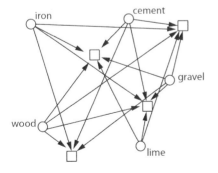
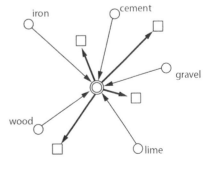

iron   cement
gravel
wood   lime

○ sources and fabrication of building materials
□ construction sites

iron   cement
gravel
wood   lime

◎ industrialized fabrication site

fabricators like Simplex Homes, it is precisely these moments of crisis that have encouraged them to even consider allowing the disruptive interventions of Res: 4 in their controlled factory environment or to pursue multi-unit housing. For architecture, a discipline in crisis, further engagement with this industry, at the scale of individual practices and through academic research, seems potentially fruitful, if not necessary, if only to question the persistent dreams of the factory-made home, which have defined it for the better part of the last century.

Notes

1   Gilbert Herbert, *The Dream of the Factory-Made House* (Cambridge, MA: MIT Press, 1984).

2   For a clear and concise definition of open and closed systems in construction, see Tom Peters, *Building the 19th Century* (Cambridge, MA: MIT Press, 1996). Peters uses American light wood-frame construction as the prime example of an open system, while, in contrast, a Sears Roebuck kit house is a relatively closed system.

3   Modular Building Institute, "PMC & RB Annual Statistical Data," in Modular Building Institute, *Modular Advantage for the Commercial Modular Construction Industry* (August 2016), 31. In the Midwest, modular constituted 4 percent of all new housing construction, approaching manufactured housing, at 5.7 percent. In the South, modular constituted only 1 percent, with 11.8 percent of all housing construction being manufactured. In the West, modular is less than 1 percent, with manufactured housing constituting 4.5 percent.

4   Based on a site visit and interview with the staff of Epoch Homes, in Pembroke, New Hampshire, on September 22, 2014, and a site visit and interview with the owners of Simplex Homes, in Scranton, Pennsylvania, on March 13, 2015. Epoch is a smaller fabricator that was founded in 1983 as a manufactured housing fabricator before shifting to modular. Simplex, one of the largest modular fabricators, was founded in 1971 as a stoker manufacturer, before briefly shifting to manufactured housing and finally modular by the end of the decade. Both discussed the difficulties they faced during the economic crisis, as well as the advantage they experienced in their recovery, versus traditional builders. In both cases, the companies complained about a general lack of knowledge about the industry, particularly about the percentage of market share. The owners of Simplex speculated that, nationally, modular housing constitutes about 4 percent of units delivered, but that in the Northeast, it may account for as much as 10 percent.

5   For more on this, see Ivan Rupnik, "Building Systems/Building Territory: Industrialized Housing Delivery and the Role of the Architect," in *Building Systems: Design Technology and Society* eds. Kiel Moe and Ryan E. Smith (London: Routledge, 2012), 86–104. In 1965, the Soviet Union recognized five systems: (1) small component systems, essentially masonry-scale units; (2) *krupnoblochnyye,* or "large-block", systems, similar to the systems Ernst May brought to the Soviet Union from Frankfurt in the 1930s and which were common by the 1940s; (3) *krupnopanel'nyye,* or "large-panel", systems, consisting of full-floor-height prefabricated concrete panels, by far the most utilized system; as well as two room-sized systems, (4) those weighing 5–8 tons, primarily prefabricated bathrooms; and (5) those weighing 15 tons, consisting of an entire room, or a cluster of rooms, which were the most similar in dimension and degree of off-site fabrication to contemporary American modular housing. Soviet engineers developed a complexity coefficient, based on a combination of factors including off-site fabrication, transport and assembly, with (1) being the most complex, at a factor of 9.5 and the room-sized

systems (4 and 5) being the least complex, at a factor of 3.15. Nevertheless, the large-panel systems (3), at 4.4, were seen as balancing overall complexity with cost, even in a planned economy. This data is included in P. N. Nedavniy, M. S. Budnikov, S. A. Voronin, O. O. Litvinov, V. N. Cherebillo, Y. G. Mel'nik, and V. N. Maydanov, *Proyektirovaniye Potochnogo Zhilishchnogo Stroitel'stva* (Kiev: Gosstroy USSR Nauchno-issledovatel'skiy Institut Stroitel'nogo Proizvodstva, 1965), 6–8.

6   For an example, see Central Intelligence Agency, "Rr Cb-61-1 Soviet Housing Drive: The First Three Years" (Washington, DC: Central Intelligence Agency, January 12, 1961).

7   E. Jay Howenstine, Philip F. Patman, Charles Z. Szczepanski, and Jack R. Warner, "Industrialized Building: A Comparative Analysis of European Experience" (Washington DC: Department of Housing and Urban Development, 1968).

8   Ibid., 5. The research committee consisted of Committee Head Philip Patman, a lawyer, Jay Howenstine, who had a background in social science, and Charles Szczepanski, a sculptor. The fourth member, Jack R. Warner, was an architect and was later a member of the AIA Research Corporation. Only passing mention of the architectural disciplines' "(a)ttempts to solve these problems" for "more than half a century" in "many countries" by architects such as "Gropius in Germany, Perret in France and Le Corbusier in Switzerland" was made, on page 17.

9   Ibid., 54. The report discusses a high degree of automation in Denmark as offering a model for the United States. By 1965, the Soviet Union was also using computer-aided automation, not only in its facilities but also in its planning institutes. Instead of improving the performance of these delivery systems, these early computational systems only exacerbated what scholars have called the "over-bureaucratization" of Soviet policies, encouraging even less interest in post-occupancy evaluation.

10 Relatively little attention has been given to this important program. The most recent and comprehensive assessment by the discipline is included in Daniel Schodek, *Operation Breakthrough: The Changing Image* (Cambridge, MA: Harvard, Department of Architecture, 1978). A more recent discussion of the program, as a "failed innovation", is included in Robert T. McCutcheon, "Science, Technology and the State in the Provision of Low-Income Accommodation: The Case of Industrialized House-Building, 1955–77," *Social Studies of Science* 22, no. 2, Symposium on "Failed Innovations" (1992). These quotes are taken from the report by Blaer B. Staats, *Operation Breakthrough: Lessons Learned about Demonstrating New Technology* (Washington DC: Comptroller General, 1976).

11 *Operation Breakthrough: Lessons Learned about Demonstrating New Technology*, 7. State and local governments proposed the sites with HUD filtering the proposals based on the size (no fewer than five and no more than 30 acres), the accessibility to major transportation (not necessarily public), and the desire to spread the sites throughout the country. Although 22 sites were planned, only nine were finally contracted, due to budget constraints. The sites were in Seattle and King County, in Washington, with 58 units at the former and 178 at the latter, Sacramento, California, with 407 units, St. Louis, Missouri, with 464 units, Memphis, Tennessee, with 374 units, Macon, Georgia, with 287 units, Indianapolis, Indiana, with 295 units, Kalamazoo, Michigan, with 245 units, and Jersey City, New Jersey, with 486 units. The projects were completed and occupied between 1973 and 1975. A number of the sites, including King County, Kalamazoo, and Jersey City, used volumetric precast concrete modules.

12 Ibid., Introduction.

13 Ibid.

14 Ibid., 4.

15 Ibid.

16 For more on this, see www.fema.gov/media-library-data/1396358023356-cd119050c31
    4328b9519fa4879227693/16+_Temporary+Housing+Units_For+FEMA_v+2_6_508.pdf
    (accessed November 24, 2016).

17 Both Epoch and Simplex began as manufactured housing fabricators before shifting to
    modular. In both cases, company representatives pointed to the growing community
    resistance towards the zoning necessary for the deployment of manufactured hous-
    ing, as well as changing consumer tastes, as the reasons for the steady decline of
    manufactured housing in the Northeast.

18 While manufactured housing is regulated by a specific regulatory framework defined
    by HUD, specifically to ensure smooth delivery, the modular industry is regulated by a
    variety of frameworks, from OSHA in off-site production to the International Building
    Code in on-site assembly and building performance. Legislation, more than fabrication
    optimization, is the most direct route to a more economical form of housing delivery.

19 As with other industries, modular housing can be purchased as a manufacturer-direct
    item, through a modular fabricator like Simplex, or through a dealer, usually a home-
    builder. In Japan, which is home to one of the largest modular housing industries,
    architects, working directly for fabricators, work as dealers, offering customization
    services to the customer.

20 Karrie Jacobs, "*Dwell* Magazine" (paper presented at the Homework: Contemporary
    Housing Delivery Systems symposium, Northeastern University, 2010), 18.

21 Ibid., 35.

22 Ibid., 18–19. Jacobs, Joseph Tanney and Peter Christensen, one of the curators of the
    Home Delivery exhibition, discussed these issues at the 2010 Homework conference.
    For more on the MoMA exhibition, see Barry Bergdoll and Peter Christensen, *Home
    Delivery: Fabricating the Modern Dwelling* (New York: MoMA, 2008).

23 My understanding of this important debate is based upon the complete set of presen-
    tations and responses included in Julius Posener, *Anfänge Des Funktionalismus: Von
    Arts and Crafts Zum Deutschen Werkbund* (Berlin: Ulstein, 1964). Stanford Anderson,
    working from Posener's assessment of the debate, as well as two of his former stu-
    dents, Francesco Passanti and Frederic Schwartz, have also reassessed this important
    moment in the formation of Modernist architecture, challenging the established reading
    of the positions represented by the two protagonists.

24 Adolf Loos, "Cultural Degeneracy" (1908), translated and republished in eds. Tim and
    Charlotte Benton *Form and Function : A Source Book for the History of Architecture
    and Design 1890–1939* (London: Crosby Lockwood Staples, 1975), 41–5.

25 Ibid. Kraus' passage is quoted in Stanford Anderson, "Critical Conventionalism in
    Architecture," *Assemblage*, 1 (October 1986).

26 Le Corbusier, "Des Yeux Qui Ne Voient Pas . . . III: Les Autos," *L'Esprit Nouveau* 10
    (1921), unpaginated. I have studied this article in my own dissertation work through
    the lens of new research on the influence of Werkbund theories, provided by the work
    of Anderson, Passanti, Schwartz, and Posener, as well as through my own research
    regarding the theories and practices of scientific management, as they were understood
    in Germany and France at that time. For more on this, see Ivan Rupnik, "Projecting in
    Space-Time: The Laboratory Method, Modern Architecture and Settlement-Building,
    1918–1932" (Harvard University, April 2015).

27 La Corbusier, "Des Yeux Qui Ne Voient Pas . . . III: Les Autos."

28 To make the point even clearer, Le Corbusier also included a year-by-year study of the
    "evolution of the form of an automobile" in the original article. The illustration was
    not used in the version of this article included in Le Corbusier, *Vers une architecture*
    (Paris: Éditions G. Crès, 1923) or in subsequent translations, including Le Corbusier,

Toward an Architecture (Vers une Architecture), trans. John Goodman (Los Angeles: Getty Research Institute, 2007). One of the most insightful analyses of this material is included in Francesco Passanti, "The Vernacular, Modernism, and Le Corbusier," *Journal of the Society of Architectural Historians* 56, no. 4 (December 1997).

29 Le Corbusier, "Maisons en Série," *L'Esprit Nouveau* 13 (1922). The title of this article has been translated as "Mass-Production Houses", emphasizing a narrow aspect of its area of focus, fabrication of products in a factory setting – a topic that is often regarded as being outside of the scope of architectural practice. The more literal translation "Houses in Series", or "Serial Houses", more directly addresses Le Corbusier's own concerns.

30 Le Corbusier, *The Marseilles Block* [*L'unité d'habitation de Marseille*], trans. Geoffrey Sainsbury (London: The Harvill Press, 1953 (1950)), 30. As Anderson and Passanti have both pointed out, this phrasing is generally relatable to the theories of the Werkbund and, most specifically, to the writings of Hermann Muthesius.

31 Allen Brooks discovered that Le Corbusier owned Maurice M. Sloan's *The Concrete House and Its Construction* (Philadelphia, PA: The Association of American Portland Cement Manufacturers, 1912). See Allen Brooks, *Le Corbusier's Formative Years* (Chicago, IL: University of Chicago Press, 1999). While that manual did include the familiar drawing of the Hennebique System, it also provided examples of much cheaper methods of reinforced concrete construction, specifically suited for low- to mid-rise housing, already in use in the United States.

32 In Howard Davis' *The Culture of Building* (Oxford: Oxford University Press, 2006), the author laments how this building system has displaced what he sees as more vernacular modes of building in places like Africa and India. For Le Corbusier, it was precisely the potential of this system to become a global vernacular that led him to use it as the foundation for his own research into spatial planning and project management norms.

33 Le Corbusier, "Maisons en Série." Actually, this particular passage was not included in the original 1922 article but was added in the chapter of *Toward an Architecture* by the same name on page 187.

34 Ibid., 1525. This passage is moved to the front of the article by the second edition of *Toward an Architecture*. By translating "maisons en série" as "mass-production houses", too much emphasis is placed on what goes on during mass production and too little on what architects need to learn in order to work with already mass-produced, and mass-consumed, objects.

35 P. Jeanneret, *Le Corbusier: Oeuvre Complete 1910–1929* (Paris: W. Boesiger et O. Stonorov, 1936).

36 Photographs of the Pope, the families of the Simplex founding partners and images of the houses they have constructed in collaboration with Res: 4 greet every visitor at the facility in Scranton.

37 Joseph Tanney, "Resolution: 4 Architecture" (paper presented at the Homework: Contemporary Housing Delivery Systems symporium, Northeastern University, 2010), 56.

38 www.onionflats.com/projects/multi-family/ridge-flats.php (accessed November 24, 2016).

39 For more on this, see Ian Volner, "Construction Stops on the B2 BKLYN High-Rise at Atlantic Yards," *Architect: The Journal of the American Institute of Architects* (2014), www.northeastern.edu/camd/architecture/portfolio/home-work (accessed December 12, 2016).

40 Gordon Stott and Jared Levy, "Modular Housing," US Patent Application Number 12/985, 514, July 7, 2011.

41 Jacobs, "*Dwell* Magazine."

42 My understanding of Japan's advanced housing delivery industry is informed by the work of Professor Shuichi Matsumura of the University of Tokyo.

43 Le Corbusier was less successful at assessing the current state of industrialization of housing delivery in the postwar period, prematurely betting on room-sized fully pre-fabricated modules becoming an established standard for his new typology, the *Unité d'habitation*. This decision was influenced by the appearance of factories producing nearly finished single-family homes during the immediate postwar years in France and in England. Here it was the need for speed more than economy that drove these systems and as soon as the immediate demand for housing dissipated, other systems proved much more economical. For more on the English system, where the French systems are also discussed, see Brenda Vale, *Prefabs: A History of the UK Temporary Housing Programme* (London: Chapman & Hall, 1995).

44 Ryan E. Smith, Gentry Griffin, Talbot Rice, and Massih Hamedani, *Sterling Prefab Manual* (Integrated Technology in Architecture Center, University of Utah Industry Report. V1.0 August 2015), 48–66.

45 Shuichi Matsumura, "How Have CAD-CAM Systems Changed Japanese Conventional Wooden Construction in These Three Decades?," in *ISARC2006* (2006), 357–60.

Chapter 5

Prefabricated housing in architectural culture

Mathew Aitchison and John Macarthur

Introduction

Architects have long been fascinated by the promise of prefabricated and modular building, in particular housing, and even more so the individual detached house. The 'prefab' house combines the promise of industrialised building with the dream of a popular mass market for architecture, and it has exercised a magnetism over architectural culture which is as strong today as it was at any point in the past. The interest originated in the mid-nineteenth century, but achieved a strong uptake in the early to mid-twentieth century, and has continued in a cyclical pattern up to the present day. This chapter attempts to describe this fascination with the prefab house and to chart some of the complications that have plagued its translation into real outcomes. This illusory chase for the holy grail of architecture Gilbert Herbert termed "the Henry Ford syndrome", a twentieth-century phenomenon whose symptoms Herbert described with the exclamation: "Why can't we mass-produce houses – standard, well-designed, at low cost – in the same way Ford mass-produces cars?"[1]

The history of prefab tells us as much about the culture of architecture as it does about the techniques and methodologies of offsite construction, and raises several questions that cut to the core of the architectural project today. How does the profession view itself and what are its core roles and responsibilities in the contemporary setting? How to measure the often colossal claims made by architects pursuing prefab against actual achievements in practice? What is the inherent value of prefab? And finally, if prefabricated, modular or industrialised building methodologies were to be implemented on the scale often promoted (indeed required) by architects, what would remain of our profession? Prefabrication is thus not only a question of technical possibilities and consequences but also of the pre-existing discursive structure of architecture and its myth of its own progress. Following Hegel's ideas of the progression of art into pure spirit,[2] since the nineteenth century architects have regularly imagined that the progress of architectural thought would reach a point where architects were no longer required and architecture would be sublated into industrialisation and social organisation.

Our interest in these questions stems from our work in researching the design and construction of prefabricated and modular housing.[3] Although this work focuses on the particularities of contemporary Australia, the search for precedents opened up the long and chequered history of high-profile attempts to make prefabrication a dominant mode of building in Australia and internationally. Throughout this research, we became aware of several longstanding tensions and unresolved conflicts surrounding the aspirations and achievements in the area. From this analysis, we make two main observations on the role played by prefabricated housing within architectural culture – first, around disciplinary frameworks and their relation to offsite construction, and second, around the role of technology in prefabricated housing and architecture more generally.

Throughout this chapter, the discussion calls on Australian instances of prefabricated housing. In many ways, the history of prefab housing in Australia is indicative of the experiences of other countries and reflects a chronology and ambition shared by most industrialised countries. The British settlement[4] of Australia in 1788 included a timber and canvas transportable house for the governor Arthur Philip, and prefabricated 'kit' houses were exported from Britain throughout the nineteenth century to facilitate colonisation. A series of gold rushes from the 1850s through to the end of the century created the demand for housing, and engendered an Australian construction industry, which provided a range of buildings to local and international markets.[5] Particularly in the northern state of Queensland, where masonry construction was uncompetitive, factory-sawn and transportable 'precut' kits for timber houses became ubiquitous and are now colloquially known as 'Queenslanders'.[6] Like those of most industrialised countries, Australia's post-World War II housing scene was dominated by materials shortages and the push towards the fuller industrialisation of housing construction. The 1950s saw wide-ranging attempts at imported and locally developed mass housing using prefabricated building techniques. From the 1960s onward, the conditions of prefabrication in housing have remained relatively constant: they are defined on the one hand by an ever-expanding suburbanisation around Australia's coastal capitals, and on the other hand by the boom–bust cycle associated with remote mining operations. In both situations, prefabrication has become a mainstream construction technique, whose attractiveness has risen sharply over the past decade within the context of Australia's national housing and skills shortages and the housing affordability crisis. Today, Australian industry is interested in exploring the transformation of the knowledge and practice of prefabrication in detached and semi-detached housing into a denser and more urban multi-storey modular approach. Recent debates around the value of computational design tools and their interaction with new modes of digital and automated 'fabrication' have proposed an overhaul of the industry and held out the promise of the attainment of many earlier and previously unmet objectives.

Terminology

The confusion around the term 'prefab', its uptake or lack thereof, and its periodic re-emergence as a breakthrough technology is partly a problem of the history of the technologies and partly of architectural culture. In a recent article, Chris Knapp provocatively called for an end to discussion of prefabrication, largely because he felt "there is not another word in the current lexicon of architecture that more erroneously asserts positive change".[7] Knapp is not alone in thinking that the problems that have coalesced around the area of prefabrication have done so because of problems of definition and the hubris associated with architect-led attempts, which have arisen under a variety of headings, including 'offsite' as proposed in this collection. Allison Arieff's *Prefab* (2002) carries a warning to the reader regarding "our definition of PREFAB", and notes that "Many of the houses presented . . . are not prefabricated in the strictest sense of the word".[8] A decade later, in an article entitled "Prefab Lives!", Arieff nevertheless avoids describing the projects as prefabricated, referring to the construction techniques as "modular building".[9]

Each of the variety of terms ('modular', 'offsite', 'indoor', 'kit', 'transportable', 'factory-built', 'manufactured' and so on) represents a significant development in building construction. 'Modular', 'systems', 'kit' or 'packaged' homes tend to point towards the flexible nature of prefabrication. 'Offsite' or 'indoor' construction refers to how and where the components are made. 'Premade' and 'prebuilt' are simply synonyms of 'prefabrication'. 'Portable', 'mobile' and 'transportable' housing highlight the moveable nature of these buildings. And finally, 'manufactured', 'factory-built' and 'mass produced' are all references to the scale and level of industrialisation involved. Knapp's frustration is that the word 'prefab' is used to cover all of these without adequately naming an underlying concept, and (we would add) not understanding the history of the processes and techniques described.

Inadequate conceptualisation is undoubtedly a problem, but it is not one that can simply be reasoned through, as it is integral to the sense that architects have of prefab being on the cusp of revolutionising construction. Endemic to this feeling of being on the cusp of revolution is the necessity to actively forget the numerous previous threshold moments and actual successes in the field. On the success front, and again returning to the Australian experience, we could note the example of the nineteenth-century timber precut Queensland house previously cited, which is not understood as a manufactured product because of the cultural pressures to see it as vernacular. Equally interesting is the mine site housing that has developed from transportable site cabins into a moderately elaborate typology of not only residential but also recreational and civil uses. Despite what the present authors see as their architectural interest, these 'dongas' (as they are customarily referred to in Australia) do not meet societal expectations of architecture, nor architects' expectations of formal or constructional novelty, and are thus not customarily thought of as architecture, or indeed worthy of architectural attention.

Prefab's supposed threshold moment is deeply linked to architectural culture. In the early twentieth century, architects believed that they needed to recognise and channel the underlying teleology of technology *per se*, which will be the subject of a fuller discussion below. It is this romance of technological progress in construction as having a single direction or end that provides a great deal of the over-determination implied by the term 'prefabrication' (as it also does of the more recent digital and automated fabrication technologies, as they are widely known).

Prefabrication and the prefab dwelling unit have particularly iconic roles because of Modernist ideas about the cultural consequences of manufacture and serial form.

One of the watershed points in architectural history is what Manfredo Tafuri refers to as the "crisis of the object".[10] Traditionally, the qualities of architecture were instantiated in a building, and to the extent that architecture was an art, this building would be considered a work of art. Modernist architects, who had determined that building was an industrial process, also decided that architecture could not lie in the qualities of any one building, but rather in the capacity to analyse, organise and produce multiple buildings. The individual building, even when seen in the singular – as with Le Corbusier's famous machine for living, the Villa Savoye – was meant to represent an instance of a series of such buildings. The simplified form of many Modernist buildings was, in part, intended to act against any sense that the building was unique. Similarly, the Villa Savoye's fit to its site at Poissy was intended to be understood as just that: the fit of preconceived generic building to a particular site.

It is this agenda of a technological breakthrough and conceptual revolution that the prefab house continues to keep alive. If manufactured housing was only about price and supply, architects would not be so interested. Rather, what interests them are the linked ideas: of a generic building that could be fitted artfully to a variety of sites while maintaining its sense of standardisation and design value; of overcoming the aggrandising effects of bespoke design with an authentic judgement of use value and forming a collective rational taste in building; that architecture would not only be seen as unique exercises in conspicuous expenditure, but also as being capable of addressing social and economic realities that lay at the supposed heart of the Modernist project; and lastly, that each prefab house would hold, and would be seen to hold, the DNA for assembly into larger buildings.

Underlying these relatively practical objectives is another issue of the self-identity of the profession: architecture remains a bespoke trade, which makes it elite, but also connected to the whims and excessive demands of individuation of the commissioning classes. The mass market for consumer goods from which architecture is apparently excluded offers not only greater impact, but also a kind of truth found in mass taste that demonstrates one car or telephone is better than another. Le Corbusier called such normalised products *objet type*, believing that the Thornet café chair and the briar pipe had evolved into final unsurpassable forms. The Pavilion of the journal *Le Esprit Nouveau* that Le Corbusier designed for the 1925 Paris International Exhibition of the Modern Decorative and Industrial Arts was intended to show how industrialisation and consumer choice would demonstrate the truth of Modernism.[11] It is sometimes overlooked that this house, like others of the period, was also a demonstration of a model of industrialised building that was also intended to be racked and stacked into much larger apartment buildings.

If architect-designed prefabricated housing has mostly remained a dream set to recur every ten to twenty years, then historical understanding of prefabricated housing and the challenges it has faced evidences a kind of amnesia. Despite a handful of excellent studies stretching back to the 1950s, there remains a distinct lack of historical awareness around the subject of prefabrication in architectural culture, which sees each new generation of architects not so much holding onto the dream, as reinventing it from scratch.[12] In the present, this dynamic is powered by the large-format high-volume picture books such as Taschen's *Prefab Houses* (2010) and FKG's *Prefab Architecture* (2012),[13] which continue to cement the role of prefabricated housing (if not in the minds of the public and industry, then on their coffee tables). In such books, we do not see the volume factory-made housing of Europe, the United States and Japan that meets a market for staid familiar house forms at moderate prices.[14] Rather, we see prototypes that are technologically articulate, formally innovative and attractive to wealthy design-literate readers, that inevitably express their technique and technology in a demonstrable way, and that rehearse the idea of the architectural prefab as an epoch in architecture and construction.

Prefabricated housing and architecture: the promised land

Architectural history provides many examples of how this fascination with prefab developed and was propagated as a wide speculation on the nature of architecture in an industrial world, while, at the same time, crowding out fundamental assessments of the inherent value and practicality of particular technologies and systems. In many ways, it would be difficult to find a more revealing description of the underlying professional and financial conditions that have motivated not only architects such as Walter Gropius as early as 1909, but the entire housing industry. As Gropius wrote of the issue:

> The reason for the malaise [in housing] is the fact that the public is always at a disadvantage, whether it builds with an entrepreneur or with an architect. The entrepreneur is justly avoided by many, because he unscrupulously hurries projects through in order to save costs, and because he does damage to his client by saving materials and wages in order to increase his own profit. The architect on the other hand who provides designs only is interested in raising the cost of a job, since final cost determines his fee. In both cases the client is the sufferer. His ideal is the artist architect who sacrifices all to aesthetic aims and thereby does economic damage to himself.[15]

Since Gropius wrote these words in 1909, architects have been repeatedly enticed by the promise of prefabricated housing solutions. Indeed, the story of this text, and the influence it has exerted over successive generations of like-minded attempts at prefabrication, have only served to underscore its importance. Gropius made these observations in a pitch delivered in March 1910 to Emil Rathenau, the then president of the German industrial giant AEG, as part of a proposal for a new version of industrialised housing that was based on the mass production of flexible, though standardised, housing. Of the company, Gropius wrote:

> The new Company intends to offer its clients not only inexpensive, well-built and practical houses and in addition a guarantee of good taste, but also take

into consideration individual wishes without sacrificing them to the principle of industrial consistency.[16]

For many years, this text was known only through a reference in Nikolaus Pevsner's 1936 *Pioneers of the Modern Movement*.[17] Later, excerpts of the text were finally published in condensed form in Sigfried Giedion's *Walter Gropius, Work and Teamwork* (1954).[18]

The latter is the most likely source for the generation of post-1939–1945 war architects, including the Australian architect and writer Robin Boyd.[19] Australia, like most other industrialised countries, adopted a large-scale mass-housing programme in the post-war period, and found in Boyd a leading advocate of the promise of prefabrication. With explicit reference to Gropius' foundational study, in his most famous book *The Australian Ugliness* (1960), Boyd wrote:

If the housing industry were to embrace modern factory methods with even half the enthusiasm of the car industry, in no time it would be producing standardized components or space-enclosures of some kind which could be assembled in various ways to suit the needs of each buyer. Gradually the family itself would become the designer of its own pattern of standardized units, as suggested by Walter Gropius as early as 1909, changing them about if necessary as the pattern of the family life developed.[20]

As the passing of time has shown, the enthusiasm of Gropius and Boyd for an architect-designed mass-housing concept was never fully realised. In Australia, despite large programmes for 'prefab' building in the 1950s, today's mass-housing market is dominated by 'project home' companies, who, to the casual observer, appear to have little regard for architect-designed houses or highly industrialised processes.[21] As Colin Davies has described in great detail, the lack of success of Gropius and other well-known twentieth-century architects, including Frank Lloyd Wright, Richard Buckminster Fuller and the engineer Jean Prouvé, up to the polemic of Archigram in the 1960s, has in no way deterred other architects and designers from similar attempts at prefabricated housing.[22] Davies points out that in some cases the reaction to failure has been quite the opposite. The case of Buckminster Fuller is illustrative, where failure in commercial terms was used to highlight creative integrity, and, we might add, created an opportunity to rehearse the wider, familiar values associated with prefabrication that we discussed above.

Gropius is significant in this debate, not only because of his early and insightful views on the potential for the mass production of houses, but because of his continued efforts in the field. Among them are: Toerten Housing in Dessau; the Weissenhof Housing in Stuttgart in 1920s Germany; his copper-plated prefabricated housing for the German industrialist Hirsch Copper and Brass Works in the early 1930s; and finally, and most spectacularly, his work with the General Panel Company with fellow German émigré architect Konrad Wachsmann in the USA in the 1940s.

The General Panel Company is perhaps the most spectacular example because its intended outcome, the Packaged House, had some of the best preconditions to create prefabricated and industrialised building by twentieth-century architects. It boasted a highly talented and influential team, large amounts of private and public funding, and the post-war housing boom that favoured mass-prefabricated housing as it did in Australia. Yet this project ultimately resulted in commercial failure, which perhaps explains why one of the most in-depth treatments of the Packaged House project, Gilbert Herbert's excellent examination of mid-century prefabrication published in 1984, is titled *The Dream of the Factory-Made House*.[23]

There are issues interior to architecture culture that have limited the potential uptake of prefabrication at the scale and modes suggested by architects. Among them are the commodification of prefab architecture mentioned above, predispositions towards a particular visual or formal style of building not widely accepted by the market, and the lack of historical awareness for previous attempts also mentioned earlier. Added to these causes is the frequent confusion around ends and means in regards to prefabrication. We would argue that prefabrication or factory-building is not inherently interesting or valuable in itself, but gains its value when compared to the cost, time and quality benefits offered by prefab construction over other methodologies, such as traditional in situ building. Perhaps the most obvious example of such confusion can be found in the multi-year campaign by *Dwell* magazine to promote the benefits of prefab housing, often using headlines like "Prefab's Promise: Good Design for Everyone" (Apr/May 2005). That many of the houses under review in *Dwell* special editions are beyond the budgets of the mass-housing market, or display conspicuous luxury usually associated with high-end custom-designed architectural commissions, portrays prefabrication as a quality to be desired in and of itself, rather than as a method for making better housing more cheaply.

Apart from such internal problems, there are also more structural issues at play in the cyclical interest in prefabricated housing. In his paper "Some Assembly Required", Martin Bignell has pointed to some of the underlying causes for Australia's staccato attempts at prefabrication.[24] Historically, interest in prefabrication in Australia has been almost universally tied to external needs, such as housing and materials supply shortages, remote working settlements, or episodes of housing need that are bounded by physical and/or temporal conditions, such as those of the Australia's mining industry.[25] Not surprisingly, this interest has tended to coincide with the boom–bust logic of these industries or the particular conditions that engendered them, ensuring no continuity of technique, technology or building experience between the discrete episodes.

Digital and automated fabrication

Over the past decade, architectural culture has become increasingly occupied with the promise of new digital and automated fabrication technologies. With specific regard to the field of prefabrication and industrialised building, many commentators see in these technologies the arrival of a long-sought-after potential to transform prefabricated housing from a generic to a highly tailored building product of the type envisioned by Gropius and Boyd. Whereas mass production previously implied the repetition of identical objects to achieve cost benefits, recent digital and automated production techniques promise individuality with similar cost benefits of mass production. The catchword of this potential is 'mass customisation', its associated production technique is 'file to factory'. Stephen Kieran and James Timberlake's book *Refabricating Architecture: How Manufacturing Methodologies Are Poised to Transform Building Construction* (2004) has played a leading role in both explaining and proselytising this potential.[26] Architecture culture, for the most part, is sympathetic to this movement, because there is a sense that these technologies will change the rules of industry itself and give architects back an agency in building that they have progressively lost. It is around this new technological revolution that familiar stories are being retold.

Despite the considerable enthusiasm for digital and automated fabrication over the past decade, it has yet to be incorporated into the historical narrative of architecture. While the younger generation of architects and scholars (after Kieran and Timberlake) are now steeped in the techniques and technologies of digital fabrication and enthusiastic about the potential it holds for the discipline, as with prefabrication there appears to be a certain amnesia regarding the long history of previous attempts to harness the forces of industrialisation within the architectural project. Take, for example, a later iteration of Gropius' call for a flexible housing system based on advanced manufacturing in 1923:

Human housing is a matter of mass demand. Just as it no longer occurs to 90 percent of the population to have shoes made to measure but rather buy ready-made products that satisfy most individual requirements thanks to refined manufacturing methods, in the future the individual will be able to order from the warehouse the housing that is right for him. It is possible that present-day technology would already be capable of this, but the present-day building industry is still almost completely dependent on traditional, craftsmanly construction methods.[27]

As noted above, practices like prefabrication, modular construction and standardisation have long offered the possibility of a fundamental transformation of architecture's relationship to industrialisation and mass production – the same transformation that Gropius invoked which turned tailoring into ready-made fashion. Both Gropius and Boyd shared the idea that the industrialisation of the design and production of housing would not only lead to improvements in housing, but would also be flexible and adaptable. This is a claim reiterated by Kieran and Timberlake, who, however, feel that modern technology has the potential to finally realise the architectural dream:

We have always customized architecture to recognize differences. Customization ran at cross purpose to the twentieth-century model of mass production. Mass customization is a hybrid. It proposes new processes to build using automated production, but with the ability to differentiate each artefact from those fabricated before and after. The ability to differentiate, to distinguish architecture based upon site, use, and desire, is a prerequisite to success that has eluded our predecessors. With the information control tools we now have we are able to visualize and manage off-site fabrication of mass customized architecture.[28]

As the history of twentieth-century architect-led prefabricated housing illustrates, architecture has tended to co-opt industrial advances to support existing ideologies. But according to Kieran and Timberlake, digital fabrication and automated construction are changing our concept of industrialisation itself, as ideas of mass customisation, free-fabrication, rapid prototyping, small batch and decentralised production are testimony. These ideas promise a deep departure from the mass production of identical objects, revealing an emergent paradigm with which architectural culture seems to have many sympathies. Lars Spuybroek's *The Sympathy of Things: Ruskin and the Ecology of Design* proposes that the combination of new manufacturing technologies, design free-ware and the internet will enable objects to evolve without designers and produce a new nature.[29] This is a form of the familiar naturalism in which architecture continually seeks authority for form-making from technology, but tellingly in Spuybroek's case, this process is supposed to return us to the values of the Arts and Crafts movement of the nineteenth century and William Morris and John Ruskin's suspicion of industrial manufacture having been overcome by the rise of digital craft. So far it appears the excitement over formal possibilities – and punditry about which architectural theory of mass customisation will prove to have been correct – has eclipsed the urge for practical application of these technologies, and thereby echoes the promise of so many mostly failed attempts at industrialisation in the past.

'Mass customisation' and 'file to factory' also carry with them a sense that new technologies will help architects painlessly bypass the problems of the mass production of Gropius and Wachsmann's Packaged House, or Boyd's automobile-industry-inspired call to arms. The repeated invocations for building to imitate the mass production of cars, aeroplanes and ships – invocations repeated by Kieran and Timberlake – not only continue a line of enquiry common in architecture since Le Corbusier's comparison of a modern car with the Parthenon, but also tend to neglect the various changes and challenges the auto industry itself has experienced as it has developed from a craft-based industry towards a modern, automated lean production system.[30] Here, a historical irony is becoming apparent in Australia, with the recent hope that an emergent manufactured housing industry can take up the place of the now departed car manufacturing.[31]

Bifurcation of the prefabricated housing industry

As is pointed out in the catalogue of MoMA's 2008 exhibition *Home Delivery: Fabricating the Modern Dwelling,* several of the observations introduced above have led to a fundamental bifurcation in the prefabricated housing industry: between architect-designed exemplars and the mass-produced housing industry. On the one hand, architect-designed prefabricated housing customarily foregrounds the 'designer' quality of the housing, usually privileging the expression of the materials, techniques and technology used to construct it, and making distinctive aesthetic and formal choices. Such examples are numerous, ranging from the polite Modernism of Gropius and Wachsmann's work with the General Panel Company (1947–1952), to Matti Suuronen's futuristic bubble pod Futuro (1968–1978) and on to Shigeru Ban's neo-modern Furniture House (1995). Architect-designed examples have continued into the twenty-first century using new materials and techniques such as automated and digital fabrication technologies introduced above, which have resulted in a range of solutions: from high-end containerised systems, to branded designs by well-known architects, such as Richard Rogers and Renzo Piano internationally, and Donovan Hill and Fender Katsalidis Architects in Australia.

What does this mean for the future of architectural practice? What implications, indeed, do prefab and offsite construction methodologies hold for the future of the discipline? In attempting to approach these questions, this bifurcation of the prefab housing industry is instructive. Whereas architects have often tended to foreground technique, technology and its expression, the mass-housing developers, on the other hand, have consistently submerged such techniques and technologies with the range of accepted (and often) historicist housing styles. Mass-housing manufacturers, who produce housing in any 'style' broadly accepted by the market, have enjoyed enormous proliferation and commercial success around the world. Many such houses are indistinguishable from their site-built neighbours: from Sears, Roebuck and Co. mail-order kit-houses from the early twentieth century, to post-war mass-produced housing such as Levittown, and on to the mass production of housing in Japan by companies like Sekisui House and Misawa House. As is pointed out in the *Home Delivery* catalogue, manufactured housing in the United States captures a third of the detached housing market, and appears to be "all but impervious to design culture".[32] What these examples and others demonstrate is that technological and commercial innovation need not always have an outward appearance of architectural invention.

This bifurcation of the prefabricated housing industry is a position explained in more depth previously by Davies, who distinguishes the bifurcation as existing between the fields of architecture and construction. Whereas the architecture field has been resistant to industrialisation, the construction industry has been quick to implement broad and sweeping changes to traditional and customary approaches to building. Davies' case in point is the mobile home industry in the United States. He describes in great detail how such exemplars are not only scorned by architects but also by the wider public, evidenced by such labels as 'trailer trash' and 'tornado bait'. But Davies also praises the leading role of this industry – more recently rebranded 'manufactured homes' – for providing low-cost housing for emerging design requirements, for its advances in construction techniques and efficiency, and for the changes it has successfully brought about in the regulatory environment, which has historically provided a barrier to many architect-led design approaches.[33]

Conclusion

It would be false to conclude this chapter with the perception that qualities like novelty, programmatic exploration, formal inventiveness, striking aesthetic choices or conceptual experiments that typically interest architects are, in fact, worthy of scorn. Or, conversely, that an unsustainable and exploitative mass-housing construction industry that continues to produce housing products that have largely evaded any spatial, material or conceptual renewal over the last century is, some-how, praiseworthy. Rather, we point towards the dramatic swings of overreach and technological over-determination on the one hand, and the often insipid and unin-spired approaches to housing on the other. A more moderate example of housing can be found in the polite Californian Modernism of the Eichler houses, which responded to new design requirements and displayed novel and sensible formal and material uses. These houses are of interest in this debate because they offered the market a balance of simplicity, good design and affordability, without the excesses of formal acrobatics, technological triumphalism and experimental expressionism prevalent in many other architect-designed houses. As Steve Jobs wrote of the Eichler houses in his neighbourhood and their formative influence on his sense of design:

> Eichler did a great thing [. . .] His houses were smart and cheap and good. They brought clean design and simple taste to lower-income people. [. . .] I love it when you can bring really great design and simple capability to some-thing that doesn't cost much. It [the clean elegance of the Eichler house] was the original vision for Apple. That's what we tried to do with the first Mac. That's what we did with the iPod.[34]

As many of the books on prefabricated architecture introduced above illus-trate, twentieth-century architect-led designs of prefabrication have placed a high value on inventiveness, often at the expense of innovation, uptake and appli-cation. Most of the examples previewed in the 'prefab' picture books convey a sense of luxury and expense. As Knapp has pointed out, this is clearly part of a broader media apparatus, whose ultimate aim is to "support the commodification of Modernism",[35] but it is also a symptom of a lack of historical understand-ing in architectural culture around previous attempts at prefabrication and at the conditions that make prefabrication of interest to the market in the first place. In attempting to design new versions of prefabricated housing, architects have tended to place an inordinate amount of effort on implementing technology or systems that are often derived from analogous construction industries (cars, aero-planes and ships), and have thus been caught up in a race with a questionable version of progress, and what Herbert referred to as "the Henry Ford syndrome".

Apart from the observations pertaining specifically to the history and future of industrialised building made in this chapter, as Colin Davies has pointed out, pre-fabricated housing also tells us much about the discipline of architecture and the challenges it faces. Issues like tectonics, space and authorship, and architecture's long-held relationship to culture and place, are the bedrock of the discipline, foun-dations that prefabrication and industrialisation, if fully realised, would promise to change irrevocably. But rather than see industrialised building as an inevitable disruptive technology that needs be invested in or hedged against, we should also recognise that architectural discourse has constructed the issues in this way. Architects' dreams of final forms, indeed of an eschatology where architecture will have been proved correct and architects lifted from the damp vagaries of culture into the clear light of socio-economic policy, continue to over-determine the practical issues that the industrialisation of construction is presenting.

Notes

1   Gilbert Herbert, *The Dream of the Factory-Made House: Walter Gropius and Konrad Wachsmann* (Cambridge, MA: MIT Press, 1984): 3.

2   Georg Wilhelm Friedrich Hegel, *Introductory Lectures on Aesthetics*. Trans. B. Bosanquet (London: Penguin, 1993).

3   This is an Australian Research Council Industry Linkage project, entitled "The Design and Construction of Quality, Sustainable and Affordable Pre-Made Housing in Australia: Optimisation and Integration", which began in March 2014 and will run for three years. Some early thoughts on the subjects under discussion are captured in: Mathew Aitchison, "Dongas and Demountables: Four Observations Concerning Prefabricated Housing", *Proceedings of Translation: The 31st Annual Conference of the Society of Architectural Historians, Australia and New Zealand*, Auckland, NZ (2014): 401–11.

4   The term 'settlement' is contentious. The British colonisation of Australia amounted to what we would conventionally call an invasion.

5   See Miles Lewis' articles on the subject: "The Asian Trade in Portable Buildings", *Fabrications* 4 (June 1993): 31–55; and "Prefabrication in the Gold-Rush Era: California, Australia, and the Pacific", *APT Bulletin* 37, 1 (2006): 7–16.

6   Donald Watson, *The Queensland House: A Report into the Nature and Evolution of Significant Aspects of Domestic Architecture in Queensland* (Brisbane: National Trust of Queensland, 1981).

7   Chris Knapp, "The End of Prefabrication", *Australian Design Review,* (October 2013), www.australiandesignreview.com/features/35295-the-end-of-prefabrication (accessed 24 November 2016).

8   Allison Arieff, *Prefab* (Salt Lake City, UT: Gibbs Smith, 2002): 4.

9   Allison Arieff, "Prefab Lives!", *The New York Times*, (23 May 2013), http://opinionator. blogs.nytimes.com/2013/05/23/prefab-lives/?_r=0 (accessed 24 November 2016).

10 Manfredo Tafuri, *Architecture and Utopia: Design and Capitalist Development* (Cambridge, MA: MIT Press, 1976).

11 Le Corbusier, *Towards a New Architecture*. Trans. Frederick Etchells (New York: Dover, 1931). Cf Peter Rayner Banham, *Theory and Design in the First Machine Age* (London: Architectural Press, 1960); Carol S. Eliel, *L'Esprit Nouveau: Purism in Paris, 1918–1925* (Los Angeles, CA: Los Angeles County Museum of Art with Harry N. Abrams, 2001).

12 A selected bibliography of these works includes: Burnham Kelly, *The Prefabrication of Houses* (Cambridge, MA: MIT Press, 1951); Arthur Bernhardt, *Building Tomorrow: The Mobile/Manufactured Housing Industry* (Cambridge, MA: MIT Press, 1980); Herbert, *The Dream of the Factory-Made House;* Arieff, *Prefab;* Colin Davies, *The Prefabricated Home* (London: Reaktion, 2005); and Barry Bergdoll, Peter Christensen, Ron Broadhurst and Museum of Modern Art, *Home Delivery: Fabricating the Modern Dwelling* (New York: Museum of Modern Art, 2008).

13 Arnt Cobbers, Oliver Jahn and Peter Gössel (eds.), *Prefab Houses* (Cologne: Taschen, 2010); Loft Publications (eds.), *Prefab Architecture* (Barcelona: FKG, 2012).

14 For a commentary on Japanese mass-produced prefabricated housing, see Mathew Aitchison, "20 Shades of Beige: Lessons from Japanese Prefab Housing", *The Conversation* (2014). http://theconversation.com/20-shades-of-beige-lessons-from-japanese-prefab-housing-31101 (accessed 24 November 2016).

15   Walter Gropius, "Gropius at Twenty-Six" [Reprint of "Programme for the Establishment of Company for the Provision of Housing on Aesthetically Consistent Principles"], *The Architectural Review* 130, 773 (July 1961): 49.

16   Gropius, "Gropius at Twenty-Six": 50.

17   Pevsner wrote: "In 1909, Gropius worked out a memorandum on standardisation and mass-production of small houses, and on advisable ways of financing such building schemes." In the attached footnote, Pevsner stated: "This was never published. Letter of W. Gropius to the author, 16 Jan. 1936." From Nikolaus Pevsner, *Pioneers of the Modern Movement: From William Morris to Walter Gropius*, (London: Faber & Faber, 1936): 42, 215. See also Herbert, *The Dream of the Factory-Made House*: 32–35, 337n20.

18   Sigfried Giedion, *Walter Gropius, Work and Teamwork* (London: The Architectural Press, 1954): 74–78.

19   Boyd must have had it from Giedion, because Gropius' full text was not published until 1961.

20   Robin Boyd, *The Australian Ugliness* (Melbourne: Cheshire, 1960): 111.

21   For an example of research on the prefabricated housing programme in Brisbane, Australia, see Alfons Vernooy, *The Dutch Houses of Coopers Plains: A Postwar Housing Debacle at Brisbane* (Kelvin Grove: Brisbane History Group, 2004).

22   See Chapter 1 "An Architectural History", in Davies, *The Prefabricated Home*: 11–43.

23   Herbert, *The Dream of the Factory-Made House*.

24   Martin Bignell, "Some Assembly Required: Component and Ensemble in Prebricated Australian Domestic Construction", *Proceedings of Translation: The 31st Annual Conference of the Society of Architectural Historians, Australia and New Zealand* (2014): 425–434.

25   On the issue of contemporary mining accommodation in Australia, see Mathew Aitchison, "The Experience of Australian Mining: Building, Planning, and Urbanization", in *The Architecture of Industry: Changing Paradigms in Industrial Building and Planning*, ed. Mathew Aitchison (Farnham: Ashgate, 2014): 163–193.

26   Stephen Kieran and James Timberlake, *Refabricating Architecture: How Manufacturing Methodologies Are Poised to Transform Building Construction* (New York: McGraw-Hill, 2004).

27   Walter Gropius, "Wohnhaus-Industrie", in *Ein Versuchshaus des Bauhaues* (Munich, 1925), cited in Bergdoll et al., *Home Delivery*.

28   Kieran and Timberlake, *Refabricating Architecture*: xiii.

29   Lars Spuybroek, *The Sympathy of Things: Ruskin and the Ecology of Design* (Rotterdam: V2 Publishing, NAi, 2011). Cf John Macarthur, "Aesthetics Redux. Review of *The Sympathy of Things: Ruskin and the Ecology of Design*, by Lars Spuybroek, Rotterdam, V2 Publishing, NAi, 2011; and *Vital Beauty: Reclaiming Aesthetics in the Tangle of Technology and Nature*, Editors Joke Brouwer, Arjen Mulder, Lars Spuybroek, Rotterdam,V2 Publishing, 2012", *Journal of Architecture* 19, 6 (2014): 1004–1009.

30   For an engaging history of the changes in car production across the twentieth century, see James Womack, Daniel T. Jones and Daniel Roos, *The Machine that Changed the World: The Story of Lean Production – Toyota's Secret Weapon in the Global Car Wars that Is Revolutionizing World Industry* (New York: Free Press, 2007).

31   Jemma Green and Peter Newman, "Building a Housing Industry from the Relics of a Car Industry", *The Conversation* (2014), http://theconversation.com/building-a-housing-industry-from-the-relics-of-a-car-industry-23195 (accessed 14 December 2014); Mathew Aitchison, "A House Is Not a Car (Yet)", *Journal of Architectural Education* 71, 1 (forthcoming).

32   Bergdoll et al., *Home Delivery*: 13.

33   Davies, *The Prefabricated Home*: 69–87.

34   Walter Isaacson, *Steve Jobs* (London: Little, Brown, 2011): 6.

35   Knapp, "The End of Prefabrication".

Part B
Offsite practices

Chapter 6

Offsite construction industry meta-analysis

Industry survey results

Talbot Rice and Ryan E. Smith

Introduction

> Instruments of labor not only supply a standard of the degree of development which human labor has attained, but they are also indicators of the social conditions under which that labor is carried on.
>
> – Karl Marx, *Capital* Vol.1

There are a series of historical events that have propelled the development of prefabrication. Examples include the climaxed development of cast iron in the Crystal Palace built in 1851; prefabricated houses driven by the California Gold Rush in 1848; precut houses, or mail-order houses, developed in the early 1900s; and precast concrete, seen in developments from Thomas Edison in 1908. Post-World War I, parts of Europe, such as Great Britain, Germany, France, and Sweden, experienced a heavy decline in the supply of skilled labor and were thus motivated to explore innovative methods of construction. On the contrary, the US was experiencing an all-time high in construction production. So, the use of prefabrication and the need for construction innovation was not in demand. The historical economic motivation to further develop and adopt offsite methods of construction is further outlined in canonical prefabrication texts.[1]

Today, offsite construction is widely adopted in the US and more present than in any period in history. In the National Institute of Building Sciences 2014 Off-Site Construction Industry Survey, it is reported that 93 percent of all construction industry respondents are using prefabrication to some level.[2] Some reasons for adopting prefabricated practices today are explained by James Timberlake in the foreword of *Prefab Architecture*.[3] First, other manufacturing industries have changed the way their products and services are delivered (i.e. the automobile, shipbuilding, and aerospace industries). Second, the critical difference in these production industries that makes factory production viable is an integrated supply chain. Third, the environmental ethic of the construction and architecture

Figure 6.1
Demand of
construction
versus supply
of skilled labor,
2005–2016
(Credit:
Cumming
Corporation)

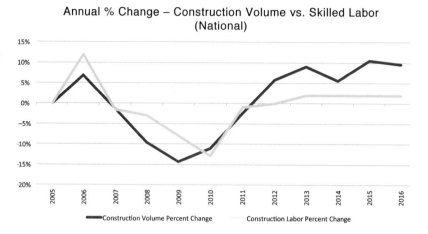

Annual % Change – Construction Volume vs. Skilled Labor (National)

━━ Construction Volume Percent Change   ━━ Construction Labor Percent Change

industries has begun to change. This is especially true since onsite construction has been estimated to waste up to 40 percent of all new products brought to site.[4]

Beyond the reasons above, there are additional causes that contribute to the growth in the use of prefabrication. One of these reasons is the rise in construction demand and a shortage of skilled labor. In Figure 6.1, it is demonstrated that the demand of construction has increased since the recession of 2008, yet the supply of skilled labor to meet that demand has not followed suit. Another reason there has been a rise in the use of prefabrication can be attributed to the development and implementation of BIM, or Building Information Modeling.[5] BIM is used widely in the construction industry to more efficiently plan, design, construct, and manage buildings and infrastructure. The offsite industry is taking advantage of BIM for design to manufacturing interoperability. As such, the prefabrication of construction components and assemblies naturally go hand-in-hand with the benefits of using BIM.

While the emergence of BIM has stimulated the popularity of prefabrication methods, the industry remains reluctant to adopt methods of prefabrication. One explanation is that there is little substantial quantifiable data to support the benefits of prefabrication in construction delivery. To enumerate the claims of prefabrication performance (i.e. cost, schedule, safety, productivity, etc.), there have been efforts to conduct industry-wide surveys and reports. Three recent surveys will be evaluated in this chapter: *Prefabrication and Modularization: Increasing Productivity in the Construction Industry* by McGraw-Hill Construction (2011); *Prefabrication and Modularization in Construction 2013 Survey Results* by FMI; and the *Report of the Results of the 2014 Off-Site Construction Industry Survey* by the National Institute of Building Sciences Off-Site Construction Council. All three publications have their own unique findings, many of which are reinforcing. This chapter is a meta-analysis of the three surveys and provides a summary of each survey and the comparative overlaps.

Surveys

Over the past half-decade, companies and organizations have developed surveys and disseminated resultant reports on the use and practice of offsite construction. The main purpose of these surveys is to identify the key performance indicators associated with offsite construction. The surveys identify barriers and substantiate claims for the industry. The following are summaries of the three surveys in chronological order.

Prefabrication and Modularization: Increasing Productivity in the Construction Industry *(2011) McGraw-Hill Construction*

Intent

The SmartMarket Report team at McGraw-Hill Construction developed this report in 2011. The aim of the report is to provide industry views on prefabrication and modularization and their impact on the construction industry broadly.

Method

This report is the result of an online survey of 809 respondents from across the AEC profession. The survey quantifies the impact of offsite construction on project schedules, costs, safety, quality, and waste reduction. The study also involved 15 in-depth qualitative interviews with owners/developers.

Table 6.1
Key findings from the 2011 McGraw-Hill Construction report

Key findings

Table 6.1 shows the key findings from the 2011 McGraw-Hill Construction report.

Schedule	66% reported that project schedules are decreased. 35% responded that the reduction is by four weeks or more.
Cost	65% reported that project budgets are decreased. 41% responded that the reduction is by 6% savings or more.
Waste	77% reported that construction site waste is decreased. 44% responded that the reduction is by 5% or more.
Usage	63% of those that responded have been using prefabrication methods for five years or more. 85% of respondents are using prefabrication today (90% of engineers, 84% of contractors, and 76% of architects).
	Only 37% have been using prefabrication at a high or very high level (more than 50% of projects).
	Within the building, respondents indicated that prefabrication most often occurs in the building superstructure (27%), MEP systems (21%), and exterior walls (20%).
	To use prefabrication methods, the following are parameters for consideration: job site accessibility (58%), number of building stories (53%), type of exterior (52%).
	Prefabrication is used in 47% of small construction firms, in 28% of medium-sized firms, and in 25% of large firms.
	Prefabrication is used by 22% of small A/E firms, 32% of medium firms, and 46% of large firms.

Barriers	The primary reason that the respondents indicated why they are not utilizing prefabrication methods on some or all of their projects is that the architect did not design them into their projects. (Architects claim that the resistance is from the owners.)
Drivers	The current drivers for utilizing prefabrication methods are as follows: 77% to improve productivity; 66% as a competitive advantage; 51% because it generates greater return on investment; 39% because of owner/client demand.
	34% of respondents indicated that using prefabrication leads to improved site safety, while 56% of respondents indicated that prefabrication is just as safe.
Markets served	The five sectors using prefabrication in over 40% of projects are: healthcare (49%), higher education (42%), manufacturing (42%), low-rise office (40%), and public (40%).

Prefabrication and Modularization in Construction 2013 Survey Results *(2013) FMI*

Intent

The authors of this study believe that the industry is following an impactful trend of adopting prefabrication techniques, sometimes fabrication facilities, into their design and construction practices. The trends identified as driving forces to adopt prefabrication techniques include:

- the constant pressure to lower prices;
- the need to achieve a competitive edge in markets increasingly calling for the use of prefabrication and modularization;
- the lack of, or impending lack of, skilled construction labor;
- the use of BIM, allowing greater coordination of design with construction;
- the need to increase productivity.

Two of the primary drivers of the survey were to identify the barriers to adopting a prefabrication facility and the extent to which prefabrication has contributed to a return on investment.

Method

The survey was sent out to contractors across the field of construction. This included GCs, CMs, MEP contractors, HVAC contractors, and so on. The questions were sent out through email and regular mail to these selected lists.

Key findings

Table 6.2 shows the key findings from the 2013 FMI report.

Usage	48% of MEP contractors accomplished more than 11% of their current project work using prefabricated methods.
	More planning for prefabricated assemblies is taking place in the design phase of construction. 35% of all MEP contractors are planning for prefabrication during design, which is a significant increase from 11% in 2010.
	81% of respondents indicated that they own their own prefabrication facilities. It was also indicated that more contractors are subcontracting prefabricated assemblies, and those who own shops are performing work for others.
	Of those who do not own their own prefabrication facilities, 17% are considering it, which is an increase from 5% in the 2010 survey.
Outlook	12% of the total annual labor hours were committed to prefabrication, but respondents would like that number to rise to 32% in five years.
	61% of respondents thought the use of prefabrication will grow more than 5% per year over the next three years.
	40% of respondents considered their capabilities in prefabrication and modular construction a part of their company's strategic initiative.
Efficiency	Most of the planning for prefabricated assemblies begins in the design phase with few exceptions. Some HVAC/MEP respondents indicated that planning occurred in the preconstruction phase.
	26% of respondents have never analyzed the efficiency of their prefabrication efforts, while only 23% reported that they do so for every project.
Cost	31% of respondents reported that they saved more than 11% on labor last year due to their prefabrication efforts.
	Most respondents indicated that they see a return on their investment within 1–3 years of adopting prefabrication methods.
	Respondents indicated that they expect to save 5–20% by using prefabrication methods.
	67% of respondents indicated that prefabrication labor is less expensive than field labor.
Drivers	The drivers for using prefabrication methods are as follows: 21% to improve construction schedule; 19% for productivity improvements; 14% to have competitive advantage; 10% improved technology allowing for greater use of prefabrication; 10% the shortage of skilled labor at the job site.

Report of the Results of the 2014 Off-Site Construction Industry Survey *(2014), NIBS*

Table 6.2
Key findings
from the 2013
FMI report

Intent

In 2014, the National Institute of Building Sciences (NIBS) Off-Site Construction Council set out to gain an understanding of how the construction sector is using offsite construction techniques by conducting a survey of the building industry.

Method

NIBS distributed the survey through its communications network, the *Building Design and Construction* and *Engineering News Record* magazines sent the survey to their subscribers, and the Association of General Contractors of America sent the survey to its membership. A total of 312 participants responded to the survey. The results demonstrate the current markets, benefits, and barriers. The respondents included construction managers/general contractors, engineers, trade contractors, architects, and owners/developers.

Key findings

Table 6.3 shows the key findings from the 2014 NIBS report.

Cost	Offsite construction has historically not been a lowest-cost solution for project delivery; however, the responses indicate that it is a cost-effective solution.
Collaboration	According to 78% of respondents, offsite construction requires moderately higher or significantly higher levels of stakeholder engagement.
	Comments also indicate that late design changes, lack of collaboration, and an adversarial climate for project delivery lead to difficulties in realizing the benefits of offsite construction.
	The majority of respondents had started collaboration among project stakeholders from design development on; however, all suggested that collaboration must happen before design development and ideally from conception.
	Respondents suggested that there needs to be a moderately or significantly higher level of collaboration on their future projects (39.5% and 37.8% respectively).
Barriers	One of the most significant barriers to implementing offsite construction is transportation, and more specifically, how far away the factory is located from the construction site.
	The most significant barrier, however, to implementing offsite construction is the design and construction culture.
Usage	Respondents indicated that the construction manager (CM) or general contractor (GC) (a combined 57.1%) is the one who most often decides to implement offsite construction. This is followed by designers, including architects and engineers (A/E) (a combined 51.5%), then clients (27.9%) and others, primarily subcontractors (20.9%).
	Precast concrete assemblies are the most used prefabricated element across the respondents, followed by HVAC, plumbing and electrical racks, and steel assemblies.
Benefits	According to the respondents, schedule reductions, quality, and cost-effectiveness were all expected benefits of using offsite construction.
	The three expected benefits above proved to also be benefits of using prefabrication.
Outlook	The respondents anticipated that they will use offsite construction methods the same or more often than they currently do (50% same and 33.2% more).

Table 6.3
Key findings
from the 2014
NIBS report

Meta-analysis

The following is a comparative analysis of all three reports. The overarching goal of this analysis is to identify the extent to which prefabricated methods of construction are used and to identify barriers to their implementation.

Schedule

A common claim among the offsite construction industry is that the schedule is reduced when prefabrication methods are employed. For instance, in modular/volumetric construction, there is a time saving attributed to constructing both the

MODULAR CONSTRUCTION

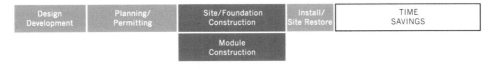

TRADITIONAL CONSTRUCTION

building and foundations at the same time (concurrent scheduling), as shown in Figure 6.2. Each of the reports addresses schedule in a unique way.

In the McGraw-Hill Construction report, it is reported that 66 percent of respondents saw building schedules reduce. About 35 percent of respondents saw a schedule reduction of four weeks or more. Thirty-one percent of respondents found a reduction of 1–3 weeks, while 28 percent of respondents found no change in reduction.

The other two surveys found similar results using a subtler question. In the FMI study, participants were asked to rank the benefits of using prefabrication. The most significant benefit category is "Reducing time to project completion." While this study did not directly ask by how many days, weeks, or months, it does suggest, with such a high rating, that there is a significant reduction in schedule. The NIBS survey asked about the benefits of using offsite construction in a similar way, but instead of a ranking system, the survey asked participants to name the most beneficial aspect of using offsite construction. This aspect is in line with the FMI study naming "Schedule advantage/speed to market" as its top response to the benefits realized using this method of construction.

Figure 6.2 Modular construction versus traditional site-built construction; conceptual schedule comparison

Cost

In the McGraw-Hill Construction report, 65 percent of respondents indicated that their project budgets decreased by employing offsite construction techniques. Twenty-four percent of respondents indicated savings on project budgets of 1–5 percent, 19 percent indicated savings of 6–10 percent, 17 percent indicated savings of 11–20 percent, and 5 percent saw a reduction of more that 20 percent. In addition, only 8 percent of respondents saw an increase in project budgets.

The FMI survey reported on cost parameters by asking questions of labor rates and cost of labor. It was found that 65 percent of respondents saved up to 10 percent of labor costs in the previous year due to the use of offsite construction practices. Thirty-one percent of respondents indicated savings of over 11 percent on the cost of labor. Seventy-three percent of respondents expected to save an average of 5–20 percent the following year. As a follow-up question, it was asked how the cost of field labor compares to that of prefabrication labor; 67 percent of respondents indicated that prefabrication labor is "less expensive." Twenty-seven percent of respondents indicated that it is "essentially the same hourly rate as field labor."

In the NIBS survey, repondents were not asked explicitly about cost savings by percentage or number; rather, we can infer the significance of cost savings from respondents' answers to the question concerning benefits. It was reported that 50.8 percent of respondents indicated that the cost-effectiveness of using offsite construction is a top benefit of this construction method.

Benefits

To continue the discussion on the previous topics of cost and schedule, the FMI and NIBS reports both addressed the benefits of prefabrication.

The McGraw-Hill Construction report did not question respondents on the benefits of prefabrication specifically.

The FMI report, as stated above, provided the participants with a ranking system for the benefits of prefabrication. The participants used a scale of 1 to 10, with 10 as the most beneficial, and 1 as the least beneficial. As a weighted average by highest rank, the highest rated to the lowest rated is shown in Figure 6.3.

The NIBS report asked two questions that target this topic. The first question was to identify the expected benefits of using offsite construction (what drove respondents to use this method of construction?), and the second was to identify the realized benefits of using offsite construction. The results, by percentage of respondents, are shown in Figure 6.4.

Figure 6.3
Ranked benefits of utilizing offsite construction (Credit: FMI report)

The results show that some of the expected benefits were actually met by the use of offsite construction, such as schedule advantage, quality, and cost-effectiveness. It is interesting to note that sustainability goals are rated low as both expected and realized benefits of prefabrication.

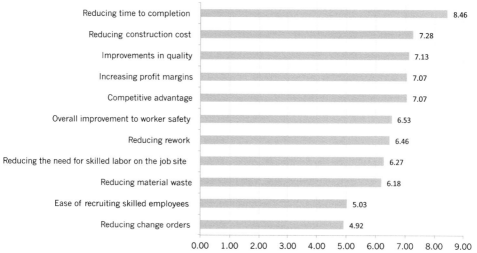

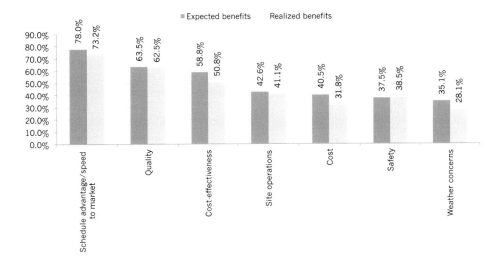

Figure 6.4
Expected
and realized
benefits
of offsite
construction
(Credit: NIBS
report)

To compare these two reports, it is important to note that schedule advantage is ranked highly in both studies, as well as the cost-effectiveness of adopting offsite construction practices.

Usage

The use of permanent modular construction, a type of offsite construction, has been noted by many sources in the industry as having a market share of 3–5 percent of the construction industry.[6] This number has been used since 2011. It is unclear as to what this number would indicate today. In the Modular Building Institute's 2011 *Permanent Modular Construction Annual Report*, the contributors predicted that the market share would double in the following five years.

Although the above market share percentage is for permanent modular construction only, it does shed light on the rest of the offsite construction industry and its market share presence in the field.

In the FMI report, 52 percent of respondents indicated that they are utilizing prefabricated assemblies in up to 10 percent of their projects. Another 32 percent of respondents indicated that up to 20 percent of their projects are utilizing prefabricated elements. Sixteen percent of respondents are using prefabricated assemblies in more that 25 percent of their projects.

In the McGraw-Hill Construction report, 63 percent of participants indicated that they are using offsite construction processes and have been doing so for the previous five years or more. It is important to note that 8–14 percent of engineers and contractors are using prefabricated assemblies in their design and implementation, more than the percentage of architects doing likewise.

The stakeholders who are responsible for selecting and implementing offsite-constructed assemblies into projects are detailed in the NIBS report. Results are shown in Figure 6.5.

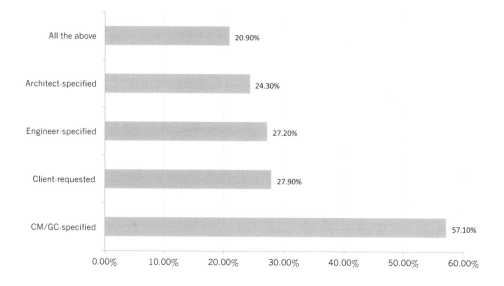

Figure 6.5

Figure 6.5
Stakeholders
responsible for
selecting and
implementing
offsite-
constructed
assemblies in
project delivery
(Credit: NIBS
report)

Outlook

The popularity of prefabrication seems to be growing according to the respondents in all three reports. In the NIBS report, it is noted that 33.2 percent of respondents will be using prefabricated assemblies more often than they are currently. Fifty percent of respondents stated that they plan to use the same amount of prefabricated assemblies. Only 9.4 percent of respondents indicated that they will use prefabricated assemblies less often. See Figure 6.6.

In the FMI report, 74 percent of the mechanical and electrical respondents indicated that the use of prefabrication will grow by 1–10 percent per year for the following three years. Sixty-eight percent of the GC/CM group predicted that

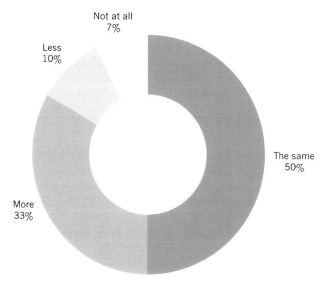

Figure 6.6
Likelihood of
utilizing offsite
construction on
future projects
(Credit: NIBS
report)

the use of prefabrication will increase by the same amount. Twenty-three percent of the mechanical and electrical group of respondents predicted a growth
of more than 10 percent per year compared to 26 percent of the GC/CM
group.

The McGraw-Hill Construction report also indicated that respondents will be
using offsite construction methods more. The level of use of prefabrication on
over 50 percent of projects was expected to increase from 37 percent in 2009 to
45 percent in 2013. It was also predicted that the use of prefabrication by current
non-users would increase immensely, with 87 percent of the current non-users
expected to become users over those next three years. It has, however, not
been verified as to what percentage of these non-users did indeed adopt offsite
construction practices in those years.

Markets served

All three reports note that there are certain market sectors (building types) that
are being served by offsite construction more often than others, as shown in
Table 6.4.

McGraw-Hill Construction report	
49%	Healthcare facilities
42%	Higher education
42%	Manufacturing
40%	Low-rise office (1–4 stories)
40%	Public
37%	Commercial warehouse
36%	K-12 school
NIBS report	
56.9%	Commercial
51.2%	Industrial
44.8%	Healthcare
37.1%	Education
24.4%	Housing multi-family
23.7%	Hospitality
FMI report	
Respondents were only allowed to choose one market sector.	
19%	Commercial
15%	Education
15%	Healthcare
14%	Office
11%	Manufacturing
8%	Hospitality
7%	Industrial

Table 6.4
**Building types
served by offsite
construction
according to
each report**

Drivers

What is the motivation to use offsite assembly? For most respondents, the drivers for employing offsite construction methods include cost and schedule reduction. However, for some, there is a motivation to increase productivity or to decrease waste. Key drivers for using prefabricated methods are shown in Table 6.5.

McGraw-Hill Construction report	
77%	Productivity improvements
66%	Competitive advantage
51%	Generates greater return on investment
NIBS report	
78.0%	Schedule reduction
63.5%	Quality improvements
58.8%	Cost reduction/effectiveness
42.6%	Site operations
37.5%	Safety
35.1%	Weather concerns
12.8%	Sustainability gains
FMI report	
Respondents were only allowed to choose one key driver.	
21%	Schedule reduction
19%	Productivity improvements
14%	Increase profits
10%	Shortage of labor

Table 6.5
Key drivers for utilizing offsite construction according to each report

Offsite elements used

The McGraw-Hill Construction and FMI reports do not include questions related to what type of prefabricated assemblies are used. It is rather important to understand, however, what assemblies are used and to what extent in order for the offsite industry to respond. The NIBS survey shed some light by asking its participants what offsite elements they use. Figure 6.7 shows those results.

Barriers

Just as these are motivational drivers, there will be barriers to adopting offsite construction. Both the McGraw-Hill Construction and NIBS reports address this question directly. The NIBS report findings – based on a weighted average of responses that included "Significant," "Moderate," "Small," and "No Barrier" to implementation – are shown in Figure 6.8.

The McGraw-Hill Construction report approached this subject in a different way by asking two discrete groups, one made up of users and the other of non-users. Table 6.6 shows the percentage of respondents by user and non-user.

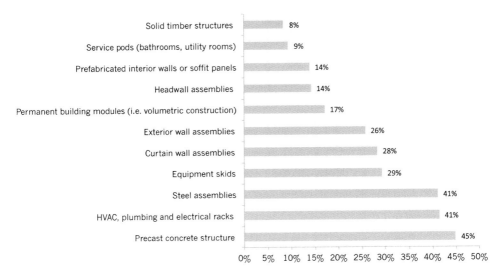

Figure 6.7 **Frequency of offsite products used (Credit: NIBS report)**

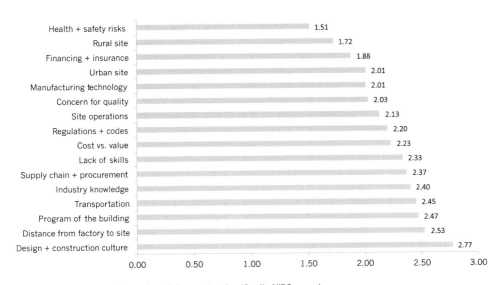

Figure 6.8 **Barriers to implementing offsite construction (Credit: NIBS report)**

The FMI survey did not ask a question on this topic directly; rather, the report includes comments from the survey regarding challenges and hurdles that users have to overcome when using offsite construction. Some of the more reoccurring answers fall into the broad categories listed below:

1. the need for early collaboration/engagement of stakeholders
2. perceptions/stigmas
3. permitting issues

Table 6.6
Barriers
to offsite
construction
by user and
non-user
(Credit:
McGraw-Hill
report)

McGraw-Hill Report – Barriers	Users	Non-Users
Architect did not design for prefab	35%	34%
Owners do not want prefabricated elements	32%	26%
Project type not applicable	30%	34%
Availability of local manufacturing facility	28%	20%
Availability of a trained workforce	19%	
Not familiar with process	18%	34%

4. design–bid–build contract structure
5. design and construction culture
6. labor unions.

Collaboration

The NIBS survey asked when respondents initiate collaboration with key stake-holders with regard to offsite work and when they recommend that such engagement should ideally begin. The results, as shown in Figure 6.9, indicate that most respondents engage with fabricators past the design development phase. This suggests that engagement must begin much earlier to benefit the most from using offsite construction methods. It was recommended that engagement with all stakeholders should begin in the concept phase of a project and before schematic design. The construction methods of prefabrication must be considered when designing and not be treated as an afterthought.

The McGraw-Hill Construction survey did not directly ask questions regarding productivity; rather, the report has key interviews with construction industry leaders. One respondent stated, "Look at contracts and contract language; that's a productivity issue. If you look at the lack of collaboration between designers, engineers, and contractors, that's a productivity issue. Delivery methods are a productivity issue." Additionally, in another interview it was stated, "We use the big room concept. We get everyone in a room to work together rather than launching things back and forth over the fence. We go through weekly schedule meetings and drill down to excruciating detail to see who is doing what and when." This approach to scheduling is not top-down; rather, it sets milestones on the riverbank, then looks upstream at the dependencies between parties and finds common solutions. BIM is used extensively as an integration tool.

The FMI report indicates that its GC/CM group plans for the use of prefabrication mostly in the design phase of a project and seldom in later phases, as shown in Figure 6.10.

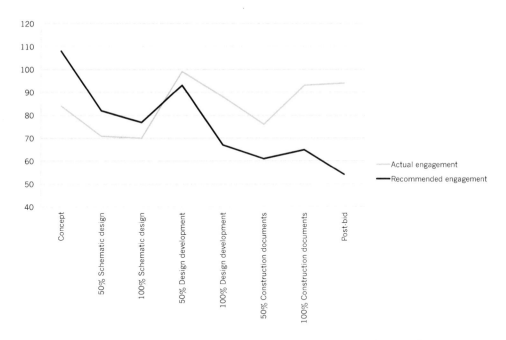

Figure 6.9 **Actual and recommended offsite fabricator engagement versus project phase (Credit: NIBS report)**

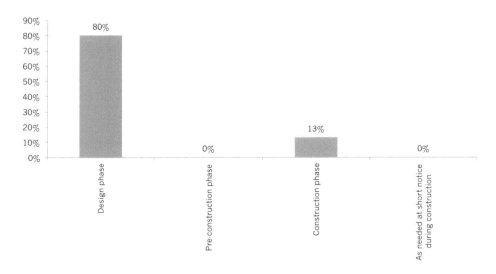

Figure 6.10 **Phase of project delivery at which offsite construction is selected as the production system (Credit: FMI report)**

Conclusions and next steps

These three surveys are positive first steps to gathering data and substantiating the claims of the offsite industry. Cost and schedule savings are among many factors that have a significant impact on the adoption of offsite construction practices for a construction project. While these reports do support some of the industry's claims, there is further work to be conducted to unravel the nuances of offsite construction. For example, in the McGraw-Hill Construction report, 65 percent of respondents found a decrease in project budget and 66 percent of respondents found a decrease in project schedule. However, there were some respondents who found an increase to both parameters (6 percent in project schedule and 8 percent in project budget). It is unclear what portions of the supply chain are contributing to this increase or decrease in cost and schedule. More in-depth analysis of construction performance is needed to clarify the added value of offsite construction given project-specific context and parameters. The Integrated Technology in Architecture Center at the University of Utah conducted one such study, which begins to unfold the subtle nuances in practicing these offsite techniques through case study evaluation (see Chapter 7 in this volume).

Notes

1   Burnham Kelly, *The Prefabrication of Houses*. The Technology Press of the Massachusetts Institute of Technology; John Wiley & Sons, Inc., New York; Chapman & Hall, Ltd., London, 1951; Lewis Mumford, *Technics and Civilization*. Harcourt, Brace & Company, Inc., New York, 1934: Alfred Bruce and Harold Sandbank, *A History of Prefabrication*. Arno Press Inc., New York, 1944; Barry Bergdoll and Peter Christensen, *Home Delivery: Fabricating the Modern Dwelling*. The Museum of Modern Art, New York, 2008; David F. Noble, *Forces of Production*. Transaction, New Brunswick, NJ, 2011.
2   Ryan E. Smith, *Report of the Results of the 2014 Off-Site Construction Industry Survey*. National Institute of Building Sciences Off-Site Construction Council, http://c.ymcdn.com/sites/www.nibs.org/resource/resmgr/OSCC/NIBS_OSCC_2014Survey.pdf (accessed 09.28.2016).
3   James Timberlake, "Foreword: Quality Assurance Quality Control," in Ryan E. Smith (Ed.), *Prefab Architecture: A Guide to Modular Design and Construction*. John Wiley & Sons, Inc., Hoboken, NJ, 2010, pp. vii–ix.
4   Ryan E. Smith (Ed.), *Prefab Architecture*. John Wiley & Sons, Inc., Hoboken, NJ, 2010.
5   McGraw-Hill Construction. *Prefabrication and Modularization: Increasing Productivity in the Construction Industry*, www.nist.gov/el/economics/upload/Prefabrication-Modularization-in-the-Construction-Industry-SMR-2011R.pdf (accessed 11.30.16).
6   Modular Building Institute. *Permanent Modular Construction Annual Report*. Modular Building Institute, Charlottesville, VA, 2011.

Chapter 7

Permanent modular construction

Construction performance

Ryan E. Smith and Talbot Rice

Introduction

Permanent modular construction (PMC) has been marketed as a more cost-effective, higher-quality, and faster-to-market solution than traditional stick-built construction (MBI). The added value of PMC, although conceptually strong, has yet to be significantly substantiated. This research aims to provide data to fill this void. The study quantifies the added value of PMC and evaluates the contextual factors by which PMC in building design and construction may be realized in North America and beyond. The research leverages 17 case studies, listed in Table 7.1, and compares a portion of them to traditional site-built benchmark projects for performance parameters including cost and schedule. The data was collected through literature review, questionnaire, and interviews. In addition, qualitative data was collected to determine the project-contextual parameters that exist to realize success in PMC delivery. Finally, a return-on-investment study is included to demonstrate some of the lifecycle benefits of PMC.

Methods

The case study method

This study utilizes the case study method for investigation. This method is a common strategy in the study of humanities, law, and business (Yin, 2014). More recently, built environment research has used the case study method, by which completed project data is collected and analyzed for generalizable results (Groat & Wang, 2013). The case study project pool was established in consultation with the Modular Building Institute Education Foundation and Canadian Foundation and the National Institute of Building Sciences Off-Site Construction Council. The selection of 17 cases documented was based on:

- access to available archival data and willingness of the stakeholders to participate and offer additional data;
- diversity of project sizes, locations, and building types, in order to evaluate PMC across sectors, countries, and cultures; and

PROJECT	LOCATION
Xstrata Nickel Rim South	Greater Sudbury, ON, Canada
High Tech High	Chula Vista, CA, USA
SOMA Studios	San Francisco, CA, USA
STEM School	Redmond, WA, USA
Nicholson Village	Melbourne, Australia
Old Redford Academy	Detroit, MI, USA
MEG Pirate's Cove Lodge	Conklin, AB, Canada
CitizenM Bankside	London, England
Mercy Hospital	Joplin, MO, USA
Starbucks	Marysville, WA, USA
Victoria Hall	Wolverhampton, UK
Whistler Athletes Lodge	Whistler, BC, Canada
Inwood Apartments (The Stack)	New York City, NY, USA
Manresa Student Housing	Manresa, Spain
Wells Fargo	Phoenix, AZ, USA
Kirkham Child Care Center	San Francisco, CA, USA
The Modules	Philadelphia, PA, USA

- architectural significance, in order to demonstrate PMC performance with respect to buildings that have a greater opportunity for continued cultural investment.

A ranking system considering these three factors was devised and provided a rudimentary process for determining the final list. Data was gathered from the architect, general contractor/construction manager, and modular manufacturer/supplier for the respective projects. For projects where there was not a response from all three parties, at least two were consulted. A questionnaire was developed and peer-review-edited to identify the quantitative data including cost and schedule. This was disseminated online and through PDF response form. Reponses were limited and therefore follow-up interviews were conducted to gather additional and clarifying metric data as well as qualitative information. Limited forthcoming data led to exclusion of some cases in portions of the study. In total, there are ten cases among the 17 that have substantial cost and schedule information. Of these ten cases, seven of them could be compared in schedule and eight could be compared in cost to traditional stick-built construction benchmark projects.

The comparative method

The data from the PMC projects was compared to benchmark projects developed by Cumming Corporation, a cost consultancy firm. Key parameters in developing these benchmark comparisons included the following:

- Data for both the PMC cases and traditional benchmark comparison cases was normalized to first quarter 2014 in US dollars and Washington DC as the building location.

- Units of cost were calculated in $/SF and it was assumed that all of the benchmark projects use a design–bid–build delivery system. When possible, estimates for the comparisons were based on actual items of work. When data was not available, precedent values from other projects were interpolated for these comparative projects.
- Unit costs were based on current bid prices in Washington DC and subcontractor overhead and mark-ups were included. General contractor overhead and profit were excluded.
- The values determined were based on the probability of cost of construction at the programmatic design stage.

For estimating the values to construct the benchmarks, the following sources were referenced: *US Department of Labor Prevailing Wage Resource Book* (US Department of Labor, 2014), *Building Construction Costs with RSMeans Data* (Gordian, 2014), and *Cumming Corporation Internal Economic and Market Report* (Gray, 2014). The items not covered in this comparison included: hazardous material abatement, utility infrastructure improvements, design/consulting fees, building permits, testing and inspection fees, and land acquisition costs.

Comparisons were developed into case study cut sheets, each serving as a stand-alone example of PMC versus traditional building benchmark counterparts. Three examples of case study cut sheets are included in the Appendix.

Limitations

The study has several limitations. The first limitation is the fact that there are few PMC cases to date that have been built relative to traditional construction. The ability to quantify a trend or make a statistical argument is difficult without more cases. Furthermore, the amount of information that was provided for particular projects by stakeholders was also limited. More often than not, participants did not share information such as cost and labor hours. With the small amount of information on the already minimal amount of case studies, it is challenging to report statistically significant results. Regardless, these cases provide timely evidence of project-specific performance.

Results

Quantitative analysis

Cost

It has been claimed that the cost of PMC is less expensive than traditional methods of construction. Further analysis in these cases demonstrates that the cost is not necessarily always lower. In fact, the cost is sometimes at a premium. Overall, the study suggests that PMC projects are on average 16 percent lower in vertical construction cost compared to conventional methods of construction (Figure 7.1).

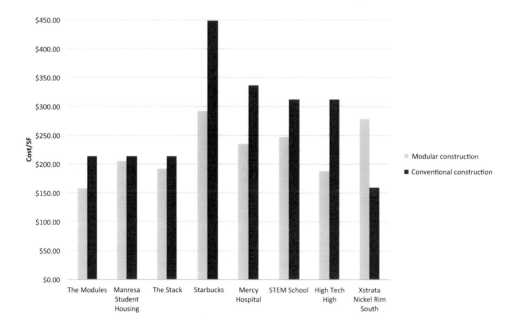

Figure 7.1
Cost of PMC
vertical
construction
compared to
benchmark
projects

It is important to note that most stakeholders reported PMC offers a greater control of cost compared to traditional build. This is attributed to the inherent ability to reduce the number of change orders in any given PMC project. In a recent study conducted in Montgomery County, Maryland, the Office of Legislative Oversight (2014) studied 17 county government projects that reached substantial completion between 2009 and 2013. The study found an 8 percent overall increase in contract costs due to change orders. Respondents concluded that the reason why modular construction is cost controlled is because the design must be nearly complete before modular production, driving the number of change orders down.

When the cost was at a premium, respondents listed the following reasons:

- additional materials required for structure and transport;
- transportation costs for large load permits and lead cars;
- time lost due to permitting;
- time lost due to transportation over long distances.

Schedule

The validity of the industry's claim that schedule reduction is a clear advantage of PMC has been demonstrated by precedent research (Smith, 2011). Across the case studies documented, the schedule was reduced by an average of 45 percent (Figure 7.2). Respondents indicated that this is due to the fact that a PMC project is built in a factory and site work is conducted concurrently. This reduces the lag time compared to traditional methods of construction, according to which onsite built work must be carried out sequentially. The time saved with PMC is also an opportunity for additional cost savings.

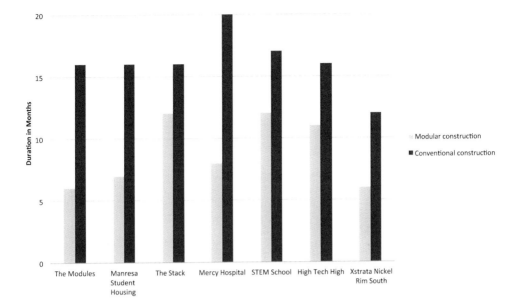

Qualitative analysis

Project stakeholders were asked for qualitative information about a range of issues to get a better understanding of how PMC performs against conventional construction methods. This information is intended to give some understanding of how PMC can be improved.

Drivers

Generally, there is a struggle to turn over construction projects on time and on budget. Based on the case studies, these survey results show that the use of PMC can mitigate cost and schedule challenges. When stakeholders were asked to name the drivers behind their use of PMC rather than conventional construction, the most common response was a motivation to reduce the construction schedule. LeRoy Stevens from Stevens Architects explained why he prefers PMC: "there is an ability to control the hard cost and schedule using PMC." All of the case studies included in this report not only met their construction deadlines but reduced the average construction schedule by an average of 45 percent when compared to traditional construction.

Software

The primary software used by all of the manufacturers, architects, and contractors are 2D drawing programs such as Autodesk AutoCAD. Remarkably, few are using BIM platforms, despite the construction culture software trend.

Figure 7.3
**Software used
in PMC delivery**

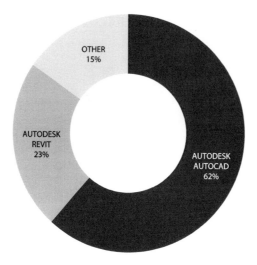

OTHER
15%

AUTODESK
REVIT
23%

AUTODESK
AUTOCAD
62%

Regulatory challenges

Of the six cases that acknowledged the issue of regulatory challenges, three noted that permitting and code issues delayed the project. Permitting and code officials are not familiar with or accustomed to this type of construction so it is imperative to start acquiring approvals and building/transportation permits early. An example of this is the Mercy Hospital in Joplin, Missouri. Because the factory was located in California, 1,500 miles and six states away, this project experienced ongoing transportation problems: "The transportation from California to Missouri was a huge hindrance to the schedule and oftentimes transportation was halted to acquire more permits" (McCarthy Building Company). Further study is needed to determine how a closer factory would impact the transportation and permit costs relative to an even faster construction schedule.

Benefits

The most significant benefit of PMC is its ability to be completed with reduction in schedule. Every survey respondent named meeting the substantial completion deadline as a success. The use of PMC, according to these case study interviews, does not entail a loss of quality compared to conventional construction. All interviewees were impressed with the substantial quality of the PMC buildings.

Early collaboration

The survey asked respondents if the utilization of PMC required earlier collaboration between project stakeholders. Only one respondent indicated that there was no need for earlier collaboration. All other responses indicated that earlier and greater levels of collaboration were necessary. There is a critical point in the project schedule where all major trades need to be well versed in the project's needs and possible mishaps. This point is far before construction begins, as the modules must be completely designed before construction starts. Such an early critical point calls for major trades to either be involved as consultants very early, or under contract from the beginning. While it is still possible to achieve this level of collaboration with a design–bid–build contract, it is very difficult and not as inherently collaborative as its design–build or integrated project delivery counterparts.

The infancy of PMC compared to traditional site building makes for many prototype projects, in which the architect, contractor, and manufacturer are experiencing their first modular build. Because of this, it is likely that the number of PMC buildings will grow exponentially in the coming years. Thorough knowledge transfer between manufacturers, contractors, and architects is crucial to the success of each of these buildings; and the failure of such knowledge transfer seems to be the largest hindrance in the success of PMC. The fast-paced nature of PMC leaves little room for error in permitting and design, both of which can lead to the downfall of the project through change orders. These items must be finalized before construction begins; therefore, the need for all key trades to be involved at the beginning of the project is critical.

It is suggested, based on these case studies, that more collaboration at the beginning of the project would be easier if there was a project delivery method in place that is more conducive to this level of collaboration, such as design–build or integrated project delivery.

Return on investment

Using PMC, the cases in this study reduced their construction time by an average of 45 percent. To put this reduction of time in terms of cost benefit, a return on investment (ROI) method was developed to account for time savings. The ROI leveraged three discrete building type pro-formas from different developers: retail, office, and charter school buildings respectively. The developer data was assessed using a schedule improvement of 25 percent and 50 percent reduction from the actual schedule. This evaluation did not include the financial benefit of early return on operational business such as sales, or social/environmental impacts. The benefits included initial cost savings on general conditions and early lease rate income associated with schedule reductions.

The pro-formas included four sections:

1. the analysis of the schedule based on 0 percent improvement, 25 percent reduction, and 50 percent reduction;
2. the cost of construction;
3. the cost of the construction loan; and
4. the generated income.

Market rate numbers for the ROI were taken from the Newmark Grubb ACRES *2014 Year End Utah/Mountain West Market Report*. The rental income numbers were based on the assumption that the building will be 100 percent occupied, reflecting the greatest possible opportunity for income. The pro-formas show two areas where there is an opportunity for cost savings using PMC. These areas include the cost of the construction loan and the money generated during the time saved.

Retail space

- The retail space at 25 percent schedule reduction shows $5,187 in saved construction loan interest and $29,333 generated in rental income for an effective gross income of $34,520.
- At 50 percent schedule reduction, $10,350 was saved in construction loan interest and $58,666 generated in rental income, giving an effective gross income of $69,017 (Figure 7.4).

Office space

- The office space shows construction loan interest savings of $52,214 and a generated rental income of $292,333 for an effective gross income of $345,547 at 25 percent schedule reduction.
- At 50 percent schedule reduction, $78,147 was saved in construction loan interest and generated rental income was $440,000, giving an effective gross income is $518,147 (Figure 7.5).

Figure 7.4
ROI for an 8,000
SF retail space

8,000 SF RETAIL SPACE - $1.55 M

40,000 SF OFFICE SPACE - $7.66 M

Charter school

Figure 7.5
**ROI for a 40,000
SF office space**

- $29,822 was saved in construction loan interest with a 25 percent schedule reduction. $134,030 was generated in rental income for an effective gross income of $163,852.
- There was a construction loan interest saving of $74,245 with a 50 percent schedule reduction. Adding rental income of $335,074 gave an effective gross income of $409,319 (Figure 7.6).

The average cost saving for a 25 percent schedule reduction across the three pro-formas is $5.81/SF in total construction cost. The average cost saving for a 50 percent schedule reduction across the three pro-formas is $10.93/SF in total construction cost.

Conclusion

Summary of results

The results from these case studies and the comparative analysis of traditional stick-built projects demonstrate that PMC offers the following quantitative benefits (Table 7.2), qualitative benefits (Table 7.3), and return on investment (Table 7.4).

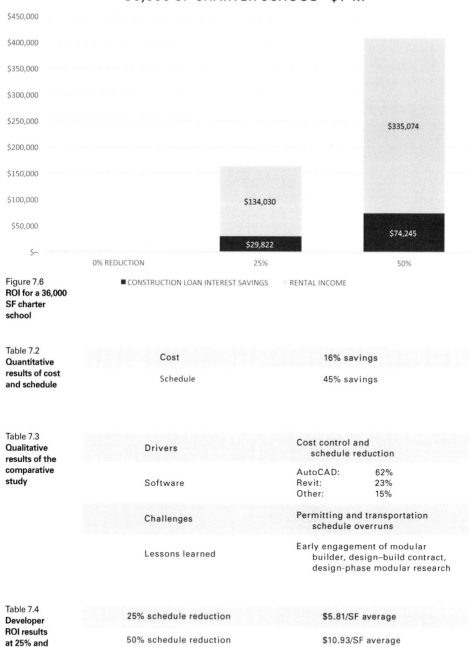

36,000 SF CHARTER SCHOOL - $7 M

Figure 7.6
ROI for a 36,000 SF charter school

Table 7.2
Quantitative results of cost and schedule

Cost	16% savings
Schedule	45% savings

Table 7.3
Qualitative results of the comparative study

Drivers	Cost control and schedule reduction
Software	AutoCAD: 62% Revit: 23% Other: 15%
Challenges	Permitting and transportation schedule overruns
Lessons learned	Early engagement of modular builder, design–build contract, design-phase modular research

Table 7.4
Developer ROI results at 25% and 50% schedule reduction

25% schedule reduction	$5.81/SF average
50% schedule reduction	$10.93/SF average

Market outlook

After the economic downturn of 2008, the demand for construction and the supply of that construction followed suit. Construction demand is high again, yet supply has stayed low and cannot meet demand (Figure 7.7). This presents a gap where modular construction can take advantage due to its lower labor requirements. The time is right for PMC.

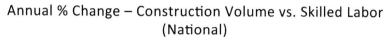

Next steps

This study is limited by the sample size, the scope of company participation, and the challenge of locating appropriate traditional construction comparisons. However, the research findings suggest helpful metrics to be developed by researchers in the future to demonstrate the value of PMC beyond initial reductions to cost and schedule. Although effective as a baseline report, construction performance metrics of cost and schedule do not take into consideration the full lifecycle benefits of offsite modular. This section discusses next steps in this research to demonstrate the performance of PMC.

Figure 7.7
US construction
volume versus
skilled labor –
gap potentially
to be filled
by modular
construction
(Credit:
Cumming
Corporation)

The study took PMC projects and gathered quantitative data for each case through literature sources and questionnaires compiled by project stakeholders. This was followed by qualitative interviews with architects, contractors, and modular manufacturers. The data collected was compared to benchmark case studies by Cumming Corporation, a cost estimation consultant. The benchmark projects were traditional site-built projects completed in the last ten years. Although cost data was normalized so the location factor was similar, it was challenging to find projects that were comparable enough to PMC cases to draw feasible conclusions that demonstrate the performance of PMC.

Identifying a traditional site-built project of similar size in overall square footage, height, and number of stories, and with similar specification is difficult. Peer review of this study suggests that future research should use two comparative methods to determine performance.

Method A

1. Locate a built project whose type is appropriate for PMC. This may include multi-family housing, student dormitory, education, retail, or other.
2. Procure the building's as-built drawings and specifications from the project stakeholder team and their permission to evaluate the project.
3. Obtain three separate bids and construction schedules from PMC builders and partnering general contractors for the project in the same locale as the site-built work, including all vertical construction costs.
4. Compare the actual traditional site-built project to the bid project data for construction performance.

Method B

1. Locate two similar buildings that are going to be built in the near term. Ensure that the buildings are appropriate for PMC, including multi-family housing or office complex, or a corporate retailer or hotel chain that is building the same brand in two different cities (e.g. Starbucks or Fairfield Inn by Marriott).
2. Convince the building owners to build one using traditional stick-built construction and the other using PMC.
3. Document the construction performance data of cost, schedule, safety, labor hours, change orders, defects, and incidents of injury.
4. Interview the project stakeholders including owners, architects, and contractors on each project to gather qualitative data.
5. Compare the site-built project to the PMC project across the construction performance parameters and determine what contextual qualitative factors from the interviews lead to successful PMC delivery.

Acknowledgments

This study was funded by an industry consortium including: Modular Building Institute Education Foundation and Canadian Foundation, Whiting-Turner, Association of General Contractors, PCL Constructors, American Institute of Steel Construction, Triumph Modular. Modular Building Institute members and the National Institute of Building Sciences Off-Site Construction Council provided peer review.

References

Gordian (2014) *Building Construction Costs with RSMeans Data*. Gordian, Rockland, MA.
Gray, S. (2014) *Cumming Corporation Internal Economic and Market Report*. Cumming Corporation, Washington, DC.
Groat, L. & Wang, D. (2013) *Architectural Research Methods, 2nd Edition*. John Wiley & Sons, Inc., Hoboken, NJ. Chapter 12.

Modular Building Institute (2010) *Improving Construction Efficiency and Productivity with Modular Construction*, www.modular.org/marketing/documents/Whitepaper_ ImprovingConstructionEfficiency.pdf 0.03 (accessed April 27, 2015).

Modular Building Institute Website, www.modular.org/HtmlPage.aspx?name=architects (accessed April 17, 2015).

Newmark Grubb ACRES (2014) *2014 Year End Utah/Mountain West Market Report*, www. ngacres.com/public/uploads/1/2015/1/newmark_yearend.pdf (accessed December 1, 2016).

Office of Legislative Oversight (2014) *Change Orders in County Construction Projects,* www.montgomerycountymd.gov/council/Resources/Files/agenda/cm/2014/140403/ 20140403_GO1.pdf (accessed December 1, 2016).

Smith, R.E. (2011) *Prefab Architecture: A Guide to Modular Design and Construction.* John Wiley & Sons Inc., Hoboken, NJ. Chapter 3.

US Department of Labor (2014) *US Department of Labor Prevailing Wage Resource Book.* US Department of Labor, Washington, DC.

Yin, R.K. (2014) *Case Study Research: Design and Methods, 5th Edition.* Sage Publications, Thousand Oaks, CA. Pp. 5–6.

Appendix

Appendix A

MANRESA STUDENT HOUSING
MANRESA, SPAIN

Architect: Xavier Tragant
Modular Builder: Compact Habit
Contractor: Constructora d'Aro

ABOUT

High quality is an inherent attribute of offsite construction. Manresa Student Housing boasts this trait while showing a schedule reduction of 56 percent and a slightly lower cost. PMC was chosen by the investor to meet a hard deadline.

(i) GENERAL   HOUSING BUILDING TYPE

2008 YEAR COMPLETED   **44,239** SQUARE FEET

75 CONCRETE MODULES   **5** STORIES TALL

($) COST   **€3.64M** CAPITAL COST

€231.5K DESIGN COST   **€2.34M** MODULAR CONTRACT

SCHEDULE

10 MONTHS FROM START TO FINISH   **7** MONTHS UNDER CONSTRUCTION   **3** MONTHS FOR DESIGN

3 MONTHS IN FACTORY   **10** DAYS TO ERECT

$204.91 PER SF   **4%** MORE COST-EFFECTIVE

56% FASTER CONSTRUCTION

LESSONS LEARNED

This building was largely a success because of the collaboration of all team members involved. It is an example of how a collaborative team can bring a complex project such as this to a more cost-effective and schedule-saving conclusion.

REFERENCES

Compact Habit.

Images: Compact Habit

	MANRESA STUDENT HOUSING	COMPARED PROJECT
CONSTRUCTION DURATION	7 MONTHS	16 MONTHS
STORIES AND CONSTRUCTION TYPE	5 STORIES CONCRETE	4 STORIES WOOD
SQUARE FOOTAGE	44,239	55,000
COST	$9M	$11.7M
COST/SF	$204.91	$213.33

Appendix B

THE MODULES
PHILADELPHIA, PA, USA

Architect: IS-Architects
Modular Builder: Build IDBS/Excel Homes
Contractor: Equinox Management and Construction

ABOUT

The Modules project is a great example of how PMC can be used to mitigate the costs of labor unions. This building was conceived and built during the recession in 2010. Aside from minor permitting problems and manufacturer difficulties, the project was a great success as it was constructed in only six months.

(i) **GENERAL** HOUSING BUILDING TYPE

2010 YEAR COMPLETED   **80,000** SQUARE FEET

89 WOOD MODULES   **5** STORIES TALL

($) **COST**   **$12.7M** CONSTRUCTION COST

$300K DESIGN COST   **$3.6M** MODULAR CONTRACT

SCHEDULE

14 MONTHS FROM START TO FINISH **6** MONTHS UNDER CONSTRUCTION **9** MONTHS FOR DESIGN

2 MONTHS IN FACTORY **12** DAYS TO ERECT

$158.23 PER SF   **25.8%** MORE COST-EFFECTIVE

135 MILES FROM FACTORY TO SITE   **63%** FASTER CONSTRUCTION

LESSONS LEARNED

PMC served this building well as it was a large factor in the success of the project. A few things could have made the project run faster with fewer setbacks. First, up-front collaboration between the contractor, architect, and modular manufacturer would have avoided the issues of onsite stitching and vapor barrier installation. The up-front collaboration also provides all parties with thorough knowledge of designing and building with modular. Second, to avoid permitting problems, it is vital to decide on the use of PMC early. The nascent nature of PMC gives rise to the importance of starting the permitting and code approval process early. Third, the project team should work with code officials early in the design process. Finally, improvements need to be made to ensure factory-based operations and site operations are clearly coordinated and knowledge is communicated between stakeholders.

Images: is-architects.com/the-modules

REFERENCES
Philips, Brian. IS-Architects. Interview with Talbot Rice on 5.22.14

Wagner, Troy. IDBS

	THE MODULES	COMPARED PROJECT
CONSTRUCTION DURATION	6 MONTHS	16 MONTHS
STORIES AND CONSTRUCTION TYPE	5 STORIES WOOD	4 STORIES WOOD
SQUARE FOOTAGE	80,000	55,000
COST	$12.7M	$11.7M
COST/SF	$158.23	$213.33

Appendix C

THE STACK
NEW YORK, NY, USA

Architect: Gluck+
Mod Manufacture: Deluxe Building Systems
Contractor: Gluck+

ABOUT

In a highly dense urban environment such as New York, it is key to construct a building as fast as possible so that the negative impacts on the surrounding community are at a minimum. Building with modular provided such circumstances for The Stack.

(i) **GENERAL**   HOUSING BUILDING TYPE

2013 YEAR COMPLETED   38,000 SQUARE FEET   8 STORIES TALL

($) **COST**

$5.4M MODULAR CONTRACT $7.3M CONSTRUCTION COST

(🕐) **SCHEDULE**

20 MONTHS FROM START TO FINISH   12 MONTHS UNDER CONSTRUCTION

4 MONTHS IN FACTORY   19 DAYS TO ERECT

$191.84 PER SF   10% MORE COST-EFFECTIVE

125 MILES FROM FACTORY TO SITE   25% FASTER CONSTRUCTION

LESSONS LEARNED

The difficulty in constructing a building with such an accelerated schedule is the collaboration between trades for permits and deadlines. In this building's case, a simple fault in insurance renewal led to a delay in schedule. In the future, there will be more involvement in the drawing, fabrication, and stitching processes. Further, ignoring small details can delay the schedule greatly. Finally, there is a need for thorough communication of information between stakeholders, from fabrication to onsite stitching.

REFERENCES

Gluck, Thomas. Gluck+. Interview with Talbot Rice on 5.27.14

Erb, John. Deluxe Building Systems.

Images: Gluck+ and Amy Barkow

	THE STACK	COMPARED PROJECT
CONSTRUCTION DURATION	12 MONTHS	16 MONTHS
STORIES AND CONSTRUCTION TYPE	8 STORIES STEEL/CONC	4 STORIES WOOD
SQUARE FOOTAGE	38,000	55,000
COST	$7.3M	$11.7M
COST/SF	$191.84	$213.33

Chapter 8

Offsite construction in education

A survey of prefabrication in design and construction academia

Ryan E. Smith, Jonathan W. Elliott, and Kevin Grosskopf

During the fall of 2014, the National Institute of Building Sciences Off-Site Construction Council (OSCC) conducted a survey in partnership member schools of the Association of Collegiate Schools of Architecture (ACSA) and the Associated Schools of Construction (ASC). The online survey was intended to determine the current state of teaching and research on the emerging practice of offsite prefabrication in the design and construction sector. In addition, the council conducted a concurrent industry survey that provided an industry practice-based comparison. This analysis of the data reveals a gap between what is being practiced in the industry versus what is being taught and researched in schools of architecture and construction management. This chapter reports on the findings of this survey to illuminate the difference between what is being practiced within the construction sector and what is being learned and researched at higher-education institutions.

Demographics

The educational survey respondents included faculty who teach in schools of architecture in the US accredited by the National Architectural Accreditation Board and faculty who teach in schools of construction management accredited by the American Council for Construction Education and/or the Accreditation Board for Engineering and Technology. The survey was disseminated through two educational trade associations, the Association of Collegiate Schools of Architecture and the Associated Schools of Construction. There was a total of 177 responses to the educational survey, 73 of which were faculty affiliated with two- and three-year Master of Architecture NAAB-accredited programs. Fifty-one of the respondents represented five-year Bachelor of Architecture NAAB-accredited programs. Forty-five of the responses were from four-year non-accredited Bachelor of Science in Architectural Studies programs. It is important to note that these B.S., B.Arch, and M.Arch programs may in some cases have been at the same institutions. Fifty-three of the respondents were from four-year Bachelor of Construction Management programs and 28 were from two-year ABET- and/

or ACCE-accredited programs. Twenty-eight respondents were from two-year accredited Master of Construction Management degree programs and nine were from four-year Bachelor of Architecture in Engineering programs.

The educational survey did not target an engineering audience, but some respondents represented institutions that offer engineering degrees within an architecture or construction management context. Four respondents were from two-year Master of Engineering programs; two were from two-year Associates Degree in Architectural Technology programs; and two were from two-year Associates Degree in Construction Management programs.

The industry survey was conducted by the National Institute of Building Sciences (NIBS) Off-Site Construction Council in late 2014 to gain an understanding of how the construction sector is using offsite construction techniques. A total of 312 participants representing architects, engineers, construction managers, general contractors, and owners/developers responded to the survey, which was conducted through *Building Design and Construction* and *Engineering News Record* magazines. The results demonstrate the current markets, benefits, and barriers to employing offsite construction. More information on and the results of the industry survey can be found in Chapter 6 of this book.

The responses were geomapped (Figure 8.1) to demonstrate the diversity of geographic regions represented by the respondents. This map does not account for duplicates from one school (more than one professor reporting from a single school). However, the survey did track IP addresses in order to ensure that one respondent did not take the survey multiple times. Because the survey was conducted during summer months when many faculty are away from the university and often travelling, IP addresses located responses from overseas.

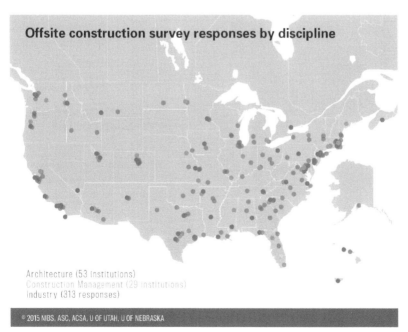

Offsite construction survey responses by discipline

Architecture (53 institutions)
Construction Management (29 institutions)
Industry (313 responses)

© 2015 NIBS, ASC, ACSA, U OF UTAH, U OF NEBRASKA

Figure 8.1
Geomapping by disciplines of IP address responses to the survey demonstrates geographically diverse responses

Frequency of offsite construction

The education survey respondents were sent the definition of offsite construction provided by the National Institute of Building Sciences Off-Site Construction Council:

"Offsite construction" is the planning, design, fabrication, and assembly of building elements at a location other than their final installed location to support the rapid and efficient construction of a permanent structure.

(National Institute of Building Sciences, 2015)

Respondents then indicated the frequency with which they address offsite construction in the classroom:

- 35.59 percent address offsite construction regularly (every year).
- 47.46 percent address it sporadically (when needed on occasion).
- 14.69 percent hardly address it (rarely).
- 2.26 percent never address it.

Of these results, architecture and construction management responses are sorted accordingly:

- 34 percent of architecture schools address offsite construction regularly.
- 66 percent of architecture schools address it sporadically or never.
- 40 percent of construction management programs address it regularly.
- 60 percent of construction management programs address it sporadically or never.

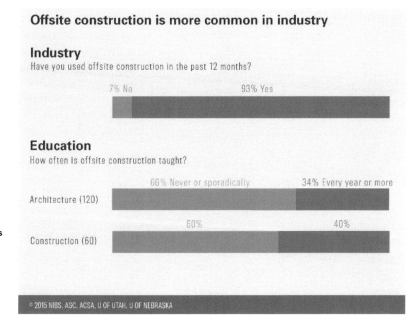

Offsite construction is more common in industry

Industry
Have you used offsite construction in the past 12 months?

7% No   93% Yes

Education
How often is offsite construction taught?

66% Never or sporadically   34% Every year or more

Architecture (120)

60%   40%

Construction (60)

© 2015 NIBS, ASC, ACSA, U OF UTAH, U OF NEBRASKA

Figure 8.2
Offsite construction as it is addressed in education compared to the frequency of use in the building industry

The industry survey found that nearly all of the construction sector respondents are utilizing offsite construction in some form. The survey suggests that 93 percent are employing the technologies. This is in contrast to the majority of architecture and construction management programs, which do not teach it each year. The education respondents who indicated they rarely or never address offsite construction noted that the subject is not relevant to their teaching or research. This disconnect between what is being taught and researched and what is being practiced is disconcerting.

Method of teaching offsite construction education

The education survey asked educators how offsite construction was taught to students. Architecture faculty indicated that students learn about offsite construction in the following venues:

- 58 percent design studios
- 51 percent lecture courses
- 50 percent hands-on design–build
- 33 percent technical courses (i.e. structures, construction)
- 30 percent guest lecturers.

Construction management faculty deliver offsite construction content to students in the following forms:

- 51 percent lecture courses
- 33 percent technical courses

Figure 8.3
The method by which offsite content is being taught

- 32 percent internships
- 30 percent competitions
- 30 percent guest lectures.

The results indicate that there is seemingly heavy reliance upon guest lecturers to deliver offsite construction content. This is likely being delivered by offsite manufacturing companies visiting the universities or students visiting the company factories to learn this content. Respondents in the comments section indicated that architecture students learning about offsite construction through design–build are engaged in the US Department of Energy Solar Decathlon competition, which has multiple student teams design and build a modular house to be set on the Washington DC National Mall.

It is important to note that 58 percent of architecture students receive offsite construction content through design studio. This is the primary required course type that is delivered each semester in an architectural education. In design studio, students apply knowledge from other courses to a building design project. Students in architecture who are exposed to offsite construction are therefore equipped to present this option to the firms in which they will work once graduated.

Offsite construction topics

The education survey questioned respondents concerning what offsite construction topics were being addressed in the classroom. The top combined architecture and construction management answers include what offsite construction is, how to implement it, and why it is important:

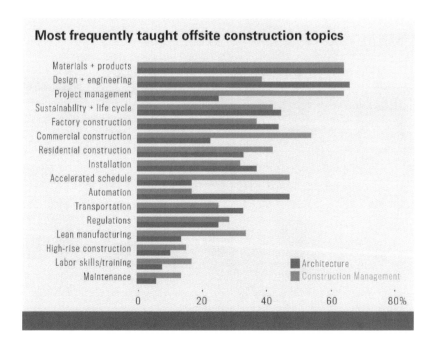

Figure 8.4
The most frequently taught offsite construction topics by discipline

- 64 percent materials, products, and systems – WHAT;
- 56 percent design, engineering, and specification – HOW;
- 44 percent sustainability – WHY;
- 39 percent factory construction processes – HOW;
- 38 percent project management and delivery – HOW.

Additional findings present gaps between education and industry. According to the survey respondents, architecture programs focus on residential offsite construction more frequently than commercial; however, although an accurate statistic of the percentage of residential construction that involves an architect has not been calculated, it is commonly understood that the wide majority of residential construction in the US does not involve an architect. This is because most residential construction in the US is single-family detached housing and does not require an architect by code. This finding may again be attributed to US Department of Energy Solar Decathlon competition or design–build projects, as indicated previously. Transportation is being addressed in 30.86 percent of the case responses. The industry survey suggests that transportation is the primary barrier to offsite construction implementation. Architecture faculty do not teach offsite scheduling with great frequency (20 percent). The industry survey suggests that reduced schedule duration is the most significant benefit realized in practice. Construction management faculty do not teach automation, CNC, and CAD/CAM with respect to offsite construction with significant frequency (20 percent). Automation is already occurring abroad in great measure and beginning to make an impact on offsite manufacture in the US.

Offsite construction typologies

According to the industry survey, the building types most frequently using offsite construction practice include, in order of most frequent to least:

- commercial
- industrial
- healthcare
- education
- multi-family housing
- hospitality
- data center
- single-family housing.

Conversely, architectural educators address the following building types, from most frequent to least:

- single-family housing
- multi-family housing
- commercial
- education

- industrial
- healthcare
- hospitality
- data center.

Construction management education programs address the following building types, from most frequent to least:

- commercial
- single-family housing
- healthcare
- multi-family housing
- education
- industrial
- hospitality
- data center.

This comparison between the industry survey responses and the education survey results demonstrates a significant gap between the building types being taught in schools and the building types utilizing offsite construction in the field. Architectural education has an opportunity to engage in additional building types when offsite construction content is being delivered. First, healthcare has been a leader in offsite methods through mechanical racks and prefabricated bathroom pods. Students should be exposed to these technologies and applications, which are rapidly becoming standard practice. Less time spent on single-family housing

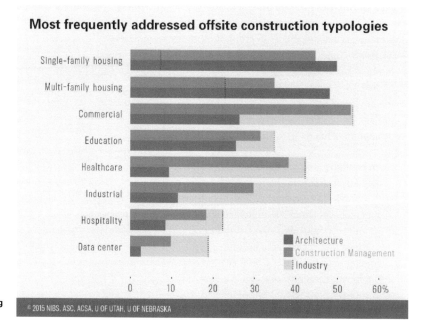

Figure 8.5
Building types taught in relation to offsite construction by discipline, in comparison to industry respondents' use of offsite construction in various building types

Most frequently addressed offsite construction typologies

in architecture and construction management education alike is perhaps warranted as the industry is not utilizing offsite construction for single-family housing in great measure.

The most alarming result of this section of the education survey is that 24 percent of respondents indicated that offsite construction is not applicable to these building types. This suggests that either offsite construction is being taught only as a solution for infrastructure construction such as bridges, roads, water, sewage, etc., or for small structures such as bus shelters, outdoor pavilions, pedestrian bridges, etc., or in fact not being taught at all. For offsite construction to become a mainstream project delivery solution, it needs to be taught in mainstream construction typologies.

Offsite construction product types

The education survey indicates that architecture schools address the following offsite construction product types, from most frequent to least:

- prefabricated exterior walls
- curtain wall assemblies (unitized curtain wall)
- precast concrete
- HVAC, plumbing, electrical
- steel assemblies
- cross-laminated timber (mass timber)
- permanent building modules
- service pods (bathroom/utility)
- prefabricated interior walls
- headwall assemblies
- equipment skids.

Construction management programs address the following offsite construction product types, from most frequent to least:

- precast concrete
- HVAC, plumbing, electrical
- steel assemblies
- equipment skids
- curtain wall assemblies (unitized curtain wall)
- prefabricated exterior walls
- permanent building modules
- headwall assemblies
- prefabricated interior walls
- service pods (bathroom/utility)
- cross-laminated timber (mass timber).

Architectural education is disproportionally teaching prefabricated exterior walls and curtain wall assemblies, as well as cross-laminated timber and service pods, compared to what is being used in industry. This is likely due to architecture's interest in new materials and technologies to augment the aesthetic and experience

Ryan E. Smith, Jonathan W. Elliott, and Kevin Grosskopf

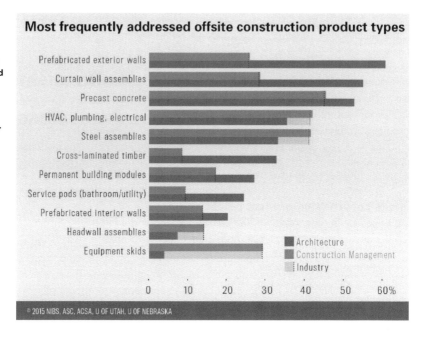

Figure 8.6
**Offsite
construction
product types
being taught in
architecture and
construction
management,
compared to
what industry
is specifying for
projects**

impact of their designs. Construction management educational product types track industry trends fairly closely with regards what industry is implementing.

Offsite construction research

The education survey respondents indicated that the majority of architecture and construction management programs are not researching in the area of offsite construction. When respondents were asked about research topics, the most common answer was that offsite construction was not suitable. For those who are conducting offsite construction industry research, R&D of new products is the most common topic, but is nevertheless addressed infrequently. Compared to the knowledge area needs identified by the industry survey, academics are not generating the data needed for industry to practice offsite construction.

For example, 19.75 percent of educators indicated that they research project delivery methods including design–build and integrated project delivery. Conversely, the industry survey illustrated that the greatest barrier to realizing offsite construction in the future is design and construction cultural challenges. Similarly, only 13.58 percent of educators indicated that continuing education and training is something they offer to the industry. However, industry respondents indicated that training in new methods of construction is one of their greatest needs. Educators are missing an opportunity for professional engagement. Additionally, supply chain management research is needed by the industry but seemingly not addressed by researchers in higher education. Conversely, academia is researching product development for the construction industry; however, the industry respondents indicated that this is a low-value need.

136

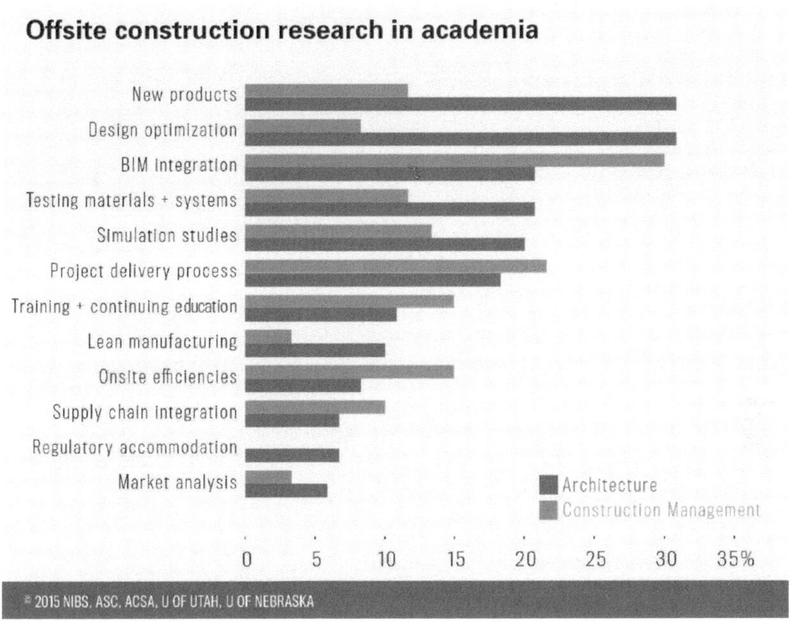
Offsite construction research in academia
New products
Design optimization
BIM integration
Testing materials + systems
Simulation studies
Project delivery process
Training + continuing education
Lean manufacturing
Onsite efficiencies
Supply chain integration
Regulatory accommodation
Market analysis
Architecture
Construction Management
0
5
10
15
20
25
30
35%
© 2015 NIBS, ASC, ACSA, U OF UTAH, U OF NEBRASKA

Figure 8.7 **Research topics addressed in architecture and construction management academia**

Additional resources

Both the industry survey and the education survey indicated that teaching tools and materials for instruction are needed in order to properly convey offsite construction information. Of the modes of content needed for teaching and researching offsite construction moving forward, respondents suggested the following, from most frequent to least:

- 75.14 percent case studies
- 61.02 percent teaching tools
- 60.45 percent financial support
- 58.19 percent guest lectures.

Conclusion

The educational survey collected responses from faculty teaching in accredited architecture and construction management programs in the US. It revealed that there are significant disconnects between what academia is researching and teaching and what industry professionals are currently practicing and requiring in the field. A summary of these misalignments includes the reality that while the construction industry is rapidly moving toward more industrialized forms of building, education is not addressing offsite construction as quickly. In order for the construction sector to progress and adopt more productive means of building, schools of architecture and construction management need to reassume their role as knowledge generators and disseminators.

In addition, there is a misalignment in the building types taught in architecture schools and those used in building practice. Residential is most often addressed in education at the expense of commercial, which is much more common in architects' day-to-day practices. Schedule is not addressed by architecture faculty; however, it is the greatest advantage documented by the industry. Positively, architecture schools address prefabricated exterior walls, cross-laminated timber, and service pods more frequently than the industry practices them, pushing the industry to adopt more sophisticated subassemblies in construction. Automation through CNC will continue to increase in the building industry; however, construction management faculty do not significantly address the topic. Transportation barriers need to be overcome in the industry in order to see prefabrication more widely adopted; however, both architecture and construction management programs are not teaching this topic widely.

Bridging the gap between education and industry is important in order to create knowledge pathways between what is being researched and taught and what is being practiced. Currently, research agendas on both sides of education and industry are mismatched, with schools focusing on product R&D and industry needing continuing professional development and training as well as supply chain management support. Aligning these needs will aid schools in making their instruction relevant and will aid industry in adopting discoveries in research at the universities. Suggestions for how this can be accomplished include university-offered continuing professional development activities, joint research projects, guest lectures from industry in education, co-ops, and internships.

Acknowledgments

This survey would not have been possible without the support of the Construction Management Association of America and the Association of Collegiate Schools of Architecture, who aided in disseminating it to their members.

Reference

National Institute of Building Sciences. 2015. *Glossary of Off-Site Construction Terms.* http://c.ymcdn.com/sites/www.nibs.org/resource/resmgr/OSCC/GlossaryOffSite ConstructionT.pdf (accessed 09.29.2016).

Chapter 9

Onsite vs. offsite

Comparing environmental impacts

John D. Quale

Introduction

Offsite construction manufacturers have often promoted their processes as a sustainable approach largely due to the waste reduction strategies in their facilities. Indeed, the amount of construction waste for a prefabricated building is typically less than that of conventional construction. This is largely due to efficient procurement processes, the convenience of recycling from one facility (in contrast with the difficulties of separating recyclables at onsite construction sites), and the ability of offsite facilities to conveniently reuse some 'waste' material in the next project going down the line.

However, this does not tell the whole story of the environmental impact of onsite versus offsite. In 2008, an interdisciplinary team of faculty members and graduate students from four universities collaborated on the first peer-reviewed study to investigate the actual differences between onsite and offsite methods when it comes to environmental impact. The study was completed in 2011, and published in the *Journal of Industrial Ecology*,[1] and the Thought Leadership and Research Proceedings of the 2011 US Green Building Council's GreenBuild Annual Conference.[2] The team included two life cycle experts, an offsite expert, and a modular construction consultant. Some of the results were a surprise to both the research team and the offsite construction community.

Contemporary building culture has seen a significant growth in offsite construction, including modular buildings, the form of prefabrication that consists of volumetric sections (often rooms) that are transported to a site and assembled into a complete structure. Modular building is utilized for various building types, including single-family homes, multi-family housing, hotels, dormitories, and various commercial and retail structures. The modules are transported to the building site 80–90 percent complete, where they are connected and the finish work is completed. (See Figures 9.1 and 9.2.) In contrast with panelized or component-based methods of prefabrication, modular buildings put many of the interior and exterior finishes in place at the factory, as well as plumbing, electrical, and mechanical equipment. Due to the efficiencies of assembly line fabrication and the fact that modules can be constructed while the site and foundation are prepared, instead of after, modular construction is thought to reduce construction

Figure 9.1
Typical modular single-family home construction, 2008. This image from a modular housing factory illustrates a standard method of modular home construction (John D. Quale)

Figure 9.2
461 Dean Street, Brooklyn, NY, elevations, 2015. This modular housing project was designed by SHoP Architects (John D. Quale)

times by 30–50 percent.[3] Some modular companies also increase their efficiency by producing several modules in parallel, cross-training their employees so there is less down time, reducing worker and machinery transportation, and using "just-in-time" material procurement strategies.

Recent research clarifies that the occupancy of buildings is responsible for a substantial proportion of US energy use and greenhouse gas emissions.[4] It is important to recognize that the amount of energy needed for heating, cooling, lighting, equipment, and appliances typically outweighs the energy demand of other stages of the life cycle of a building, such as construction and the production of building materials. It is likely that the overall relationship between these two categories will change with time as buildings continue to become more energy efficient. Wider implementation of best practices for sustainable construction could see the proportion of environmental impacts from the occupancy of buildings fall sharply. Therefore, as the relative impact of the construction phase of buildings begins to increase, the importance of understanding this impact will also increase. A study by Gustavsson and Joelsson documents that for a highly energy-efficient building, the manufacturing of materials and the construction phase account for 60 percent of life cycle energy consumption.[5]

The size of the modular industry nationally in the US is approximately 2–3 percent of residential construction, with wide variation among regions.[6] Use of modular construction for commercial buildings varies even more widely depending on location and building type. Commercial modular is more common in repetitive housing (dormitories, hotels, or multi-story housing), laboratories, and educational facilities than in other types of buildings.[7]

For both onsite and offsite construction, the site development phase is essentially the same. This includes site preparation, utilities, excavation, and foundation construction. The process of fabricating buildings in a factory requires energy and water, and energy is also required for transporting the modules. However, offsite has potential material, water, and energy efficiencies. This essay is based on a study the author co-authored with four other researchers. Until this study was completed, environmental trade-offs between modular building and conventional onsite construction had not been thoroughly investigated. The study used life cycle analysis to compare these two methods of construction. The research team studied both single-family detached modular homes and a commercial building consisting of 22 affordable housing units organized as 11 attached duplex three-story townhomes as a basis of comparison.

Life cycle analysis (LCA) research on buildings

The majority of LCA research on buildings and construction involves the investigation of energy consumption and greenhouse gas (GHG) emissions.[8] There are also some research projects that have taken on other topics such as water use, habitat disruption, or impacts from emissions and harmful manufacturing processes. Scheuer et al. completed one of the most comprehensive process-based LCAs for an institutional building, finding that impacts of global warming, ozone depletion, eutrophication, and acidification potentials followed the same basic pattern as energy use where the use phase of the building was the dominant source of impact.[9] To date, the published literature indicates that the use or occupancy phase is responsible for the majority of environmental impacts in a building's life cycle. This is especially true for energy use and GHG emissions, but not always true for other impacts. In some cases, the construction phase was found to contribute the majority of impacts for certain impact categories. For example, in a study of residential buildings, Ochoa et al. found that the construction phase contributed 57 percent of toxic air emissions and 51 percent of hazardous waste generated over the building life cycle.[10] Similarly, Junnila and Horvath found that the impacts of producing building materials dominated the release of toxic metals category over the building life cycle and also contributed significantly to smog-forming emissions.[11] The current literature suggests that the construction phase is the second most important phase to investigate when assessing the environmental impact of buildings, although it is possible that that may change in the future.

A variety of construction phase impacts have been investigated. Gangolells et al. found that transportation, water use, energy use, construction equipment, and waste production all had significant environmental consequences, implying that any improvements in these areas could be priority targets for reducing the overall life cycle impact of the building.[12] Research by Bilec et al. revealed that the transportation of precast elements for a concrete parking structure was the most substantial contributor to the environmental burden of the building.[13] A study by Guggemos and Horvath and corroborated by Junnila and Horvath found that the structural frame had the largest impact during construction due in large part to the heavy use of diesel equipment.[14]

Previous construction LCA research had focused mostly on comparing the environmental impacts of various structural systems, with very little emphasis on the contribution of construction methods on these impacts. At the time of this study, a search of English-language literature did not reveal any previous peer-reviewed articles comparing the impacts of offsite construction methods to those of conventional site-built construction. In a review in 2016, it appears that aspects of this team's study have been cited in several articles, although no research team has attempted to take on the same scope to further verify the outcomes. The life cycle impacts of a modular and a conventionally constructed home were assessed by Kim in a study that found transportation energy, solid waste generation, and overall GHG emissions are significantly lower when modular construction is used.[15] However, this study was not peer reviewed, and it did not include actual data from multiple onsite and offsite homebuilders. The author used a number of broad assumptions.

Methods of assessment

This study compared the environmental impacts stemming from offsite and onsite methods of construction. There are obvious differences between these methods of construction, but there are also less obvious, indirect differences that touch other phases of the building life cycle: the creation and transportation of construction materials required, for example. The researchers aimed to capture differences across the life cycle, and therefore the team considered impacts from material production and transportation, offsite and onsite energy use, worker transportation, and waste management. The only other significant stage in the life cycle of buildings is the use phase, which the team omitted because it would vary depending on the design of the building. Design and construction practices and quality vary tremendously, and a modular building is not inherently more or less efficient than one constructed through conventional onsite means. Energy and water efficiency during the use phase fall more into the realm of design and less into the category of construction, assuming the quality of design and construction is similar. Therefore, until a robust, longitudinal survey of energy use in modular buildings is conducted, the team felt it more useful to assume that the construction method for comparable buildings will not affect energy use once occupied, and to examine instead the more certain differences between onsite and offsite construction. The team did not study the end phase either. The demolition or recycling phase is less relevant when it comes to the construction method, although a case could be made that an offsite building could more easily be disassembled and repurposed in a different configuration. This topic should be investigated. However, anecdotally, when Japan, one of the most sophisticated offsite construction cultures in the world, attempted to initiate an offsite home recycling program, they realized that the only realistic and practical scale of material reclaim and reuse was to fully disassemble the buildings.[16]

The first step of the project was to collect construction data for both offsite and onsite construction methods. The team selected several northeastern US modular companies, generally representative of both the single-family home modular industry and the commercial modular industry. The team extensively interviewed them, visited their facilities, and gathered data. The commercial modular industry is substantially different from the modular homebuilding industry. Commercial modular builders work on a much broader array of projects, both in scale and building type. Very few projects are repeated, although many companies will create repetitive units within the same building. They also tend to use more steel and concrete. All the residential modular builders involved in the study offer a line of homes that can be adapted and personalized almost at will. The concept of mass customization is relevant in this context, and means that clients can select everything from finishes to floor plan configuration. The efficiency comes from the consistency of construction methods, and the use of typical details and adaptable configurations.

The modular companies supplied extensive data on a completed project for this study. Most of them included utility bills for their facility, employee home ZIP codes and commuting methods, receipts for building materials, documentation on actual recycling and waste generation, construction schedules, employee schedules, and other relevant information. The multi-story, multi-family affordable housing project was installed in 2009 in the same metropolitan area where the modular company is located. As for the modular homebuilders, the homes were completed between 2007 and 2010.

One of the greatest difficulties in conducting LCAs in the building sector is in proving equivalence between buildings. Buildings are occupied and operated in many different ways, and in general it is difficult to make side-by-side comparisons

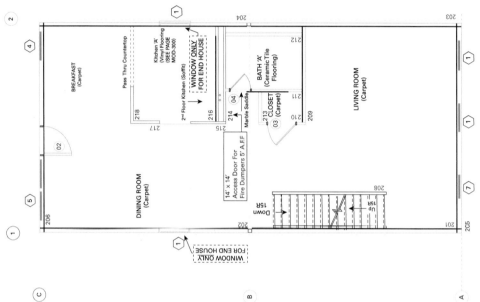

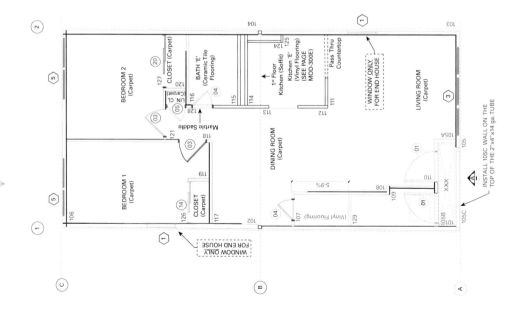

Figure 9.3
Floor plan of the multi-family modular housing project used for the research study (name of modular company withheld)

under the assumption that two buildings provide exactly the same services to their inhabitants. In this study of construction methods, it was a challenge to identify two equivalent structures that had been constructed using the two construction methods. It was not surprising to the team that no such structures were found. In order to work around this precise issue, much of the previous comparative building LCA literature makes use of construction schedule and cost consultants to provide hypothetical construction information on an alternative version of an existing building.

For the multi-family commercial modular project, the research team estimated material and energy use data for a site-built version of the buildings by having a construction consultant create a detailed schedule based on data and documentation for the offsite building. The consultant was provided complete drawings and specifications of the modular building and asked to estimate the construction schedule, equipment and energy needs, and required number of staff and subcontractors, including their commuting information (Figure 9.3). The consulting firm was selected because it has 43 years of experience creating cost estimates and construction schedules in the metropolitan area of the project, and has worked on both modular and conventional construction projects. The firm has often been called on to assess a building design and recommend modular or conventional construction. After speaking with two of the firm's clients and with the president of the firm, we were able to determine that the firm does not have a vested interest in promoting either method of construction. In a process similar to what this firm would do for a commercial client, the consultant documented the specific steps required to construct an onsite version of the building from site preparation through final cleanup, and assessed the differences in materials, energy, and employee transportation. All data for the real offsite building and the hypothetical onsite building were then fed into an LCA model using SimaPro 7.3 software, utilizing the most commonly used life cycle inventory database, US-EI LCI, and the BEES 4.02 impact assessment method.

For the single-family residential assessment, the work was similar. However, due to the availability of more substantial data, and with the information coming from five modular companies in the same region, the data set was more robust. To compare results from the modular companies with hypothetical onsite homes, the team hired three onsite residential contractors to pretend they were building the same home for a client. A survey was created laying out the general steps required to construct a building from site preparation through final cleanup. They were asked to estimate the construction schedule and the required number of staff and subcontractors, including their commuting information. The data from the surveys were divided into the categories discussed above and aggregated by type for analysis. This survey furnished data pertaining to worker transportation and energy for construction. Respondents were asked to estimate the number of days needed for each phase of the job and where those workers would drive during their workday, as well as any external power or equipment needed for the job. Vehicle types and estimated actual mileage were included. The local contractors were selected based on their knowledge of the process of building similarly sized homes in the region. They were provided the construction drawings and

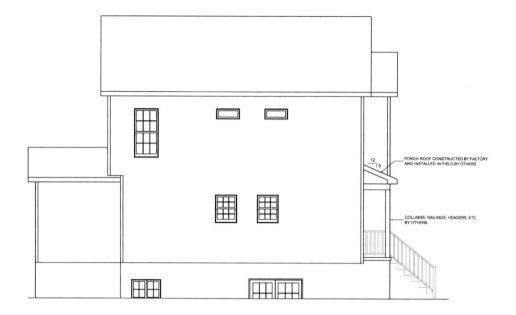

PORCH ROOF CONSTRUCTED BY FACTORY
AND INSTALLED IN FIELD BY OTHERS

COLUMNS, RAILINGS, HEADERS, ETC
BY OTHERS

FACTORY-SUPPLIED/FIELD-
INSTALLED RIDGE VENT

EXTERIOR STAIRS
BY OTHERS

Figure 9.4
**Elevations of
single-family
modular
home used for
the research
study (name
of modular
company
withheld)**

specifications, and were asked to assume their typical subcontractors would be building the home with them.

In onsite single-family residential construction, there is no central facility for which utilities are paid and where workers arrive each day, so a different tactic was needed to acquire the travel data needed. The contractors were asked to use the previous year's climate data and their own budgets, expenses, and financial records for similar projects, as well as human resource documentation, to determine how to include information about energy usage at the contractor's office and at the construction site. Equipment and fuel types were identified, along with the number of hours the equipment would likely be used. Each contractor was also asked to realistically assess the building material procurement process for the majority of their projects. It is not uncommon for contractors to make additional trips to building suppliers or hardware stores to purchase something at the last minute. Modular homebuilders have material delivered to their factory, and will not begin a project until the procurement of all materials is complete. Most of the onsite contractors assumed at least four or five of these trips in their pickup trucks a week.

Analysis and characterization of impacts was conducted on the basis of a standardized functional unit. For the single-family home study, this was a 2,000-square-foot, two-story home that is a production model for one of the companies involved in the study (Figure 9.4). The other factories had a very similar model, so in order to accurately compare across factories, the data from the other companies were scaled to the production of 2,000 square feet of space.

In some ways, the multi-family commercial modular aspect of the research was similar to the single-family. The main difference between the two construction methods is that modular designs used approximately 25 percent more galvanized steel (for commercial) or lumber (for single-family) for structural framing to support the modules during craning and transportation. Building with modular boxes requires additional structure that would not necessarily be included if the building was built onsite (Figure 9.5).

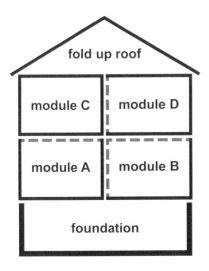

structure required for both modular and conventional construction

- - - - - - -
structure required for modular construction only; this structure can be temporary

Figure 9.5
Schematic diagram of a four-module home showing redundant structure (John D. Quale)

It was assumed that materials were transported either to the factory site or the construction site using the average fuel mix and load factor for US trucks (from US-EI LCI). Similar data were used for the transportation of the modules from the factory to the building site.

Onsite homebuilders typically order materials and products as needed for one building at a time (for the purposes of this study, the surveyed homebuilders assumed the lot was discrete and not part of a larger housing development), and may make many ad hoc trips to building supply stores to procure materials as needed. Conventional homebuilders generally lack sufficient dry or climate-controlled storage space at the construction site to store building materials and have fewer staff to develop efficient procurement strategies. The homebuilders surveyed for this study agreed that an "order-as-you-go" strategy is less efficient and can also lead to additional material and employee transportation impacts. In addition, there is anecdotal evidence that onsite builders routinely order a surplus of 5 percent to 15 percent to make up for wasted material.

In comparing the modular and onsite methods, only those building materials whose amounts differed between construction methods were considered. For example, dimensional lumber for wall framing was included, while doors and windows, which appear identically in both versions of the building, were not. Material types and quantities came from both bills of materials and estimates based on the construction drawings for the building. Based on surveys of contractors, it was determined that the foundation and roof structure would not appreciably differ between the two construction methods.

Offsite energy use data for the modular companies were derived from annual utility bills for electricity and heating fuels, which were converted into energy units and scaled by annual production volumes. Onsite energy use was determined in a bottom-up fashion from the construction schedule estimate. For each job in the schedule, both worker-hours and required equipment were specified. Typical power ratings were then gathered for hand tools, power tools, diesel generators, gas-powered mixers, and other equipment. These power ratings were multiplied by the number of worker-hours for each job to determine total energy use. Based on information from the onsite builders, it was assumed that temporary heating using typical natural gas blowers was assumed eight hours a day during 50 percent of the construction schedule.

The commercial modular companies provided records on employee transportation to the factory site, located on public transport routes. The companies provided data on employees they believed were commuting on public transport, and on those who drove to the faculty. Using that information, onsite construction commuting was determined from the construction cost estimator, who provided a schedule of all workers and assumed an average commute of 22 miles, based on employment records. For the onsite single-family homes, worker transportation was calculated based on data supplied in the homebuilder survey. For each task (interior painting, for example), each respondent was asked to estimate the number of people needed, the number of days to finish the task, and the city of origin of those workers. Round-trip commuting distances were calculated as:

Onsite worker-miles = Round-trip distance × People needed for task × Duration of task in days × 1.5

The 50 percent factor of safety was determined from contractor interviews, as surveys indicated that scheduling delays or tasks that must be repeated are commonplace during onsite construction projects. For example, the plumbing subcontractor may arrive prior to completion by the framing subcontractors or the inspector must make multiple trips to permit various aspects of the project. This parameter is considered later in the team's uncertainty analysis. All onsite worker-miles were modeled as small-truck transportation, except in the cases where large equipment or material was being delivered (such as an excavator for site preparation or a cement truck). In these cases, larger truck sizes were assigned as appropriate and the trucks were assumed to be loaded to 50 percent of capacity for those miles.

In the case of modular construction, worker transportation to the facility was determined using data on where employees live in relation to the factory and the number of workdays per year. Transportation and craning of the modules were also assessed. With the actual commuting distance of each employee, weekly days of work, and an assumption of 50 working weeks a year, total annual worker-miles were calculated as:

Offsite worker-miles = Round-trip distance × Number of employees × Workdays/week × 50 weeks

Using annual production of a factory in total square feet of built area, a normalized worker transportation metric was determined for each company, which was then scaled to the functional unit of a 2,000-square-foot building. It was assumed that miles driven by workers at modular factories were 50 percent by small car and 50 percent by van or truck, based on conversations with the modular companies and photographs of their parking lots.

Recycling and disposal data were gathered from the modular construction companies for drywall, metal scraps, and mixed waste. The onsite cost estimation assumed an average wastage rate of 10 percent, which was adopted.

Commercial modular results

Table 9.1 shows the comparative results between commercial construction methods for GHG emissions, suggesting that modular building has moderately lower impacts overall. The differences are most marked for emissions from onsite energy use and worker transportation. The increase in the amount of steel needed for redundant framing in the commercial modular project greatly increases the materials-related GHG emissions of the project. Energy use for conventional construction is greater than that for modular, even when including the fuel needed to transport the modules from the factory to the building site. This reflects the fairly small delivery radius for the modular company, as well as the reliance of onsite builders on gas-powered generators and diesel equipment. The last significant

COMMERCIAL MULTI-FAMILY HOUSING GLOBAL WARMING POTENTIAL measured in carbon dioxide equivalent (CO₂e)	MATERIALS PRODUCTION	MATERIAL TRANSPORTATION	OFFSITE CONSTRUCTION	MODULE TRANSPORTATION	ONSITE CONSTRUCTION	WORKER TRANSPORTATION	WASTE MANAGEMENT	TOTAL CO₂e
OFFSITE	24,200	227	3,390	365	872	961	38	30,053
ONSITE	22,400	224	0	0	6,980	3,380	38	33,022

Table 9.1 GHG emissions from the commercial modular analysis, 2011. Average results from offsite and onsite construction, using the BEES 4.02 impact assessment method (NIST 2007; Quale et al.)[17]

difference between the two methods is for worker transportation, which is much higher for the onsite case. Again, the modular company's location in a dense metropolitan area means that employees can live close to where they work and have access to public transport.

When considering other types of environmental impacts, however, the results are mixed. While commercial modular construction appears to have fewer impacts for global warming, acid rain formation, criteria air pollutants, smog formation, and ozone depletion, onsite conventional construction has lower impacts for the other categories assessed, including eutrophication, several toxicity metrics, and water use. While the production of building materials remains the largest source of impacts for most categories, energy use in the modular building facility is also a significant source, particularly for the eutrophication and water use categories. This drives the preference toward onsite conventional construction in the LCA results for those two categories.

Single-family residential results

Table 9.2 *opposite* Overall results in various impact categories from the single-family home analysis, 2011. Average results from offsite and onsite construction, using the BEES 4.02 impact assessment method (NIST 2007; Quale et al.)[18]

The analysis for the three modular and five onsite companies reveals that impacts from modular construction are, on average, lower than those from onsite construction, but that there is significant variation within each. For example, Offsite Company 1's GHG emissions were the highest of the three of the offsite companies, and also higher than three of the five onsite companies (Table 9.2). This particular facility is located in a rural area with a commute that is more than twice as long as for the other modular facilities, when normalized for production volumes. This factory also reported higher levels of electricity use than the others and was heated with fuel oil, again leading to increased levels of emissions. On average, however, GHG emissions from conventional construction were about 40 percent higher than for modular construction. Given that the production and transportation of several building materials were omitted from the analysis, as they were identical between construction methods, it is more appropriate to consider the absolute rather than relative difference in GHG emissions, which were found here to be nearly six metric tons of carbon dioxide equivalent (CO₂e) higher for onsite construction, per 2,000-square-foot home. It is important to note again that

SINGLE-FAMILY HOMES

	IMPACT CATEGORY	GLOBAL WARMING POTENTIAL	ACIDIFICATION	HUMAN HEALTH: CANCER	HUMAN HEALTH: NON-CANCER	HUMAN HEALTH: AIR POLLUTANTS	EUTROPHICATION	ECOTOXICITY	SMOG	NATURAL RESOURCE DEPLETION	WATER INTAKE	OZONE DEPLETION
	Unit of Measurement	CO_2 eq	H+ moles eq	C_7H_7 eq	C_7H_7 eq	microDALYs	N eq	2,4-D eq	NOx eq	MJ surplus	liters	CFC-11 eq
OFFSITE	Offsite 1	18,916,847	8,201,640	10,236	28,095,778	2,163	7,652	48,725	151,961	32,271	3,545,617	2.88
	Offsite 2	11,890,024	5,646,300	9,434	24,778,993	1,424	*5,991*	38,542	*105,326*	*21,309*	*3,545,532*	2.83
	Offsite 3	*10,967,100*	*5,048,326*	*8,887*	*23,329,368*	*1,211*	6,014	*33,751*	108,260	21,828	3,545,653	2.79
	Offsite Average	13,924,657	6,298,755	9,519	25,401,380	1,599	6,552	40,339	121,849	25,136	3,545,601	2.83
ONSITE	Onsite 1	*22,508,216*	*14,248,730*	*238,924*	*337,070,760*	3,673	*148,738*	93,126	*180,305*	*54,803*	5,833,206	*9.5*
	Onsite 2	14,363,727	9,254,642	234,931	316,807,249	2,411	146,419	82,132	118,724	34,245	5,818,876	6.42
	Onsite 3	16,186,337	10,067,765	234,676	317,157,036	2,859	146,656	86,072	126,973	38,034	5,817,912	6
	Onsite 4	19,911,804	12,280,798	230,825	303,440,273	*4,070*	146,744	*94,227*	139,353	51,351	*6,225,381*	*2.37*
	Onsite 5	17,236,292	11,877,891	231,987	305,285,143	3,323	146,271	84,118	119,023	45,236	5,950,351	3.8
	Onsite Average	18,041,275	11,545,965	234,269	315,952,092	3,267	146,966	87,935	136,875	44,734	5,929,145	5.62
	MAXIMUM	*22,508,216*	*14,248,730*	*238,924*	*337,070,760*	*4,070*	*148,738*	*94,227*	*180,305*	*54,803*	*6,225,381*	*9.5*
	MINIMUM	*10,967,100*	*5,048,326*	*8,887*	*23,329,368*	*1,211*	*5,991*	*33,751*	*105,326*	*21,309*	*3,545,532*	*2.37*

NOTE: *BOLD ITALICS INDICATES MAXIMUM OR MINIMUM*

this difference is likely to be modest compared to the emissions associated with building occupancy, but also that the relative importance of construction impacts will increase as the use of buildings becomes more efficient.

Differences in the materials needed for the two construction methods did not significantly affect results, largely due to the fact that the additional dimensional lumber needed to give structural support to the modular units during transportation was nearly equal to the extra lumber needed to make up for wood scraps typically generated during onsite construction. Material transportation and waste management were also small contributors to overall GHG emissions. Energy use onsite and worker transportation to the site were the most important categories for GHG emissions from conventional construction, which is intuitive as both represent direct combustion of fossil fuels. Therefore, reducing unnecessary worker trips, idling of equipment, and temporary heating through effective management practices remain the most important goals of the low-carbon construction of homes.

Uncertainty associated with selected input parameters is shown in the error bars of Table 9.2. There is moderate overlap between the sets of modular and conventionally built homes, and a much larger uncertainty range for the latter set, which reflects the sensitivity of the overall results to assumptions of temporary heating and redundant worker trips.

Table 9.2 also shows impacts from each construction stage for the other impact assessment categories included in the BEES 4.02 methodology. The distribution of impacts among construction processes for most other impact categories is similar to that of GHG emissions: onsite construction has higher impacts (20 percent to 70 percent) than modular construction, with factory and onsite energy use being the primary drivers of impacts.

As seen in Table 9.2, modular construction has fewer impacts, on average, than onsite construction for all environmental impact categories, although again the uncertainty associated with these values is significant. Examining the three modular and five onsite homes individually, the home from Offsite Company 1 has high impacts relative to the other modular homes, stemming in part from its rural location, as explained above. Onsite Company 1 home has low impacts relative to the set of conventional homes. In this particular case, the contractor who supplied the information in the study worked with a local crew and so reported relatively short distances for worker transportation to the construction site, which is a major driver of impacts for most categories. This contractor also reported lower consumption of all fuels and electricity onsite than reported by other contractors. The variability of the responses serves to highlight the site- and company-specific nature of this study, as well as the potential for error in drawing general conclusions from single building case studies.

The environmental benefits of a compressed construction schedule for modular construction are implicit in the model inputs, as they were scaled to annual production volumes, but still bear discussion. This analysis assumes energy inputs averaged over the year; however, location and time of year will significantly affect the results for each of the two construction methods, particularly as they will determine the number of heating-degree days needed both for the modular factory and for temporary onsite heating.

Commercial modular buildings tend to have more energy-intensive structural materials (steel, aluminum, and concrete, as opposed to wood), and therefore the additional structural material required for modular construction may have a more significant impact. In addition, there is greater variety in the percentages of construction completed offsite for commercial or institutional modular projects compared to single-family residential projects.

Uncertainty

Several of the input parameters used here are significantly uncertain and their associated error was calculated for each factory and building site. The percentage of uncertainty was estimated and propagated for onsite waste generation (+/– 25 percent), transportation distances to the modular facility (+/– 25 percent), onsite ad hoc trips (+/– 25 percent), and onsite temporary heating (+/– 25 percent). Uncertainty associated with the choice of emissions factors, the contractor surveys, and human error in reporting is certainly present, but is not considered here.

Conclusions and suggestions

Based on this research, it is clear that both modular and conventional construction could be improved when it comes to reducing environmental impacts. Construction and worker transportation impacts, while lower for modular, could clearly be improved in both methods. It should also be noted that modular factories (both commercial and residential companies) are typically located in uninsulated high-bay industrial buildings that often need to be heated or cooled year round for employee comfort. Weatherizing and insulating their own facilities would substantially reduce the embodied energy of the buildings created by these companies. As for conventional contractors, the use of more efficient strategies for onsite heating, cooling, and energy generation would reduce impacts. Other strategies to be considered include more efficient building material procurement procedures, strategic scheduling of subcontractors, the use of portable renewable energy systems, and carpooling.

It appears likely that the amount of time required for onsite work plays an important role in assessing the impact differences between modular and site-built. Commercial modular companies can provide everything from mostly complete modular rooms to small modules for bathrooms and kitchens integrated into buildings that are otherwise conventionally built. The results indicate that the shortened schedule is the primary advantage of modular construction, and if smaller components that require more onsite construction time are used, it is likely to increase environmental impact.

Note

This chapter combines and expands upon content from two peer-reviewed articles and a white paper the author co-authored with Julie Zimmerman, an Associate Professor at Yale University; Matthew Eckelman, an Assistant Professor at Northeastern University; Kyle Williams, a former Yale and Stanford graduate student, and currently the Conservation Director at Athens Land Trust in Athens, Georgia; and Greg Sloditskie, Principal at MBS Consulting in Walnut Creek, California.

Acknowledgments

This research project would not have been possible without the time commitment made by the onsite and offsite construction company employees who participated. Partial funding for this study and chapter was provided by the University of Virginia School of Architecture, the University of New Mexico School of Architecture + Planning, and a grant from the Modular Building Institute (MBI), a commercial modular industry trade association. MBI made suggestions to the research team for companies to contact, but none of these companies provided data used in the research. University of Virginia graduate students Rachel Lau and Emily McDermott and University of New Mexico graduate students Victoria Cousino and MhD Alaa Eddin Arar also contributed to the research.

Notes

1   Quale, J., M.J. Eckelman, K.W. Williams, G. Sloditskie, and J.B. Zimmerman. 2012. Construction matters: Comparing environmental impacts of building modular and conventional homes in the United States. *Journal of Industrial Ecology* 16(2): 243–253.

2   Quale, J.D., M.J. Eckelman, K.W. Williams, G. Slotidskie, and J.B. Zimmerman. 2011. Two recent life cycle analysis (LCA) studies for buildings: on-site versus off-site construction and building material reuse. *GreenBuild Thought Leadership and Research Proceedings*, US Green Building Council Annual Conference.

3   Smith, R. 2010. *Prefab Architecture: A Guide to Modular Design and Construction.* Wiley, New York, NY.

4   US DOE: EERE. 2008. *Energy Efficiency Trends in Residential and Commercial Buildings.* United States Department of Energy, Washington DC.

5   Gustavsson, L. and A. Joelsson. 2010. Life cycle primary energy analysis of residential buildings. *Energy and Buildings* 42(2): 210–220.

6   Hallahan Associates. 2011. Personal communication with Fred Hallahan, Principal.

7   Modular Building Institute. 2011. *Permanent Modular Construction 2010 Annual Report.* Modular Building Institute, Charlottesville, VA.

8   Ortiz, S., F. Castells, and G. Sonnemann. 2009. Sustainability in the construction industry: A review of recent developments based on LCA. *Construction Building Materials* 23(1): 28.

9   Scheuer, C., G.A. Keoleian, and P. Reppe. 2003. Life cycle energy and environmental performance of a new university building: Modeling challenges and design implications. *Energy and Buildings* 35(10–11): 1049–1064.

10 Ochoa, L., C. Hendrickson, and H.S. Matthews. 2002. Economic input–output life-cycle assessment of US residential buildings. *Journal of Infrastructure Systems* 8(4): 132–138.

11 Junnila, K. and A. Horvath. 2003. Life-cycle environmental effects of an office building. *Journal on Infrastructure Systems* 9(4): 157–166.

12 Gangolells, M., M. Casals, S. Gasso, N. Forcada, X. Roca, and A. Fuertes. 2009. A methodology for predicting the severity of environmental impacts related to the construction

process of residential buildings. *Building and Environment* 44(3): 558–571.

13 Bilec, M., R. Ries, H.S. Matthews, and A.L. Sharrard. 2006. Example of a hybrid life-cycle assessment of construction processes. *Journal of Infrastructure Systems* 12(4): 207–215.

14 Guggemos, A.A. and A. Horvath. 2006. Decision-support tool for assessing the environmental effects of constructing commercial buildings. *Journal of Architectural Engineering* 12(4): 187–195.

15 Kim, D. 2008. Preliminary life cycle analysis of modular and conventional housing in Benton Harbor, Michigan. Master's Thesis, School of Natural Resources and Environment, University of Michigan.

16 Personal communication with Professor Shuichi Matsumura, University of Tokyo, Department of Architecture, 2010.

17 Quale, J., M.J. Eckelman, K.W. Williams, G. Sloditskie, and J.B. Zimmerman. 2012. Construction matters: Comparing environmental impacts of building modular and conventional homes in the United States. *Journal of Industrial Ecology,* 16(2): 243–253.

18 Ibid.

Chapter 10

High-performance affordable modular homes

A university and modular industry collaboration

John D. Quale

As the modular housing industry in the US continues to recover after the great recession, it has become increasingly focused on sustainability. The concept of a low-energy modular home is gaining traction, with companies like Unity Homes, Blu Homes, Method, and LivingHomes offering high-performance models. These carefully designed homes are finding buyers willing to spend more money to get a home that uses less energy, and therefore costs less to operate.

However, it is low-income families who experience the most substantial benefit from the reduced energy costs of a high-performance home, especially those that qualify for subsidized affordable housing. Low-income families often pay more than 30 percent of their household income on housing costs (rent or mortgage payments, utilities, insurance, and other housing-related expenses). Anything over 30 percent of household income puts these individuals and families in the category of cost burdened, and over 50 percent is defined by the federal government as severely cost burdened.

Projections that appear in a 2015 report prepared by the Joint Center for Housing Studies at Harvard University and Enterprise Community Partners indicate the number of severely burdened US households will increase from 11.8 million in 2015 to 20 million by 2025. As of 2013, almost 50 percent of renters fell into the cost-burdened category, roughly double the percentage in 1960. In 2013, slightly more than 25 percent of renters were severely cost burdened, which is also twice the percentage from 1960.[1]

Financially, modular housing has advantages over site-built homes. One aspect of this is the shorter construction schedule for modular homes compared to site-built, which reduces the carrying costs. In addition, the material and labor costs are generally lower due to efficient procurement processes and the fact that many modular construction employees are trained in more than one trade. When comparing modular vs. site-built homes using the same materials and specifications, the cost differences can vary from 10 to 25 percent. This kind of cost saving is particularly important for affordable housing projects, because non-profit affordable housing organizations are often working with a schedule and budget defined by the type of funding used to finance the project. In addition, the typical cost overruns one might find with a site-built home are eliminated with modular, or at least minimized. This is because the procurement process occurs at the beginning of construction, not continuously throughout the construction phase. In general, it is fair to say that a modular home, with as much 85 percent built off site, is more predictable when it comes to schedule and budget.

Pushing the boundaries of high-performance affordable

The ecoMOD project is a research and design/build/evaluate initiative, focused on high-performance new modular homes as well as energy-efficient renovations of existing homes. The project was founded at the University of Virginia in 2004, and moved to the University of New Mexico in 2014.[2] Since the beginning, interdisciplinary teams of students and faculty have created a series of highly energy-efficient affordable housing units (see Figure 10.1). All phases of the projects are embedded in the curriculum and structured to maximize the educational opportunities. To date, over 470 students (and about a dozen faculty members) have helped to create a total of eight modular housing units on six sites. Once occupied, student evaluation teams monitor and evaluate the homes carefully, with the results guiding subsequent designs. The current version of the ecoMOD project is a partnership between various academic departments, including architecture, civil engineering, construction management, law, landscape architecture, planning, historic preservation, and management. The goal of the project is to provide a valuable educational experience, while demonstrating the environmental and economic potential of prefabrication and renovation. ecoMOD teams work

Figure 10.1 ecoMOD South, South Boston, Virginia, 2013. Late stage of onsite construction for two of the ecoMOD South homes, Passive House standard home on the left, and house built to code on the right. Trent Bell Photography

directly with affordable housing organizations to ensure sustainable housing is no longer a luxury reserved for the wealthy.

The project teams strive to address the two most important challenges facing the next generation of designers: the significant environmental impact of the built environment, and the growing economic divide between high-income and low-income individuals. The projects have been recognized nationally and internationally as a model for sustainable architectural and engineering education, and have won over 30 major awards for design or curriculum.[3]

The evaluation phase is structured to monitor and analyze completed housing units. It is essential to the project because it can contribute to building both confidence and humility in students. The evaluation teams typically assess the environmental impact, efficiency, affordability, and occupant satisfaction of each housing unit. The monitoring systems deployed by the engineering teams often measure indoor and outdoor air temperature and relative humidity, as well as electricity, gas, and water usage.

The University of Virginia, and now the University of New Mexico, have registered the copyrights for the designs of the completed homes. Since the beginning, the intent was to allow affordable housing organizations to benefit from the convenience of getting a high-performance home delivered for a reasonable construction cost. By taking the ecoMOD designs into production, our intent is to give affordable housing organizations quick, well-designed, low-cost, and sustainable infill housing options that cost less to operate.

Background

In the summer of 2011, the Tobacco Indemnification and Community Revitalization Commission (TIC Commission) of the Commonwealth of Virginia approved a $2.45 million research and development grant for the ecoMOD project (shared with another UVA project, focused on post-disaster transitional housing). The ecoMOD half of the grant was structured to create a collaborative partnership between ecoMOD, a modular homebuilder, a structural insulated panel (SIP) manufacturer, and two non-profit organizations to create a commercially viable high-performance modular home design. Both commercial partners and both non-profit organizations are in small towns in southern Virginia within the footprint of the TIC Commission. The majority of the funding was provided to the non-profit and commercial partners for materials, new technology, and training.

Known collectively as the ecoMOD South team, the partners decided to commercialize one of the ecoMOD project's previous homes, ecoMOD4, completed in 2010 for Habitat for Humanity of Greater Charlottesville. The original house was a two-story, two bedroom home with just over 1,000 square feet, and is home to a refugee couple from Afghanistan. It has a donated photovoltaic array, which, when combined with a well-insulated and carefully air-sealed building envelope, allowed the designers to target net-zero energy. The home has achieved several months of net-zero living, although not consistently. It is believed that the energy habits of the homeowners, and the fact that the construction budget did not allow for high-performance windows, contribute to energy use that is slightly higher than anticipated. However, the home's energy use remains substantially lower than a comparably sized conventional home in the area.

Cardinal Homes was the ecoMOD South modular homebuilder. Cardinal is located in Wylliesburg, a small rural hamlet in the south central part of Virginia, known as Southside. Wylliesburg is close to South Boston, Virginia, where two of the three ecoMOD South homes are sited – next door to each other. The non-profit partner in South Boston is Southside Outreach, an organization with substantial experience in affordable housing in the region. The third home is sited in the small town of Abingdon in southwestern Virginia. Located in Washington County, the non-profit partner in Abingdon was People Inc., a large community action agency.

The collaboration with Southside Outreach and People Inc. was productive. The most significant challenge the research team faced working with these two experienced affordable housing non-profits is the fact that they are quite different from each other. Southside Outreach consists of two full-time staff and a community board. Despite their limited size and resources, they have been able to have a significant impact on the communities they serve. In addition to developing new affordable housing, they also repair and renovate housing, and offer educational programs to help clients learn how to prepare themselves for homeownership. They work in six counties in Southside, and have been in existence for 20 years.

By contrast, People Inc., 50 years old in 2014, is one of the largest community action agencies in the nation. It currently counts 12 counties in southwestern and northern Virginia as primary service areas, with an additional 11 counties in southwestern Virginia as secondary areas. Affordable housing is just one of their interests. The organization has over 200 staff members, and runs a wide variety of programs. Examples include efforts to support elder care, child daycare, preschool and head start programs, after school programs, tutoring, community development, business development and financing, consumer loans, weatherization and repairs of homes, transitional housing, Section 8 housing, health care, dental care, court-appointed special advocates, domestic violence support programs, drop out prevention programs, and workforce development programs of various types.

The towns of South Boston and Abingdon were both established in the late 1700s. The populations of the two cities are the same (approximately 8,000 people in each), yet their character is substantially different from each other. Located on a flat, low-lying area along the Dan River, South Boston was one of the important hubs for the tobacco trade in southern Virginia. It is about 300 feet above sea level, and is prone to flooding. Abingdon, at almost 2,000 feet about sea level, is sited in the foothills of the Blue Ridge Mountains in the far southwestern part of Virginia. While hard to imagine for most Virginians, it is located further west than the Midwestern city of Detroit. Long considered a trading post for travelers and local settlers, Abingdon is now a local tourist destination, with an emphasis on outdoor activities and Appalachian arts and crafts.

The climate data for the two cities is somewhat similar. They each have average annual high temperatures in the high 60s and lows in the 40s, with similar precipitation. However, the important climatic difference is that due to Abingdon's higher elevation. On average, it gets four times as much of its precipitation in snow compared to South Boston.[4]

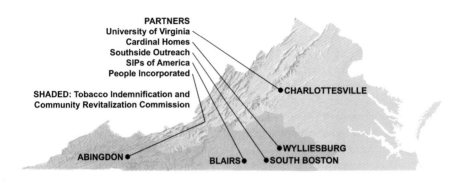

UNITED STATES	VIRGINIA	CHARLOTTESVILLE	ABINGDON	SOUTH BOSTON
POPULATION: 311,591,917	POPULATION: 8,096,604	POPULATION: 42,475	POPULATION: 8,183	POPULATION: 8,102
RACE/ETHNICITY: 78.1% White 13.1% Black 5.0% Asian 16.7% Latino/Hispanic	RACE/ETHNICITY: 68.6% White 19.4% Black 5.5% Asian 7.9% Latino/Hispanic	RACE/ETHNICITY: 70.7% White 19.1% Black 6.8% Asian 5.1% Latino/Hispanic	RACE/ETHNICITY: 93.8% White 3.1% Black 1.0% Asian 2.6% Latino/Hispanic	RACE/ETHNICITY: 46.2% White 50.2% Black 0.6% Asian 2.3% Latino/Hispanic
BELOW POVERTY LINE: 13.8%	BELOW POVERTY LINE: 10.3%	BELOW POVERTY LINE: 27.1%	BELOW POVERTY LINE: 22.2%	BELOW POVERTY LINE: 25.5%
MEDIAN HOUSEHOLD INCOME: $51,914	MEDIAN HOUSEHOLD INCOME: $61,406	MEDIAN HOUSEHOLD INCOME: $42,240	MEDIAN HOUSEHOLD INCOME: $33,525	MEDIAN HOUSEHOLD INCOME: $28,692

Figure 10.2 ecoMOD South partners, locations, and demographics. Information from the 2010 US Census and www. dataplace.org

The differences in the demographics is likely related to the differences between a city built on tobacco in an era of slavery versus a city that was once on the edge of the frontier. The differences in income level between the two are related to industries in each town. Poverty is clearly a concern in both cities (see Figure 10.2).

Design phase

The first important design decision was determining how to ensure the ecoMOD South homes would be truly high performance. Three previous ecoMOD homes (two modular, one rehab) had achieved a Platinum certification in the US Green Building Council's Leadership in Energy and Environmental Design (LEED) system. ecoMOD South is based on one of those houses, ecoMOD4. Rather than aiming for another LEED Platinum for a similar house, we felt we needed to stretch ourselves and target another standard. We wanted a standard that rigorously addressed energy efficiency to ensure the design would significantly reduce the utility bills for the occupants. We did not want to include renewable energy technologies, preferring to address the challenge with design, not technology. That decision eliminated the idea of a net-zero home, which typically includes some form of renewable technology. In the end, we selected the Passive House (PH) standard, which is exclusively focused on minimizing energy utilized for heating and cooling the building. The standard is simple to describe and easy to understand conceptually, but is very difficult to achieve, especially for a home that would arrive on site in large chunks.

To make the design challenge even more difficult, we wanted to build more than one home – so we could measure and compare performance. We decided to create designs for two identical versions of the PH home, and to site one of them in South Boston and the other in Abingdon. The South Boston PH home is rented to low-income individuals and the Abingdon PH home is also rented out, but will eventually be purchased by low-income homeowners. A third house was designed and constructed to look exactly the same from the outside, and was placed next door to the PH unit in South Boston. Serving as the "control" in this experiment, the insulation, window specifications, air barrier, and mechanical systems of this "code unit" were designed to go no further than meet the basic energy requirements of the standard building code. The performance of all three homes is being monitored, and in the end, there will be an assessment of the return on investment of the added cost to achieve PH standard.

The TIC grant-funded effort was not directly integrated into the curriculum in the same way as the previous design/build/evaluate efforts, although students contributed to some aspects of the work, including the development of the monitoring system. The majority of the work was completed by a design and research team of former students acting as paid research assistants, three of whom had previous experience with ecoMOD.

Figure 10.3
**ecoMOD4,
Charlottesville,
Virginia, 2010:
front façade.
Scott Smith
Photography**

Figure 10.4
ecoMOD South,
South Boston,
Virginia, 2013:
front façade.
Trent Bell
Photography

The design process took considerably longer than originally anticipated. With the schematic design from the original ecoMOD4 home already in place, the team assumed a relatively straightforward process to add a third bedroom. However, during the simulation of the design to achieve PH standard, it was decided to increase the size of the home to four bedrooms. The decision was intended to improve the ratio of exterior surface to interior volume, which increased the overall energy efficiency in the PH simulation. Three of the bedrooms are on the second floor, and one is fully accessible and on the first floor. The house looks almost the same as the original from the front (see Figures 10.3 and 10.4).

It took a full year and a half to adapt the ecoMOD4 design to become the ecoMOD South four-bedroom, 1,800-square-foot home. In addition to the redesign process, the team critiqued the materials and construction processes used in the original, and spent many months researching material choices, construction details, landscape design strategies, and PH modeling and creating simulations of energy use, air flow, heat gain, daylighting, and thermal bridging (see Figures 10.5 and 10.6). The effort was led by the ecoMOD Director, working closely with the research assistants. Three other faculty members with expertise in engineering, landscape architecture, and building simulation participated as well. A PH-certified consultant managed the PH modeling process, and a PH-certified engineer designed the mechanical system.

One of the most difficult challenges was the need to adjust the design of the building envelope to respond to the PH standards. This required close collaboration with Cardinal Homes to understand their typical construction process, so that adjustments could be made. All the partners agreed on the goals of achieving high-performance housing on a limited budget, but not surprisingly, the difficulty was in finding a shared understanding of the meaning of "high performance" and "limited budget." In the end, the team had the opportunity to extend the grant period to ensure we could come up with the best possible project within the budget available.

Over time, the ecoMOD South team, working with the PH consultant, researched a wide variety of insulation and air-sealing ideas, glazing specifications,

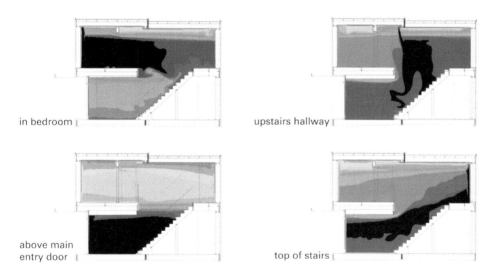

Figure 10.5 **Early ecoMOD South mechanical airflow studies. Michael Britt**

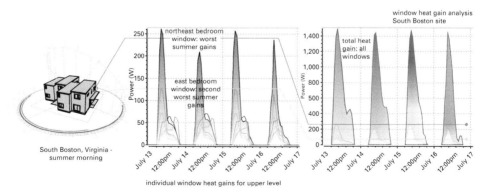

Figure 10.6 **Early ecoMOD South heat gain studies. Michael Britt**

and building materials. A particularly difficult challenge was testing the PH design variations on both sites. Fairly often, a small change to a detail or material selection meant the design would fail to achieve PH certification in the simulation at one site but not the other. This issue was complicated by the fact that the designs are identical, but the sites are not. The orientation of the Abingdon home is rotated 170 degrees from the two homes in South Boston. The designers had to ensure the proper balance of glazing (for heat gain) and insulation (for heat flow resistance) on all facades.

For Southside Outreach, the ecoMOD South initiative was an important project and consumed a significant percentage of staff time. For People Inc., ecoMOD South was just one of many housing initiatives that they are working on. The Southside Outreach staff and the housing team at People Inc. know each other well, and had even partnered on a project in the past. Yet, the team worked with the two organizations in very different ways. The team made sure to understand not only the differences in administrative processes, but also the unique interests and preferences of each organization. The two PH homes are exactly the same for the two organizations, but the methods of financing the community partner's portion of funding, and individual size and configuration preferences, led to a compromise design and required a unique working process for both.

The first serious attempt at cost estimating the project was an important moment. The team discovered that the construction budget was not sufficient. Initially the team was planning on creating four homes – two units built as an attached duplex for each of the non-profit partners. The budget for the grant, created several months before, was not based upon actual construction costs for these homes, but on what seemed to be the maximum request to the funder. Since the estimate was roughly 30 percent over budget, the research team suggested simply eliminating one of the homes. The site that People Inc. had selected in Abingdon was proving to be too narrow for the two-unit duplex, and changing to a single-family detached home also made more sense in that urban context. Southside Outreach was willing to change to two single-family homes, and actually would have preferred that from the beginning. Another upside of this significant change is that it helped to clarify the research questions. Rather than dealing with the ambiguity of townhomes, which at that stage were assumed to have structural insulated panel (SIP) construction in one home and a double-wood-stud wall in the other, the research team was pleased to have the clarity of two PH homes of exactly the same construction on two separate sites, as well as a code unit that looks the same. The variables had been reduced and clarified, and the evaluation of the performance of the homes will more clearly document the advantages and disadvantages of the PH standard for affordable housing in the mid-Atlantic region.

From the beginning, the team sought certification under the PH standard, while remaining limited to an affordable housing budget. The portion of the grant funding available for construction allowed the housing organizations to exceed their typical budget compared to a similarly sized home. This allowed for the integration of very high-performance glazing in the windows and doors, as well as an upgrade to the typical air barrier/vapor retarder products. The total cost of modular production of the PH units is about $105/SF, with the code unit coming in about

$70/SF. This does not include site and landscape costs, which vary considerably due to radically different topographic and site conditions. The Abingdon PH home is infill housing in a somewhat dense urban context on a very steep lot, with a much more expensive foundation and little opportunity for landscape development. The PH home and code unit in South Boston were placed on a mostly flat empty lot, with 13 more adjacent lots that have been zoned and may someday be filled by other ecoMOD designs.

These per-square-foot costs, while higher than similarly sized affordable housing in Southside and southwestern Virginia, are in line with the affordable housing market in the rest of the state, including central Virginia and the Richmond area. They are also below the cost of similar affordable housing in most of northern Virginia near Washington DC. Therefore, the homes are unlikely to be duplicated by these partners as PH homes, but there is clearly a market to sell them as PH units to housing organizations in other parts of the state, as well as to affordable and market-rate homebuyers throughout the state and region. The ecoMOD project, recognizing its inability to achieve a truly PH design that can be replicated for

Figure 10.7
ecoMOD Ranch exterior rendering. ecoMOD Ranch team

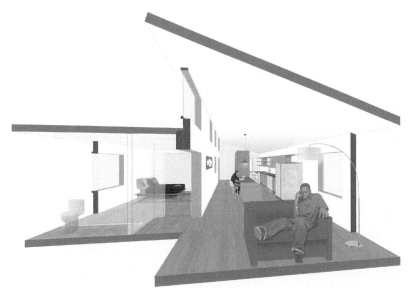

Figure 10.8
ecoMOD Ranch interior rendering. ecoMOD Ranch team

double 2x4 stud wall - separated

r-value (thermal resistance through clear wall) = 42.3

TECHNICAL	Low Maintenance:	How often does the assembly require maintenance?
	Well-Established Technology:	Does the assembly use a well-established technology?
	Constructability:	Is the assembly easily constructed?
	Labor Force Compatibility:	Is the labor force prepared to install this material?
	Emerging Technology:	Is the material using emerging sustainable technologies?

SOCIAL	Educational Opportunities:	Will the use of the assembly provide educational opportunities?
	Occupant Health:	Will the assembly avoid negative health impacts?
	Local Development:	Will the use of the assembly contribute to local economies?
	Modular Commercialization:	Does the assembly support prefabricated commercialization?

| FINANCIAL | Low Initial Cost: | What is the cost of the overall assembly, including labor? |
| | Return On Investment: | Do the projected savings yield a return on the initial investment? |

ENERGY	Low Embodied Energy:	What is the embodied energy of the assembly?
	Insulating Properties:	How does the wall assembly perform?
	Locally Produced-Structure:	How far away are the structural components produced?
	Locally Processed-Insulation:	How far away are the insulation components processed?

| ENVIRONMENTAL | Ethically Produced: | Is the assembly ethically produced in regards to the environment? |
| | Low Toxicity: | Does the assembly avoid the use of toxic materials? |

10 inch structurally integrated panel (sip) wall

r-value (thermal resistance through clear wall) = 50.5

TECHNICAL	Low Maintenance:	How often does the assembly require maintenance?
	Well-Established Technology:	Does the assembly use a well-established technology?
	Constructability:	Is the assembly easily constructed?
	Labor Force Compatibility:	Is the labor force prepared to install this material?
	Emerging Technology:	Is the material using emerging sustainable technologies?

SOCIAL	Educational Opportunities:	Will the use of the assembly provide educational opportunities?
	Occupant Health:	Will the assembly avoid negative health impacts?
	Local Development:	Will the use of the assembly contribute to local economies?
	Modular Commercialization:	Does the assembly support prefabricated commercialization?

| FINANCIAL | Low Initial Cost: | What is the cost of the overall assembly, including labor? |
| | Return On Investment: | Do the projected savings yield a return on the initial investment? |

ENERGY	Low Embodied Energy:	What is the embodied energy of the assembly?
	Insulating Properties:	How does the wall assembly perform?
	Locally Produced-Structure:	How far away are the structural components produced?
	Locally Processed-Insulation:	How far away are the insulation components processed?

| ENVIRONMENTAL | Ethically Produced: | Is the assembly ethically produced in regards to the environment? |
| | Low Toxicity: | Does the assembly avoid the use of toxic materials? |

Figure 10.9 **ecoMOD Decision Analysis Tool (DAT). A sample of DAT used to assess one of several wood wall systems for ecoMOD South. Michael Britt**

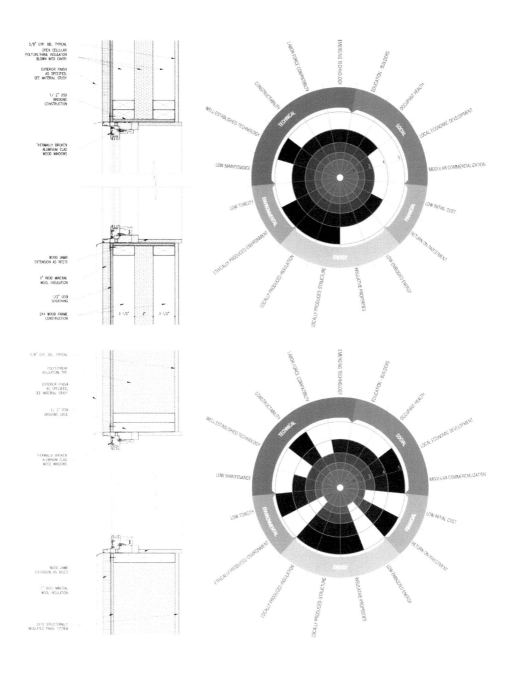

these two partners in their primary services areas, offered a design studio and engineering seminar in the fall of 2012 to design lower-cost, one-story, Energy Star-rated homes that will meet the necessary budget for future affordable housing development in South Boston and Abingdon. Cardinal Homes will be able to sell both the ecoMOD South PH and non-PH design, as well as these one-story home designs, called ecoMOD Ranch because they are a reinterpretation of the standard American ranch house (see Figures 10.7 and 10.8).

Across the street from the South Boston homes, there are six two-story apartment buildings (approximately eight units per building) that are owned by the same non-profit partner, Southside Outreach. Another ecoMOD team completed a schematic design for energy upgrades and aesthetic improvements to these buildings. The ideas were handed over to a professional architecture/engineering firm from the South Boston area.

Making decisions

For the UVA research team and the staff of Cardinal Homes, the design process was an important educational opportunity for both sides. The ecoMOD South team had to learn about the normal process of designing, engineering, and building a home with Cardinal Homes (each modular homebuilder is somewhat different), and the Cardinal staff were exposed to innovative building materials they had not previously procured, and learned how to build a modular home to meet PH standards. Early in the collaborative process, it became clear the expectations on both sides did not align with each other. Cardinal was used to operating as a for-profit company that provides a service to a client. The ecoMOD team was expecting a collaborative research lab experience, while Cardinal was looking for clear-cut direction from the UVA team. Once this misalignment of expectations was identified, both sides were able to adjust and find a process that was mutually agreeable.

One of the most difficult challenges of working collaboratively is making decisions. Among the individuals involved in this complex project, there are a wide variety of backgrounds, priorities, and responsibilities. This topic has been a difficult challenge since the founding of the ecoMOD project in 2004. The very first ecoMOD team struggled with making decisions and developed a decision-making process that involved a research database, and the use of spider diagrams to allow the team to visualize their priorities. This process helped the team to ensure that all relevant research on any individual decision was being discussed, and also helped them to set priorities when it came to selecting design strategies, building materials, and technologies. These diagrams became known as "Decision Webs" among the ecoMOD teams over the years. The points of the webs were organized into six major categories: Energy, Environmental, Social, Financial, Aesthetic, and Technical. As a system of graphic representation, Decision Webs allowed for the quick appraisal of several components at once, and provided a concise statement of values to be handed to the community partner, or to the next design team if the project was stretching across semesters. Two ecoMOD students, who later got married, used the webs to make a decision about purchasing a new car, and jokingly referred to Decision Webs as their method for choosing their first child's name.

One of the unexpected benefits of using paid research assistants to help run the ecoMOD South project (rather than students in design studios and engineering seminars) was the further development of Decision Webs into a much more sophisticated database and ultimately a web-based tool that can be shared with others. The ecoMOD South research team developed an online database system to collect information on construction materials, partner surveys, design strategies, and equipment, as well as a web interface that can generate diagrams to use in discussions. The tool, known as the Decision Analysis Tool and nicknamed DAT, is a graphic system that represents information, major categories, sub-categories, and scoring data in a terse radar graph format (see Figure 10.9).

The driving goal for the development of the ecoMOD DAT was to accumulate research on sustainable building components, and display this information in an accessible way. Comparable tools include the Pharos project, organized by the Healthy Building Network, which aims to increase product transparency by providing a score according to several "impact categories" to explain information to consumers, and Arup's SPeAR diagram, a propriety application used by Arup consultants to clarify sustainability priorities with their clients. Besides the unique graphic interface that the team has developed, the DAT differs from these precedents in that it can be adapted to any decision or situation. Already it has been used to assess the values of the different partners in the ecoMOD South project, and to evaluate complex components such as wall systems. Additionally, it has been utilized in a couple of public meetings to help visualize the priorities of the members of the audience.

Build phase

After months of research, design, collaborative decision making, cost estimating, and material procurement, the ecoMOD South project finally went into production in late December 2012. Once on Cardinal's shop floor, the work progressed quickly (see Figures 10.10 and 10.11). The obvious advantage of offsite construction is that the modules were under construction in Cardinal's manufacturing facility while the house foundations and site work were underway simultaneously. Minor problems arose – mostly related to a couple of building materials that had been selected but were mistakenly replaced with choices that are typically used by Cardinal. The communication of the desired choices was more thoroughly distributed to the appropriate Cardinal staff, and the ecoMOD South team remained flexible about some items if they did not impact the performance or aesthetics of the design.

There were two major problems during the construction phase. The first was related to the delivery of the SIPs. One of the partners in the grant was a SIP manufacturer based in Southside. This company was the recipient of a very substantial portion of the grant funding to acquire sophisticated digital fabrication equipment to allow them to use CAD/CAM technology for routing SIPs. After a long delay in the final assembly of this equipment in their facility, the company was forced to meet the ecoMOD South deadline and assemble the SIPs for the project using conventional tools. The SIPs were delivered to Cardinal, but were

Figure 10.10
Staff of Cardinal Homes in a meeting about coordination of moisture and air barriers.
John D. Quale

Figure 10.11
Cardinal Homes factory during production of ecoMOD South homes. John D. Quale

deemed to be below the quality standard required for the energy-efficient building envelope of a PH standard home. Rather than wait for the company to get their new equipment working, or switching to a double-stud wall construction method, Cardinal recommended asking another SIP manufacturer to build replacement SIPs. Unfortunately, the company is based in Georgia rather than Virginia, but they were able to produce excellent-quality panels in a very short time. The three homes were placed on their foundations in March 2013.

The second major concern was the fact that one of the onsite contractors had no experience with modular construction, and little understanding of energy-efficient construction, let alone the PH standard. Cardinal was responsible for the modular part of the homes, but the rest was the responsibility of a contractor in South Boston and of People Inc. (which is a licensed contractor) in Abingdon. The South Boston contractor was responsible for building the foundations, connecting the homes to utilities, and sealing up the joints where the modules come together. The foundation was designed by a local civil engineer, working as a consultant for Southside Outreach and the City of South Boston (who had donated the land). The contractor ignored the engineer's design, and built what he was accustomed to building. While structurally sound, it did not include any drainage for water along the footings, or waterproofing on the foundation walls. The team discovered this when we arrived one day to find standing water in the crawlspaces, which is just about the worst thing to imagine for any home, let alone one built to the PH standard, where trapped moisture is a serious concern. Southside Outreach, the city manager, and the local civil engineer worked together to address this serious concern. It was a reminder that the best of intentions can be ruined by sloppy work and lack of coordination or communication. It became clear that the remainder of the work on site needed to be carefully managed by one of our team members, to ensure there would no more errors. One of the research assistants stayed in South Boston for a couple of weeks to inspect each aspect of the "buttoning-up" of the modules. She was able to "train" the contractor on the importance of a drainage plane, and on sealing up all gaps in the building envelope. She is roughly 30 years younger than the contractor, but she was able to handle the situation smoothly – pointing out every minor mistake as the work was progressing, and insisting he fix each one. By the end of the experience, he was texting her pictures of work completed in her absence, to confirm he had lapped the air barrier properly, and maintained a drainage plane for moisture.

Final observations

Besides the exciting opportunity to deliver high-quality homes for three affordable housing families, the most important aspect of this project will be the results from the monitoring and post-occupancy evaluations. The ecoMOD South engineering team assembled an affordable, wireless monitoring system that gathers data about local weather; indoor air temperature, humidity, and quality; energy use; and building envelope heat flow with sensors in all three homes, including sensors inside the wall and roof sections of the homes.

The effort also contributed to an ongoing interest in the environmental impact of conventional versus offsite construction. The ecoMOD Director co-authored a study that determined that this is evidence of a lower impact for offsite strategies, although not for reasons previously understood. This day-in, day-out interaction with a modular homebuilder helped reinforce some of the evidence examined in that study.[5]

One of the most interesting questions is whether it makes financial sense to build PH-standard housing for affordable housing organizations in the kind of mixed climate found in the mid-Atlantic region. The research behind PH was developed in the northern part of the US in the 1970s, but funding for the research ended in

Figure 10.12
Interior of
ecoMOD South.
Andrea Hubbell
Photography

the 1980s. As a formal standard, PH emerged from Germany and other parts of northern Europe where heat and humidity are less of an issue. The Passive House Institute of the US (PHIUS) went through a process of recalibrating the standard to the wide range of climates in the US – a process that is likely to take several years to perfect. The ecoMOD South project has the opportunity to contribute data for analysis to assist PHIUS with this process, but this could also be an important precedent to allow affordable housing organizations, modular homebuilders, and individual market-rate homeowners to understand the possible return on investment for PH-standard homes in this region. We have already proven that the additional costs associated with high-performance windows, doors, and other components of the building envelope that achieve PH standard put the price for these homes beyond the amount considered to be accessible for affordable housing organizations in the southern part of Virginia. Yet, the ecoMOD South project has the potential to create economic development with the sale of well-designed homes to market-rate homebuyers and affordable housing organizations in other parts of the state and the region.

Acknowledgments

The ecoMOD South research team consisted of John D. Quale, ecoMOD Director; Michael Britt, ecoMOD South Project Manager; and ecoMOD South Research Assistants Liz Jennings, Erik de los Reyes, and Beth Bailey. The team also owes a great deal to Phil Parrish, the university's Associate Vice President for Research; Paxton Marshall, ecoMOD Engineering Director; Nancy Takahashi, ecoMOD

Landscape Architecture Advisor; Eric Field, ecoMOD Simulation Advisor; and the staff of the UVA Office of Sponsored Programs. Barbara Gehrung was the Passive House consultant, and Galen Staengl provided mechanical engineering consulting. The staff members at Cardinal Homes, Southside Outreach, and People Inc. were important collaborators in this effort, and the team is deeply appreciative of their advice, hard work, and creativity. The team also acknowledges the faculty and staff of the University of Virginia School of Architecture, and School of Engineering and Applied Science.

Portions of this chapter were originally published in another form in a peer-reviewed paper for the Architectural Research Centers Consortium.[6]

Notes

1 Allison Charette, Chris Herbert, Andrew Jakabovics, and Ellen Tracy Marya, *Projecting Trends in Severely Cost-Burdened Renters: 2015–2025* (Cambridge, MA: Joint Center for Housing Studies at Harvard University and Enterprise Community Partners, 2015).
2 John D. Quale, *Sustainable, Affordable, Prefab: The ecoMOD Project* (Charlottesville, VA: University of Virginia Press, 2012).
3 Gideon Fink Shapiro, "2013 R+D Awards Winner: ecoMOD," *Architect Magazine,* August 2013: 108–111, www.architectmagazine.com/awards/r-d-awards/2013-r-d-awards-winner-ecomod_o (accessed December 4, 2016); Wanda Lau, "The Path to Designing ecoMOD, an Affordable and Energy-Efficient Housing Module," *Architect Magazine,* March 27, 2015, www.architectmagazine.com/technology/the-path-to-designing-ecomod-an-affordable-and-energy-efficient-housing-module_o (accessed December 4, 2016).
4 www.usclimatedata.com (accessed December 4, 2016).
5 John D. Quale, Matthew J. Eckelman, Kyle W. Williams, Greg Sloditskie, and Julie B. Zimmerman, "Construction Matters: Comparing Environmental Impacts of Building Modular and Conventional Homes in the United States," *Journal of Industrial Ecology,* 16(2): 243–253; John D. Quale, Matthew J. Eckelman, Kyle W. Williams, Greg Sloditskie and Julie B. Zimmerman, "Two Recent Life Cycle Analysis (LCA) Studies for Buildings: On-Site versus Off-Site Construction and Building Material Reuse," *GreenBuild Thought Leadership and Research Proceedings* (US Green Building Council Annual Conference, 2011).
6 John D. Quale, Michael Britt, Erik De Los Reyes, and Elizabeth Rivard [Jennings], "Commercializing Energy-Efficient Affordable Housing: The ecoMOD South Project," *The Visibility of Research* (Charlotte, NC: Architectural Research Centers Consortium, 2013): 553–560.

Chapter 11

A case study of multi-trade near-site factory assembly

Kihong Ku and Paul Broadstone

Introduction

Prefabrication or offsite fabrication has continued to lead to new possibilities in architecture and construction. From the early Modernist vision of affordable mass housing to twentieth-century applications of offsite-produced structural components, cladding systems, and modular spatial units, and the more recent use of digitally manufactured complex-shaped building components, the impact of this approach has been obvious. In the past two decades, offsite fabrication means and methods have been adopted by designers or constructors to achieve better quality, with a reduced schedule and/or less cost.

A range of terms including 'modularization,' 'preassembly,' and 'industrialization' are associated with the concept of prefabrication or offsite fabrication (Gibb, 1999; Smith, 2010) which describe the multi-dimensional and diverse aspects of its development and strategies that have been explored throughout its evolution. Smith (2010) and White (1965) explain the ambiguity of the term 'prefabrication' and point out that the origin of the term comes from a time when there was a body of work that occurred before onsite fabrication or onsite assembly commenced. The other term, 'offsite fabrication,' broadly includes construction techniques ranging from simple elements including a prefabricated brick to panelized components or entire buildings such as modular houses or whole office buildings such as the De Bolder in the Netherlands (Maas and van Eekelen, 2003). Gibb compiled definitions from the Construction Industry Institute (CII) and the Construction Industry Research and Information Association (CIRIA) as follows:

> In a CII report, Tatum et al. define prefabrication as a manufacturing process, generally taking place at a specialized facility, in which various materials are joined to form a component part of the final installation and preassembly as a process by which various materials, prefabricated components, and/or equipment are joined together at a remote location for subsequent installation as a sub-unit, generally focusing on a system. CIRIA defines preassembly as the organization and completion of a substantial proportion of its final assembly work before installation in its final position, including many forms of sub-assembly, taking place on or off site and often involving standardization.
>
> (Gibb, 1999: 1)

Based on these descriptions, Gibb (1999) uses the term 'offsite fabrication' to include both prefabrication and preassembly, and defines offsite fabrication as a process that involves the design and manufacture of units or modules, usually remote from the work site, and their installation to form the permanent works at the work site. In its fullest sense, offsite fabrication requires a project strategy that will change the orientation of the project process from construction to manufacture and installation incorporated.

The next section takes a closer look at the various strategies of offsite fabrication that have evolved over time. The degree of prefabrication has resulted in various physical sizes and volumetric or non-volumetric shapes at the scale of components, systems, and entire buildings. Considering the economic and logistical impact of travel distance from factory to job site, in some cases the factory environments have been moved closer to or onto the job site. Another aspect of offsite fabrication is the level of integration of the trades involved in the process, involving single-trade to multi-trade fabrication.

Classifications and near-site/onsite fabrication

The elements of offsite construction can range from materials to components, to panels and modules (Smith, 2010). Gibb (1999) classifies offsite fabrication into non-volumetric, volumetric, and modular buildings. These classifications can be correlated. For example, materials, components, and panels are non-volumetric, while modules can all be considered volumetric. The distinction between the types within each classification is often relative. Applications often involve multiple types such as volumetric modular subassemblies that incorporate non-volumetric materials such as structural components, cladding, partitions, ductwork, etc. Other designs might include large-scale volumetric modules (for a medium-rise office, apartment building, or hotel) that in turn include non-volumetric components or smaller volumetric modules for restrooms or mechanical rooms.

These classifications can be extended to consider the distance of the factory to the job site. In this chapter, examining an emerging trend of near-site factories, the discussion of offsite fabrication concentrates on prefabrication or preassembly approaches staged near or on site.

The cost of transportation is an integral part of offsite fabrication that determines the feasibility of the specific applications. Generally, the growing distance between the job site and prefabrication facility makes offsite production less effective compared to conventional construction (Warszawski, 2003). Warszawski suggests a distance of 150 km to 200 km (approx. 93 miles to 124 miles) allowing one transportation cycle per day as an economic limit. Seaker and Lee (2006) note 150 miles to 200 miles (approx. 241 km to 322 km) as an economic limit beyond which offsite fabrication is not viable (Smith, 2010). Ku and Cardenas (2008) describe the Pulte Home Sciences panelization system and facility, which set 125 miles as its economical transportation range. According to industry expert opinions from a UK engineer at Buro Happold and Pulte Home Sciences in the US, about 200 km or 125 miles from the plant are proposed as the limit of cost-effective shipping, which coincides with the regional distribution of modular builders

(Smith, 2010). As such, transportation is an important factor in determining the viability of prefabrication approaches. Not only does it impact the size and shape of elements (linear, flat components vs. volumetric modules) that can be economically shipped but in some cases, near-site assembly approaches may also offer advantages over shipping large assembled products over longer distances.

Near-site or onsite fabrication can be further categorized by the scope of trade involvement (i.e., single-trade vs. multi-trade).

Near-site and onsite fabrication

Near-site or onsite factories have been applied in projects for reasons including the economic travel distance from the factory to the job site, enhanced quality control, schedule compression, simplification of packing, handling, and transporting products, and the lack of infrastructure in developing countries or remote sites. Table 11.1 lists a few near-site or onsite examples distinguished by single- or multi-trade.

Near-site factory approaches have been employed to take advantage of the main benefits of offsite fabrication including reduced time, improved quality, and sometimes reduced cost. For single-trade contractors, specialty contractors like A. Zahner, a leading architectural metal fabricator sought for their unique capabilities to produce complex sheet-metal envelopes, have been dealing with the complications of creating custom crating for long hauls, and the size limitations of transportable units, which impact onsite erection and joint sealing time (Brandt, 2008). Larger preassembled panels are beneficial despite the fact that they can be cost prohibitive when shipping long distances. Brandt explains that in the BOK Center project in Tulsa, Oklahoma, A. Zahner manufactured the curved complex sheet-metal components at their headquarters in Kansas City, Missouri, and separately fabricated more linear components at their Fort Worth, Texas facility. All components from both locations were flat-packed and shipped with other accessories to a rented warehouse near the site to preassemble, seal, and insulate them.

Recently in the US, since around 2009 there have been a number of hospital projects that have applied the use of multi-trade ceiling racks that are composed of a unistrut frame integrating mechanical ducts, pipes, electrical conduits, and sometimes fire sprinkler pipes. Table 11.1 lists a few example projects that have adopted multi-trade near-site strategies. These have involved near-site preassembly of components into modular racks that are installed on site. A similar approach was developed earlier in the 1990s in the UK and case studies on a mechanical and electrical contractor (Crown House Engineering) have been introduced (Gibb 1999). The primary drivers for such modular preassembly have been reduced schedule and improved quality. In the US, general contractors have been primary proponents of this approach as it involves integration of multiple trades including mechanical, electrical, and drywall contractors.

Daewoo Corporation of Korea developed and used a multi-room modular construction system in the 1980s and 1990s which prefabricated near or on the job site three-dimensional precast concrete structural modules of individual dwelling units for multi-story high-rise residential buildings (Pollalis, 1997; Gibb, 1999). A typical project involved a four-month mobilization period to set up a prefabrication

	Near-site	Onsite
Single-trade	Architectural metal cladding • A. Zahner (BOK Center, Tulsa, OK)	Steel roll-forming mobile factory • FRAMECAD • Scottsdale • M.I.C. Industries Onsite containerized CNC fabrication for homes • Facit[1] • ROB[2] mobile fabrication unit
Multi-trade	Multi-trade ceiling racks; headwalls; bathroom pods: • Skanska USA Building (Miami Valley Hospital, Dayton, OH) • Mortenson (Exempla St. Joseph's Hospital, Denver, CO) • Beck Group (Texas Health Harris Methodist Alliance Hospital, Fort Worth, TX) • Balfour Beatty (Parkland Replacement Hospital Project, Dallas, TX) • Whiting-Turner (Ohio Health Neuroscience Institute at Riverside Methodist Hospital, Columbus, OH) • Haselden (University of Colorado Hospital, Denver, CO) • Crown House Engineering (UK) Modular units: • FC Modular (B2 Brooklyn Building)	Precast volumetric spatial module • Daewoo (multi-room modular construction system in Hawaii)

1 http://www.architectureanddesign.com.au/news/revolution-for-prefab-homes-moving-digital-fabrica
2 http://gramaziokohler.arch.ethz.ch/web/e/forschung/135.html

facility, on or near the job site, to manufacture precast concrete modules that were crane lifted into position at a rate of one floor per day. Daewoo reported that this system was financially feasible for projects with more than 500 units with its primary benefit being speed of construction, about half the time of conventional construction. The project cost was about 1 percent more than conventional construction, with a cost breakdown of 10 percent for structural elements, 70 percent for construction of the modules, and 20 percent for transportation and installation. The labor was about 70–80 percent of the resources required for conventional construction.

Table 11.1
Examples of near- and onsite fabrication by trade involvement

There have been limited applications of mobile or containerized factories of steel roll-forming applications that accommodate forming and cut machinery on a trailer bed or in a container. These applications are advantageous for remote sites with little infrastructure.

At a smaller scale, digital design and manufacturing demonstration and research projects have explored the possibilities of robotic assemblies or CNC routing incorporated into a mobile container. Facit Homes in the UK is a firm that focuses on prefabricated homes incorporating enhanced customized design control to fabrication. The ROB mobile fabrication unit has demonstrated the use of a containerized robotic arm that allows for assembly or manufacturing of specific forms from digital design environments. Such research demonstrations of mobile factory approaches raise questions about the financial feasibility, logistics, and design, material, and fabrication implications for mainstream applications in construction.

Productivity is the primary driver of using prefabrication and modularization (McGraw-Hill, 2011). A survey conducted in 2011 by McGraw-Hill highlights that the highest level of usage is driven by fabricators, mechanical contractors, and design-builders. The report lists the primary barriers to prefabrication as not being part of the architectural design and owner's resistance. Hence, there is a need to better define the parameters of prefabrication strategies to assist designers and owners to adopt appropriate prefabrication strategies. Precise dimensional control and coordination abilities through BIM technologies and growing awareness of lean construction processes facilitate prefabrication approaches.

Despite the overall benefits of prefabrication, a number of factors including transportation costs, shipping limitations on the unit size of building assemblies, packing and shipping costs, construction tolerances of site-assembled joints, onsite joint sealing errors, and safety and ergonomics issues during site erection, have led fabricators, general contractors, and designers to consider near-site fabrication solutions.

To better understand the innovations and implications of near-site multi-trade prefabrication, a detailed case study on the Miami Valley Hospital examines the preassembly of modular integrated building service ceiling modules, patient room bathroom pods, and patient room headwall assemblies.

The Miami Valley Hospital case study

Miami Valley Hospital (MVH) is part of the Premier Health Partners (PHP) health care system based in southwest Ohio. In December 2010, MVH opened their new 484,000-square-foot, $155 million addition, consisting of a 12-story tower with a new patient/visitor entry lobby, two levels of underground parking, overhead pedestrian walkways, 178 new patient rooms, and room for 72 additional patient rooms in the future. The MVH Southeast Tower Addition was awarded as a design–bid–build project, designed by NBBJ and constructed by the joint venture of Skanska USA and Shook Construction. The project has been awarded LEED Silver certification. The MVH Southeast Tower Addition is one of the first major hospital projects in the US to incorporate all of the following areas of prefabrication: bathroom pods, MEP ceiling racks, patient room headwalls, modular nurse stations, and exterior panels.

Prefabrication and design strategies

Prefabrication initiatives

Both NBBJ and Skanska sought ways to improve hospital construction. NBBJ began to identify systems that would be good candidates for prefabrication with an emphasis on areas that were complex and repetitive. Skanska was also search-ing for ways to improve hospital construction by researching the prefabrication methods that Skanska UK had been using for years in London. The Skanska team visited St. Bartholomew's Hospital and the Royal London Hospital and observed how they were using multi-trade prefabrication to create mechanical, electrical, and plumbing (MEP) ceiling racks. MEP ceiling racks have been used for years in Europe, and Skanska UK has a special division with dedicated facilities and personnel to support prefabrication in London. According to the Skanska team, this prefabrication facility has allowed Skanska UK to vertically integrate the prefabrication and perfect it over the last eight to ten years.

As a result of the research being done by NBBJ and Skanska, the project team decided to proceed with five prefabrication initiatives on the MVH project. The first three initiatives were accomplished by procuring prefabricated components through third-party vendors:

1. *Unitized curtain wall*: the curtain wall is comprised of modular units that can be manufactured to higher standards and installed on site in a faster and safer manner.
2. *Modular, demountable caregiver workstations*: these are flexible workstations found in each of the three patient wings, on the seven patient room floors that allow the hospital to easily adapt the furniture and workstations to their needs.
3. *Temporary bridge*: to construct the new tower, three existing buildings were demolished but the hospital needed to maintain access to the surrounding buildings with a temporary elevated walkway. The solution was to use a jetway manufacturer that was able to prefabricate the walkway, install it in three days, and cause no disruptions to hospital activities.

The last two initiatives were accomplished by establishing a multi-trade, offsite prefabrication warehouse, arranged and managed by Skanska Shook, within three miles of the project site to manufacture components that could be easily transported to the site:

4. *Patient rooms (bathroom pods, headwalls, and case work)*: to establish stand-ardization but maintain flexibility, NBBJ designed the patient bed tower rooms with prefabrication in mind.
5. *Integrated MEP racks*: due to the complexity and congestion of the MEP systems that could be routed in the corridor ceiling of the patient room floors, the MEP ceiling racks were identified as an excellent candidate for the pre-fabrication techniques that the Skanska team had researched in London with Skanska UK. These units were designed and detailed by Korda Nemeth Engineering, the building systems consultant.

The original project duration, without multi-trade prefabrication, was 30 months but a sandy seam that was missed during soil test bores forced the removal of ten newly placed footings and the redesign of some of the foundations. This rework delayed the project by 15 weeks and further encouraged the project team to implement their prefabrication ideas to save time. Premier Health says that at an early stage Skanska Shook and NBBJ were able to collaborate on the prefabrication ideas and recover seven to eight weeks of construction time. The multi-trade prefabrication initiative allowed the subcontractors to work concurrently on construction tasks such as site work, foundations, structural steel, and/or concrete.

Skanska led the ceiling rack initiative to get everyone on board while NBBJ pushed for the prefabricated patient room. The owner project representative, and mechanical electrical subcontractors visited London to see Skanska UK's prefabrication operation. After this visit, the Premier Health management was convinced to allow the team to move forward with prefabrication. The owner representative mentioned that they had gone through two other jobs with Skanska Shook and they had a lot of faith in their abilities.

Prefabrication was a major goal when designing this project but the NBBJ designer notes that they did not want the prefabrication to dictate how the building would look and operate. They considered the functionality and aesthetics first before making a decision to go forward with prefabrication. It was important to Premier Health, NBBJ, and Skanska Shook that nobody would be able to tell which items were prefabricated on the project.

Same-handed room design

The design team adopted the same-handed room design instead of the typical mirror-image patient room in which the headwall and everything including the bathroom, casework, and equipment of one patient room backs up to the headwall of the room next to it. Mirror-image rooms are typically more economic because MEP services are concentrated in the headwall and bathroom of every other wall rather than every wall. The same-handed design has been recently advocated to promote patient safety and standardization but also proved to be conducive for prefabrication because each patient room could be defined by a single 'blade' that consisted of the bathroom pod and headwall assembly (Herman Miller Healthcare, 2011). According to Herman Miller's report, the hospital is able to standardize not only the design and construction of the room but also its medical staff processes and workflows, resulting in fewer errors and increased efficiency from patient caregivers.

Subcontractor design–assist

Chapel Electric and TP Mechanical were brought on board as design–assist subcontractors before the decision was made to go ahead with offsite multi-trade prefabrication. With the assistance of the subcontractors, the project team was able to route utilities such as electrical, plumbing and medical gas through the corridor rather than along the perimeter of the building. Routing the systems down the corridor increased the materials required to complete the installation but allowed the project team to maximize the utility of the MEP ceiling racks (Figure 11.1). The more systems the team was able to install in the racks in the warehouse, the more they were able to take advantage of the safer and more comfortable working environment, resulting in increased productivity and cost savings.

Use of BIM

In order to coordinate the available spaces in the ceiling racks, the subcontractors used Building Information Modeling (BIM) for spatial coordination and clash detection. NBBJ and Korda Nemeth provided a structural, architectural, and MEP model to be used by the subcontractors to model their systems. The NBBJ and Skanska teams both agree that despite their previous experience with prefabrication, the complexity of the systems that are in a hospital and a patient room made it difficult to resolve the three-dimensional systems without the use of a very robust building information model.

NBBJ used Bentley MicroStation Triforma to create their model, while the structural engineer was using Autodesk's Revit Structure. NBBJ has since switched to the Revit platform for their models. Many of the subcontractors used different software packages, which required them to re-create the models provided by NBBJ. The different software packages and different subcontractors contributing to the models required more collaboration than typically found amongst the trades. Subcontractors worked together to establish the level of detail required for each system, the space each subcontractor would be allowed to use, and rules to resolve any clashes. Larger pieces of equipment and equipment requiring tighter tolerances were modeled in detail but smaller components such as an electrical conduit were designated with a 'box-out.' For example, Chapel Electric was not required to draw each conduit but rather draw a box that represented the space

Figure 11.1
Eight-foot-wide installed ceiling rack and components for the Smyth County Community Hospital, Marion, VA

in which they needed to place their conduit. This technique saved them a lot of time when modeling, but also provided flexibility if another subcontractor required additional space in particular places. The sheetrock contractor, Dayton Walls & Ceilings (DWC), was also involved to provide the proper cut-outs for beam pockets.

Autodesk NavisWorks was used to integrate all of the models by Skanska Shook in regular coordination meetings. The subcontractors also used NavisWorks to solve coordination issues within their own models and between other trades in between the formal coordination meetings.

Mock-ups

Once the decision was made to proceed with offsite multi-trade prefabrication, Skanska and NBBJ constructed full-scale mock-ups of the MEP ceiling racks and a patient bathroom to get buy-in from the clients (Figure 11.2).

Figure 11.2
A bathroom pod assembly for the MVH South project in the warehouse

Skanska and Korda Nemeth staff explained that this also allowed the prospective bidders to physically walk around the mock-ups and get an idea of how they would be constructed so that they could estimate what would be involved in constructing 178 bathroom pods and 120 ceiling racks.

Construction considerations

Procurement strategy

The MVH Southeast Tower Addition was procured as a traditional design–bid–build project but the implementation of offsite multi-trade prefabrication required that each party worked together in a more collaborative manner. The NBBJ project leader explains that this project was not formally an Integrated project delivery (IPD) type of a project but that the IPD process lends itself very well to prefabrication, emphasizing the need for a true partnership between the design team and the construction manager.

Project leaders were concerned from the beginning about having the trades work alongside each other in the warehouse in a production line setting, especially with a union electrician (Chapel Electric), a union fire protection subcontractor (Dalmation), an open-shop drywall subcontractor (DWC), and an open-shop mechanical subcontractor (TP Mechanical), but they had confidence in the subcontractors and worked with them to make sure that only employees who were open-minded and excited about prefabrication were involved. A Skanska team leader explained, "a lot of it had to do with the right people . . . not only did we have the right contractors, we had the right people within the contractors too." The union workers and non-union workers realized they were performing the same tasks in the warehouse that they normally would do in the field and that neither was taking work from the other. The teamwork of the subcontractors working in the warehouse was so successful that they tried to keep as many of the same employees on a subsequent MVH project.

Near-site warehouse

The selection of a warehouse to use for prefabrication dictates the largest expense in using multi-trade prefabrication. Skanksa Shook was able to secure a 35,000-square-foot warehouse less than three miles away from the site for prefabrication. However, the delay from the soil conditions and higher than expected production rates forced Skanska to lease an additional 70,000-square-foot warehouse three miles in the opposite direction (Post, 2010). According to the contract arrangements, TP Mechanical was responsible for the cost of the warehouse but was reimbursed by Skanska. The only major expense for setting up the warehouse was the leasing of the space and general utilities. No special equipment was required for the subcontractors to complete their tasks and Skanska purposely requested that they did not want to have anything in the warehouse that they did not have on site. The components could be maneuvered throughout the warehouse with small dollies and loaded onto the truck with a standard loading dock.

Building codes and seismic considerations

To prevent any delays or concerns with the local inspectors, the prefabrication team decided to involve the different inspection departments in the entire process. During the design phases of the project, NBBJ and Korda Nemeth communicated the process to the local authorities. The inspectors were invited to the warehouse for initial inspections and pressure testing, and the standard inspection after installation. After the installation on site, they conducted an additional pressure test.

The International Building Code requires the use of seismic restraint for hospitals and healthcare facilities even in areas of the country without significant seismic activity. Premier Health knew about the requirement and was satisfied when it turned out the ceiling racks could be used as seismic bracing.

Construction and installation

Installation of the prefabricated components began once the concrete deck and corridor walls had been laid out, hanging clips for the racks had been installed, and fireproofing had been sprayed. It was necessary to haul and hoist the components on Saturdays in order to use the site's tower crane without interrupting the ongoing steel erection. The 8'×20' size of the racks allowed the team to transport them on flatbed trucks without having to obtain any additional permitting. Tower cranes were the only option for hoisting due to the extremely limited lay-down area around the site and the 'landlocked' orientation of the building (Post, 2010). The racks were easily managed by the site's tower crane, with the heaviest rack weighing approximately 2,000 pounds.

The ceiling racks were hauled to the site and lifted to the correct level, and TP Mechanical took a week to a week and a half to move and lift each rack into its final location. The ceiling racks were hoisted into the building using straps to a landing platform that extended out from the building. Once inside the building, TP Mechanical could move each rack into position using the same dollies from the warehouse and then lifting the racks with lifts (Figure 11.3). A lift was positioned at each corner of each rack in order to prevent damaging the rack.

During the installation of the first set of racks, the team discovered that they had not taken into account the thickness of the fireproofing on the face of the columns and it was causing the racks to hang out of square. With the help of the BIM model the team was able to alter the remaining 72 racks to avoid future problems, by simply altering the sheetrock and metal studs that were attached to the racks. As a result of the BIM coordination, every beam pocket, located every eight feet, was exactly where it was needed and did not require any modifications in the field.

To ensure that the racks were going to work, Skanska asked TP Mechanical to practice jacking up and connecting the racks together in the warehouse. The copper piping uses the same hard piping and soldered connections that would be found in the field, and requires soldering after the racks are hung. The electrical conduit is connected from rack to rack with a flexible conduit. Chapel Electric found that the flexible conduit serves its purpose but that change in material causes some trouble when trying to pull wires through the rack system compared to a traditional, hard-piped connection. In the UK, electricians do not use a conduit to house their wiring so there is no need for a slip connection. Slip connections are currently available and allowed for other MEP systems but Bridgeport, the vendor, has to write the UL specifications and seek approval in order for the product to receive a UL listing.

The bathroom pods and headwall units were transported to the site and hoisted into the building. The crew was able to haul and lift 33 bathroom pods in one eight-hour day and three to four more days to level and secure each pod. Once inside the building, the pods could be maneuvered using the same metal dollies as the ceiling racks.

Figure 11.3 **Lift used to position MEP ceiling rack during installation in the Smyth County Community Hospital, Marion, VA**

Benefits of multi-trade prefabrication

Schedule reduction
Multi-trade prefabrication saved seven to eight weeks in this project and the Skanska team leaders estimate that they could have saved up to four to six months from the schedule and delivered higher quality more safely if the team had decided to prefabricate from day one.

Cost savings and quality improvements
Total cost savings were reported across the three multi-trade prefabricated elements: pods, headwalls, and racks. The 360-degree access of the units on a shop floor allowed easier access and inspection of the work and therefore better quality control. The three subcontractors – mechanical, electrical, and drywall – vary in terms of their labor savings. While overall material savings were reported across all trades, the cost of leasing the warehouse, transportation, Unistrut, and

additional fireproofing expenses balanced the savings. The electrical contractor attributed labor savings to a 300 percent increase in productivity. The drywall contractor reported a 10 percent labor saving and 5–10 percent overall cost saving. The mechanical contractor averaged about 14 percent labor saving and about 5 percent overall cost saving.

- *Ceiling racks*: the production of the racks exceeded initial estimates of five to eight racks per week by completing 12–15 racks per week after three weeks of production in the warehouse. This is equal to completing the ceiling racks for an entire wing of the hospital in a week. The MEP ceiling racks resulted in a 2 percent increase in labor hours per rack but still achieved an overall cost saving of 10 percent. The mechanical contractor explained that the ceiling racks in comparison to the bathroom pods resulted in a labor increase because they did not include all the necessary Unistrut bracing material in the estimate.
- *Bathroom pods*: the bathroom pod provides utilities for the adjoining patient, rough-ins for the caregiver wash station, and media and data connections. While a number of third-party companies manufacture bathroom pods for hospitals, the project team decided to construct the pods in the warehouse to ensure accountability, and to achieve a level of standardization and customization that third-party vendors could not provide. Overall labor savings and cost savings were reported by all three trades involved, achieving about 32 percent savings on the overall labor hours and about 25 percent savings on the estimated costs.
- *Headwalls*: this wall section extends from the bathroom pod to the exterior wall of the patient room and provides medical gases and electrical and data outlets. The drywall was applied on site. Overall labor savings of about 55 percent and cost savings of 52 percent were reported.

Safety and productivity

There were zero injuries in the prefabrication warehouse throughout the duration of the project and only a small number of recordable injuries on the site during construction. This is significantly lower than is reported on similar projects. This improved safety can be attributed to improved working conditions in the warehouse and the overall reduction in the number of workers on site throughout construction. According to the Skanska USA Building Project Executive for Field Operations, there were only 18 workers in the warehouse throughout the entire prefabrication process.

Anecdotal evidence provided by the electrical contractor shows a 300 percent increase in productivity.

Environmental impact

As a result of the efficiencies achieved in the warehouse, only one dumpster was used throughout the entire fabrication stage of the project. According to data provided by Skanska, a typical hospital project of this size would accrue a total dumpster cost of approximately 0.14 percent of the total $155 million project cost. Actual dumpster costs for the MVH Southeast Tower Addition were only 0.09 percent. Data on the reduced environmental impact as a result of energy savings from reduced labor hours and fewer workers traveling to the construction site are not available.

Challenges of multi-trade prefabrication

Procurement

In this project, the subcontractors were allowed to keep any savings that were realized as a result of prefabrication. Skanska Shook felt that it was the best way to allocate potential risks and rewards. In an effort to pass on and share some of the expected savings from the subcontractors, the mock-ups were constructed with the hopes that the subcontractor's bids would be lower. Unfortunately, most of the bids did not reflect savings over a traditional installation. From a CM-at-Risk perspective, a number of the Skanska team members believe that one of the biggest areas for improvement is Skanska's in-house preconstruction estimates and budgets for prefabricated elements, used to compare against subcontractor bids. Having more accurate preconstruction budgets would allow Skanska to pass any savings on to the owner.

The owner representative shared that going forward he believes that projects could be bid on in two different ways. The first does not require the use of prefabrication but allows using the time savings and any other benefits as a competitive advantage. If construction managers choose this path, he fully expects them to be able to show the expected cost savings in their bid. The other pricing strategy involves building prefabrication into the specifications and allowing every potential construction manager to bid on the project with a prefabrication plan.

Design–engineering interfaces

Project requirements present different challenges for prefabrication. For example, in another hospital project by Skanska, the plans were based on eight-foot corridors as opposed to the 16-foot corridors seen in the MVH project and the patient room adopted the common mirror-image layout. This resulted in less favorable conditions to apply bathroom pods and headwall units. The issues of tolerance and product connectors also need to be addressed during design.

Manufacturing vs. construction

The experiences from the first MVH project highlighted the need for more informed scheduling decisions. With more realistic production rates, construction can achieve just-in-time delivery for the prefabricated elements and eliminate the leasing of additional warehouse space. To achieve a leaner process, the construction manager may need to take on more control of the entire process, including the manufacturing logistics in the warehouse.

Performance measurement

Prefabrication requires re-examining the productivity in multi-trade environments. More accurate performance metrics that reflect the productivity gains achieved through eliminating idle time and non-value-adding activities from the site need to be measured. Transportation activities need to be carefully studied as near-site fabrication not only impacts the coordination within the factory but also the packaging, storing, unloading, and staging on the construction site.

Conclusion

The case study offers some insights into the benefits of near-site fabrication and the challenges of coordinating multiple trades in a factory environment. While the time savings, quality improvements, and safety benefits through preassembly of larger elements are obvious from the case study, it was illustrated that realizing the full potential of this new approach requires changes in performance measurements, cost models, design and engineering capabilities, and business models. The warehouse environment requires little capital investment but mobilizing and optimizing the assembly line process requires managerial processes that differ from conventional construction processes. Questions about who controls the processes and how to monitor labor and cost savings are critical to achieving broader acceptance and efficiencies through near-site fabrication. While examples from the healthcare sector seem to be the frontrunners of this new near-site multi-trade prefabrication approach, lessons from these projects could lead to near-site assemblies of customized cladding systems and modular building systems, or the development of mobile factories of other building components that have to deal with the constraints of long-haul transportation from centralized factories.

As the building industry keeps pushing forward with novel prefabrication approaches to build faster, better, and cheaper, it is expected that innovative near-site or onsite fabrication applications will evolve. In parallel, the construction industry will see new delivery methods, new leaders in design, construction, and fabrication, and overall improved performance as an industry.

Acknowledgments

Portions of this chapter were originally presented at the ACSA Fall 2012 conference and subsequently published in the conference proceedings.

The primary research sources of the case study were structured interviews and project documentation to collect data.

The authors thank Skanska USA Building for providing funding through their Innovation Grant Program. We are also thankful to the case study participants from Skanska USA Building, NBBJ, Premier Health Partners, Korda Nemeth Engineering, Chapel Electric, TP Mechanical, Dayton Walls & Ceilings, Draper & Associates, and GSP for their participation in the interviews.

References

Brandt, J. (2008). *Mobile Production of Composite Building Envelopes with Complex Geometries*. Doctoral Dissertation, Harvard University Graduate School of Design.

Gibb, A.G.F. (1999). *Offsite Fabrication*. Caithness, UK: Whittles Publishing.

Herman Miller Healthcare (2011). *Patient Room Design: The Same-Handed, Mirror-Image Debate Research Summary*. www.hermanmiller.com/MarketFacingTech/hmc/research/research_summaries/assets/wp_Same_vs_Mirror.pdf, accessed December 6, 2016.

Ku, K. and Cardenas, C. (2008). Flexibility in prefabrication approaches: Lessons from two US homebuilders, *2008 ACSA Northeast Fall Conference Proceedings*, September 25–27, 2008, University of Massachusetts Amherst.

Ku, K., Broadstone, P., and Colonna, A. (2012). Towards on-site fabrication: A case study on multi-trade prefabrication. In R.E. Smith, J.D. Quale, and R. Ng (eds.), *Proceedings of the 2012 ACSA Fall Conference, Offsite: Theory and Practice of Architectural Production, Philadelphia, PA, September 27–29, 2012*. Philadelphia, PA: ACSA, pp. 52–57.

Maas, G. and van Eekelen, B. (2003). De Bolder, an Unusual Example of Offsite Construction. *NIST Special Publication*, 143–148.

McGraw-Hill (2011). *Prefabrication and Modularization: Increasing Productivity in the Construction Industry*. SmartMarketReport, www.nist.gov/sites/default/files/documents/el/economics/Prefabrication-Modularization-in-the-Construction-Industry-SMR-2011R.pdf, accessed October 2, 2016.

Pollalis, S.N. (1997). *Country Club Village, Hawaii: A Case Study on Daewoo's Multi-room Modular Construction System*. Unpublished. Harvard Graduate School of Design, Cambridge, MA.

Post, N.M. (2010). Racking up big points for prefab. *Engineering News-Record*, http://enr.construction.com/buildings/construction_methods/2010/0908-PrefabPotential-1.asp, accessed December 6, 2016.

Seaker, R. and Lee, S. (2006). Assessing alternative prefabrication methods: Logistical influences. In M. Pandey, W.-C. Xie, and L. Xu (eds.), *Advances in Engineering Structures, Mechanics and Construction: Proceedings of an International Conference on Advances in Engineering Structures, Mechanics and Construction, Waterloo, Ontario, Canada, May 14–17, 2006*. Dordrecht, Netherlands: Springer, pp. 607–614.

Smith, R.E. (2010). *Prefab Architecture: A Guide to Modular Design and Construction*. Hoboken, NJ: John Wiley & Sons.

Warszawski, A. (2003). *Industrialized and Automated Building Systems: A Managerial Approach (2nd edn)*. New York: Routledge.

White, R.B. (1965). *Prefabrication: A History of Its Development in Great Britain*. London: HMSO.

Chapter 12

Prefabricated housing in Japan

Dana Buntrock

Japan's strong role in the factory-built housing industry emerged as a response to World War II. In 1945, 63,153 hectares across 115 cities were in ruins, 2.3 million houses had been lost, and the nation's total housing shortage was a whopping 4.2 million homes, since colonizers were also returning from Japan's far-flung and short-lived empire.[1] Reconstruction was neither smooth nor quick: the economy was shaky, materials and labor were scarce, and supply chains were non-existent. Things began to improve in the early 1950s, due to global economic demand caused by the Korean War; many of today's major "house-makers" (the Japanese term for companies building homes off-site) were founded in these early years after World War II: Daiwa House began producing prefabricated housing in 1955,

Figure 12.1
Midget house

PanaHome in 1959, Sekisui House in 1960, and Misawa Homes in 1962. Rivals also emerged – but quickly failed in the face of volatile economic conditions.

Construction labor shortages seesawed from a "low" of 16–21 percent in 1960 to a high of 48 percent in 1962 (during a frenzy of preparation for the 1964 Olympics), then dropped to a forbidding 26.5 percent in 1966.[2] Under acute pressure to rebuild – and with unusually low opposition from builders working on site – the Japanese government was free to encourage the emerging factory-based housing industry. The Ministry of International Trade and Industry (MITI) established the Japan Prefabricated Construction Suppliers and Manufacturers Association (JPCSMA) in 1964 to promote best practices, develop and disseminate research, and form industry standards. MITI also subsidized efficient factory-based construction practices: Misawa Homes, for example, received $6.6 million during the 1970s to develop low-cost, lightweight autoclaved ceramic (PALC) components.[3] The Japanese government's Housing Loan Corporation simultaneously bolstered consumption with preferential loan rates.[4] Sales of manufactured housing soared tenfold in three years, from 5,000 units in 1962 to 50,530 in 1965.

It did not stop with that initial and amazing expansion; by 1970, 137,300 factory-built homes were sold in Japan – nearly one-tenth of housing starts that year.[5] As residential demand boomed, new contenders again entered the field: Sekisui Heim (a separate corporate entity from Sekisui House)[6] exhibited its first model in 1970; Asahi Kasei began to market the Hebel House in 1972; and in 1975 Toyota Motors, aware that leading house manufacturers based their production on strategies adopted from the automotive industry (and particularly from Toyota itself), also began to produce housing. In the years right after World War II, Toyota experimented with precast concrete homes – but suspended the effort when cars emerged as a more lucrative opportunity.[7]

Economic policies between the 1950s and the mid-1970s nurtured many oligopolies. All of today's leading "house-makers" were active by 1975; seven still dominate the field. Ranked, they are Sekisui House, Asahi Kasei, Sekisui Heim, Daiwa House, Misawa, PanaHome, and Toyota.

These companies were not established by builders. Sekisui Chemical spun off Sekisui House to create a market for plastics. A Matsumoto-area lumber supplier started Misawa. Asahi Kasei marketed construction materials made from lightweight autoclaved aerated concrete. PanaHome's parent company, Matsushita, produced household electronics.[8] Yet with the exception of Asahi Kasei and PanaHome (offering "Smart Homes for Smart People"), these origins are often unseen – or even repudiated: Sekisui House explicitly states it does not use PVC in construction.

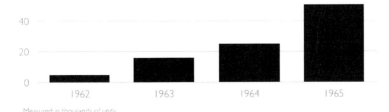

Figure 12.2
**Annual sales
of factory-built
housing, Japan,
1962–1965**[9]

Dana Buntrock

Company	Total homes sold	Sales value ¥10,000,000	Single-family	Apartment (multi-family housing of two stories or fewer)	"Mansion" (multi-family housing of three stories or more)
Daiwa House	43,203	2,007,989	9,881	30,514	2,808
Sekisui House	45,098	1,613,816	16,191	27,869	1,038
Hebel House (Asahi Kasei)	15,791	486,200	10,721	5,036	n/a
Sekisui Heim	13,860	469,036	10,610	3,250	n/a
Misawa	13,130	394,696	10,190	2,275	665
PanaHome	10,446	289,402	6,065	4,381	n/a
Mitsui Home	5,540	218,387	3,975	1,361	n/a
Toyota Home	5,878	150,000	4,626	n/a	n/a
Yamada SXL	1,489	39,860	1,458	31	n/a

Source: "2012 Nendo Ōte Jūtaku Meikā Rankingu Hyō [FY2012 Major House-maker Ranking]", *Jūtaku Sangyō Shinbun* [*Housing Industry Newspaper*] n. 1670 (December 13, 2013) p. 6.

Table 12.1
House-maker sales and ranking, 2012

Japan frequently experiences large earthquakes, which killed tens of thousands in the last half-century. Since 1981, building standards have ratcheted upwards in response to new knowledge; older buildings were rightly thought unsafe. Thus throughout the late twentieth century, improving living standards and technical innovation boosted residential demand, forging a market more likely to tear down and replace homes than to renovate. The useful life of a house became measured in mere decades. Only 13.5 percent of homes sold in Japan in 2008 were previously occupied; comparable figures in the US in 2010 and in England in 2012 were 89.3 percent and 88 percent respectively. An aging house in Japan drives down the cost of land if not removed before the property is put up for sale. Style, size, or type of construction rarely impact land value. Older houses are liabilities; newer ones offer increased luxury and safety. Housing, whether built in a remote plant or on site, is simply a commodity – not an investment.[10]

Japanese prefabricated housing tends to be sturdy, even overbuilt; steel frames are used in 80 percent of prefabricated housing and concrete is also widely used.[11] In light of the rising cost of steel, companies now offer deconstruction and recycling services for their early products. Promotional literature portrays shaker table tests, base isolation (now standard at connections to foundations), and fat structural components. Technical literature also emphasizes durability, resistance to weathering, and performance in typhoons. The exteriors of factory-built homes frequently feature lightweight concrete or ceramic finishes with high fire resistance; this was especially true in the first decades of the industry's expansion, when many could still recall firebombing. Motion detectors turn on security lights; exterior glass is laminated to resist break-ins; wireless security systems allow owners to check houses remotely – all standard on factory-built housing.

Sunlight and natural ventilation, justified for health reasons, are also featured prominently in pamphlets. Air systems incorporate HEPA filters; some even monitor carbon dioxide. Heat exchange and natural convection are integrated into

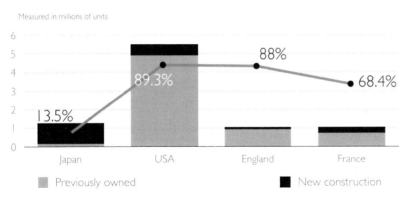

Figure 12.3
**Residential
reselling is rare
in Japan; most
homes sold are
newly built[12]**

Measured in millions of units

88%

89.3%

68.4%

13.5%

Japan USA England France

Previously owned New construction

exterior detailing with an eye to air currents and watertightness. Some industry leaders recently shifted from rigid foam insulation to glass wool in response to indoor air-quality concerns.

Small local builders lack the economies of scale required to offer similar materials at competitive prices and rarely have the sophistication or scale of production to justify carefully planned ventilation. Japan's loose enforcement of building codes, evidenced in several scandals, also damaged homeowners' confidence in smaller builders.[13] Today, the qualitative difference between site-built homes and factory-built products strongly favors factory-built production.

Where once factory-built housing tried to compete on cost savings due to streamlined production and economies of scale, since the 1970s, the industry has competed on quality. Factory-built homes have a strong share of the high end of the market. A 2010 marketing plan from Sekisui House showed the company's market share was strongest for large homes. In 2008, this single company built nearly 7 percent of all homes in Japan larger than 180 square meters – and it had ambitions to increase its share to one out of every 12 homes of that size.[14]

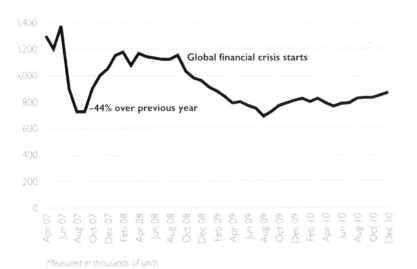

Global financial crisis starts

−44% over previous year

Measured in thousands of units

Figure 12.4
**Market
response
to a 2007
construction
scandal,
followed by
the global
economic
downturn[15]**

Figure 12.5
Market
share for
prefabricated
homes
generally
increases with
construction
cost and
quality[16]

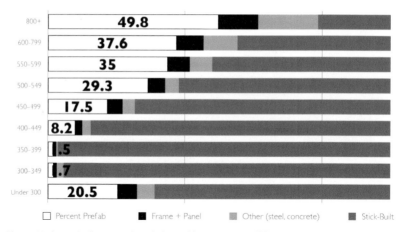

Measured in thousands of yen per *tsubo*, equivalent to 3.3 square meters (1992)

The cost of factory-built residences is about 8 percent higher than for compara-ble site-built structures.[17] In the postwar period when industry leaders emerged, a refrigerator, a small black-and-white television, and a car were considered the marks of success; today, prefabricated houses are sold with far flashier features. Models feature elevators, saunas, jet baths and outdoor hot tubs, remote-controlled toilets, and systems kitchens – priced competitively, thanks to house-makers' corporate ties with suppliers. Universal design is also highlighted in promotional materials, with wide corridors and doorways, roll-in showers, and grab bars.

Prefabricators leverage their higher product quality by offering strong war-ranties and post-occupancy maintenance programs involving sophisticated technologies. Daiwa House pamphlets feature a nifty robot used to check small spaces, for example. The JPCSMA long required members to offer ten-year war-ranties. But since 2000, local builders have also been legally required to offer ten-year warranties, so JPCSMA members extended the length of theirs.[18] Sekisui House schedules check-ups at three months after move-in, and again at 12 and 24 months; product literature notes the 24-month visit will involve close inspec-tion and complimentary light repairs. Customers can take advantage of a free ten-year inspection; if they commission any recommended repairs, Sekisui House automatically extends its warranty on the home to 20 years.[19] PanaHome follows a two-year "Aftercare Service" with "Maintenance Support" for as long as 60 years (with additional fees required after 25 years). Daiwa House offers contracts with coverage for up to 50 years.) PanaHome Owners' Club members can get other kinds of support, including relief funds after natural disasters and special discounts for services. At one point, the company also offered these members 30-year warranties and up to 35 years of free maintenance. Companies promise 24-hour, 365-day customer response by phone. Maintaining original product inven-tories allows them to anticipate replacement parts and paint or product colors for service calls.

Purchasers can preview houses in model home parks (Jyūtakutenjijō), a prac-tice initiated by Asahi Broadcast Company, a leading TV broadcaster, in 1966.[20]

Figure 12.6
**Daiwa House
robot**

Figure 12.7
**Model home
park**

Larger operators manage multiple sites: ABC Housing claims to be the largest, with 24 exhibition parks showing around 350 houses in two densely populated regions.[21] A 2000 academic paper identified 405 model home parks throughout Japan, displaying roughly 5,000 houses; Sekisui House exhibited about 600 model homes across the country.[22] This appears consistent across major industry players: a survey in 2002 found each producer had about 500 model homes on display every year, at considerable expense to the companies involved.[23] Model home sites also offer informational seminars on purchasing a factory-built home and family-friendly promotions such as free toys and prizes. A newspaper article on one visit to a model home park began, "We went for the six-pack of beer, which the manufactured-housing company was giving away to the first ten people who came to inspect its new model homes."[24] Misawa even has a mascot, "Miffy."

Model home parks are not limited to factory-built housing, however. ABC's website, for example, lists 46 companies; over 30 are not JPCSMA members. Industry leaders therefore maintain their own model home parks and showrooms where consumers can examine large-scale samples of finish materials. Buyers can also tour factories – and even spend the night in a PanaHome model.[25]

Figure 12.8
Misawa material featuring Miffy

Producers of factory-built housing demonstrate considerable effort to promote brand loyalty. Sekisui House claims its in-house magazine *Kizuna* (*Emotional Ties*)[26] has built up a list of 650,000 subscribers since it was established in 1975.[27] Articles, archived online, picture seasonally appropriate minor maintenance (e.g., removing door or window screens) and offer tips on entertaining or refreshing interiors. New services are also introduced:

> I read an article about the Everloop program in *Kizuna*, Sekisui House's magazine for homeowners. I soon contacted Sekisui House, inquired about the Everloop program, and decided to sell our home under this program. – Everloop home seller[28]

Industry leaders publish to keep brands in the public eye and expand product awareness. Misawa Homes' irregular serial publication received an award from the Ministry of Construction in 1992 and was recently re-published in a handsome three-volume collection.[29] In 2012, Daiwa House's CEO wrote columns that ran for one month in the morning *Nihon Keizai Shimbun* (*Japanese Economic Newspaper*), later compiled into a book as well. Perhaps reflecting Asahi Broadcasting's early ties to the industry, prefabricators also aggressively use television to promote their products: Daiwa House, likely reaching out to a younger consumer, produces some extremely funny commercials, with the actual product playing only a minor role – if any! – in storylines.

Although perhaps not an intended outcome, the aggressive marketing of prefabricated homes within Japan and the ample promotional material available is likely one reason why the industry is better known abroad than, for example, Northern European prefabricators.

At times, companies commission homes by well-respected architects. In the 1980s, Sekisui House commissioned a row of homes by Toyō Itō, Kunihiko

Figure 12.9
Daiwa House commercial

Hayakawa, Itsuko Hasegawa, and two other architects. They were built "as far as possible" using the company's IS structural system with a patented concrete formwork setting a 500mm construction module.[30] Owners worked with the architects to fine-tune the prototypes, causing greater grief and expense than originally anticipated; Hiroshi Watanabe reported, "Hasegawa is reluctant to admit to having had any connection to the project." Hayakawa's experience was more positive and influenced new approaches Sekisui House used in subsequent models. Five houses were still in use by their original owners 26 years later and apparently well cared for; the home Hayakawa designed was torn down in 2004 to allow the land to be sold.[31] Generally, though, architect-designed models serve a promotional role, offered in one-off or limited-edition lines.

Like architects, prefabricators aggressively pursue recognition for the high quality they offer. The Good Design Award has gone to a number of factory-built houses: PanaHome (1994 and 2009) and Sekisui House (2004 and 2007), for example. The smaller company Sanyo Homes received a Good Design Award for a factory-built house in 2004 and MUJI, a relatively new contender, has already received it three times for its precut products: in 2006 (Box House designed by Kazuhiko Namba), 2008 (Window House designed by Kengo Kuma), and 2009 (*Asahi* (Morning), or A, House).[32] Daiwa House received an award in 2014 for a condominium project, an emerging market where they have taken a stronger position. Starting in 1991, Misawa Homes received the award 16 years straight, and over 24 years a whopping 47 Misawa designs snagged the Good Design Award. Companies also go for product or component awards: Sekisui House, for example, received the Good Design Award for unit bathrooms in 2009 and 2010 and for features as mundane as a hose reel (2004) and a laundry-folding stand (2007). Model home sites are lavishly embellished with Good Design marks.

In addition to developing brand awareness, industry leaders segment the market through product differentiation. PanaHome, as noted earlier, ties its offerings to sophisticated electronic products such as hands-free water faucets in bathrooms; Toyota, highlighting technology transfer from the automotive industry, recently rolled out an experimental home that can be temporarily powered by a plug-in hybrid or electric car to assure comfort following a disaster.[33] Hebel House, built by Asahi Kasei, is specifically designed for urban areas, which limits the impact of higher transport costs for aerated concrete. The company emphasizes that concrete enhances security and strength, fire resistance, and quiet – and the houses also respond to the urban market with space-saving strategies like compact, sliding bookshelves and a line of pet-oriented options: small doors and shelves positioned for cats to roam, tiny interior rooms for dogs, and places to bathe animals.[34]

Many of these options are, like the choices available when ordering automobiles, localized and result in minimal impact on overall production costs, while allowing for personalization and flexibility.

At the whole-house scale, though, each company has developed a carefully limited menu of potential variants listed in tiered packages priced to reflect production costs. Sales staff, often working in model homes displayed at exhibition sites, guide consumers through these choices without making them feel limiting. Even though industry leaders use the internet for marketing, consumers cannot explore product variation through online plug-and-play systems that might encourage greater demand for variation. The modularity of traditional Japanese architecture, which used larger measuring units – the *tatami* mat, measuring roughly one meter by two meters; the *tsubo*, the size of two *tatami* mats – may also make a modular approach more acceptable.

Available customization varies by company, too. Among the industry leaders, Sekisui House offers the greatest flexibility and number of models. Heavy, concrete

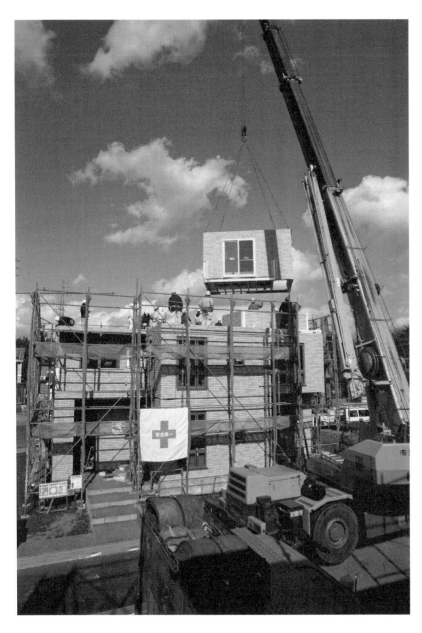

Figure 12.10
**Sekisui Heim
volume**

関西
滋賀県 | 京都府 | 奈良県
大阪府 | 和歌山県 | 兵庫県

関東
東京都 | 神奈川県
千葉県 | 埼玉県
栃木県 | 茨城県
群馬県 | 山梨県

西日本
岡山県 | 広島県
山口県 | 福岡県
佐賀県

東海
静岡県 | 愛知県
三重県 | 岐阜県

Figure 12.11
Hebel House
distribution
areas

panels mounted on boxy steel frames leave Asahi Kasei's Hebel House little room for major modifications.

Sekisui Heim offers eight unit sizes, working with two set widths (1.2 and 2.4 meters) and established lengths between 2.3 and 5.4 meters; as a result, their homes take less time to complete. Even so, in 2006 a Sekisui Heim employee noted that each residence involved about 30,000 parts from a catalog of 300,000 in stock.[35] Failures associated with the postwar Lustron House in the US are often blamed on the large number of necessary parts; perhaps this is less of an issue in an era of computer inventories and bar codes. In the early 1980s, Japanese companies were in the vanguard of pursuing digital planning, computer-controlled inventory, and CNC production, described collectively as "robotic" systems. Their digital know-how preceded the wide use of computers in design practice and received considerable attention in scholarly and popular publications.

Material choices impact the path from production to delivery as well. Because Asahi Kasei's houses use its signature autoclaved concrete (an expensive technology involving a large kiln), the company is limited to a single factory. The weight and volume of each building unit limits sales territory, while competitors sell across the nation. Sekisui House, on the other hand, contracts with corporate affiliates who actually build its product. Daiwa House uses preselected subcontractors, who build under the supervision of a Daiwa House superintendent. Misawa sells kits to independent dealers or builders, perhaps easier because their wood structures use technologies familiar to small homebuilders.

Production choices set efficiencies. Sekisui Heim produces three to four houses per employee each year, at a rate of about 135 homes each day.[36] Sekisui House sold 52,231 residences in 2009 with 16,215 employees, coming in at a slightly lower three units per employee. But many employees are involved in sales and marketing, too. Misawa Homes, for example, employed about 9,000 people in FY2011, and yet it sold only 13,000 homes – even though Misawa does not use its own employees to build on site.

With strong and consistent demand for new homes, Japan's industry leaders can tap into competitive financing during times of slow demand. The housemakers even attract foreign investment (as much as a quarter of capitalization) and float bonds internationally. Sekisui House first issued a foreign convertible bond (in Deutschmarks) in 1976. In over half a century, Sekisui House has sold more

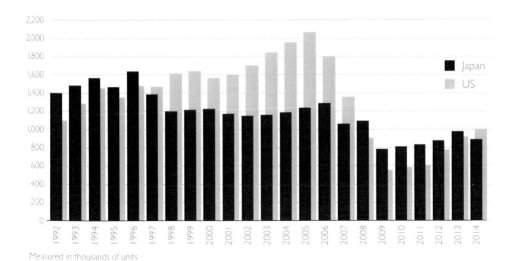

Measured in thousands of units

than two million homes, longevity that results from easy access to financing – at home and abroad – to compensate for the recessions that often drive fabricators out of business in other nations.

Over the last two decades, housing starts in Japan outpaced housing starts in the US about half the time, in spite of sizable differences in population. (There is also greater stability in Japan's residential market in comparison to the US.) In 2012, with a population of about 127 million, there were 882,797 housing starts in Japan, or one new residence built for every 144 people.

That year, about 15 percent of housing starts, or 132,244 homes, were pre-fabricated, using a narrow definition of the term. "Prefabricators" must belong to the JPCSMA – and to do so, they must produce at least 300 homes a year.[38] Kengo Kuma's detached houses for MUJI, for example, are a precut product assembled on site, and not officially "prefabricated." Including precut lumber kits and smaller-scale house-makers, prefabricated housing served 25 percent of the

Figure 12.12
US and Japanese housing starts[37]

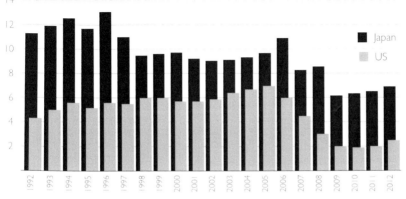

Measured in 100,000 of units per capita

Figure 12.13
US and Japanese housing starts, population adjusted[39]

detached home market in 2008.[40] Even under tighter JPCSMA guidelines, prefabricated housing production consistently turned out between 12.4 and 16 percent of Japan's new homes each year for the last decade – but the nation's thirst for housing is dwindling, affecting factory-built housing demand, too.

Japan's population is shrinking and aging; the economy has also been in the doldrums for at least two decades. This impacts house-makers. Misawa Homes, once the largest producer of factory-built housing, was restructured between 2003 and 2006 in the face of more than half a billion dollars of debt.[41] Toyota, struggling to grow beyond modest sales (it sold only 4,300 houses in 2004), purchased a major stake in Misawa and the two share research and development. Customers visiting model homes today will get a hard sell; flyers push special limited-time prices or limited-time discounts on add-ons like towel warmers, heated floors, and mist saunas.

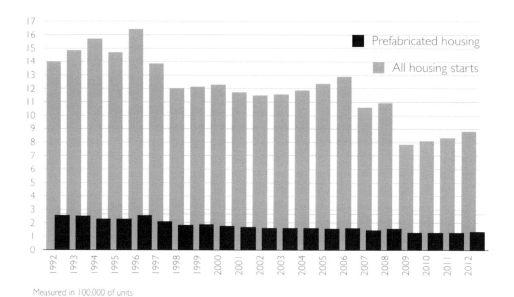

Measured in 100,000 of units

Figure 12.14 **Japan's prefabricated housing starts vs. total housing starts**[42]

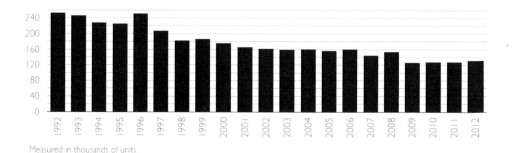

Measured in thousands of units

Figure 12.15 **Declines in Japan's prefabricated housing**[43]

Sekisui Heim's largest factory can produce 800 homes a month; not so long ago, Sekisui House was producing 750 houses a month in its Kanto factory.[44] But overcapacity has become a problem with dropping demand, and at least one major plant was closed to increase efficiency.[45] Since many factories are already highly automated (and have been since the 1970s or early 1980s), there is little opportunity for savings on the production line. Companies have addressed market decline by reducing choices, reining in inventory and production costs; Sekisui House, for example, offered 110 models in 1997 but only 50 three years later.[46]

Japan is divided into 47 prefectures, which function something like states; JPCSMA data allows a nuanced understanding of prefabrication's market penetration.

Table 12.2
Prefabricated housing sales and market share, by prefecture

Prefecture	Housing starts (2012)	Prefab units sold	Market share	Prefab plant located in prefecture?	Single-family	Town-house	Multi-family
National	882,797	132,244	15.0%		60,561	24,826	46,857
Hokkaido*	35,237	1,366	3.9%		1,139	157	70
Aomori	5,578	718	12.9%	✓	264	336	118
Iwate	7,752	1,131	14.6%		403	368	360
Miyagi	20,609	3,314	16.1%		1,604	923	787
Akita	3,668	349	20.6%	✓	235	58	56
Yamagata	4,716	766	22.7%		370	241	155
Fukushima	11,353	2,334	20.6%		1,114	804	416
Ibaraki	22,482	5,095	22.7%	✓	2,179	1,184	1,732
Tochigi	14,814	3,174	21.4%	✓	1,417	1,095	662
Gunma	12,114	2,532	20.9%	✓	1,239	618	675
Saitama	59,605	10,499	17.6%		3,532	1,676	5,291
Chiba	46,013	8,587	18.7%		3,298	1,925	3,364
Tokyo	140,862	18,205	12.9%		4,091	4,231	9,883
Kanagawa	67,606	11,203	16.6%		3,821	384	6,998
Niigata	11,953	1,437	12.0%		653	332	452
Toyama	5,192	593	11.4%	✓	206	285	102
Ishikawa	6,164	897	14.6%		305	344	248
Fukui	3,614	507	14.0%		237	186	84
Yamanashi	4,286	688	16.1%		485	91	112
Nagano	10,483	1,832	17.5%		1,238	352	242
Gifu	10,603	1,798	17.0%		1,308	102	388
Shizuoka	24,722	5,547	22.4%		3,725	1,109	713
Aichi	56,280	10,828	19.2%	✓	6,963	1,216	2,649
Mie	9,554	1,956	20.5%	✓	1,513	112	331
Shiga	9,271	1,739	18.8%		1,107	250	382
Kyoto	15,408	1,723	11.2%	✓	841	147	735
Osaka	61,617	6,130	9.9%		2,347	509	3,274
Hyogo	33,695	5,190	15.4%	✓	2,733	1,026	1,431
Nara	6,740	1,230	18.2%	✓	675	200	355

Prefecture	Housing starts (2012)	Prefab units sold	Market share	Prefab plant located in prefecture?	Single-family	Town-house	Multi-family
Wakayama	4,961	1,067	21.5%	✓	565	288	214
Tottori	2,101	316	15.0%		166	91	59
Shimane	3,037	333	11.0%		85	186	62
Okayama	12,500	3,043	24.3%		2,054	554	435
Hiroshima	16,487	2,705	16.4%	✓	1,306	593	806
Yamaguchi	8,494	1,920	22.6%		830	455	635
Tokushima	3,616	344	9.5%	✓	211	117	16
Kagawa	4,976	742	14.9%		503	195	44
Ehime	7,535	1,085	14.4%		615	352	118
Kochi	2,761	420	15.2%		231	130	59
Fukuoka	36,111	3,756	10.4%		1,978	668	1,110
Saga	4,524	852	18.8%	✓	410	203	239
Nagasaki	6,344	802	12.6%		495	97	210
Kumamoto	11,521	1,246	10.8%		665	190	391
Oita	6,670	923	13.8%		552	188	183
Miyazaki	6,754	529	7.8%		318	103	108
Kagoshima	9,701	655	6.8%		397	155	103
Okinawa	12,713	138	1.1%		138	0	0

* Hokkaido is not a prefecture, but functions similarly.

Source: Japan Prefabricated Construction Suppliers and Manufacturers Association, www.purekyo.or.jp/3-1.html, accessed July 20, 2013.

Table 12.2 continued

Ticks in Table 12.2 indicate prefectures where one or more factories are located; prefabricated housing generally has greater market share nearby, reflecting transportation savings. Demand for factory-built housing weakens furthest from plants: it is very low in Hokkaido and Okinawa (at the extreme north and south) and also relatively low at the southern tip of Kyushu, in Miyazaki and Kagoshima. Demand is also somewhat lower along the western coast, which is not as well connected by major transportation routes; highways and rail lines are more developed on Japan's eastern coastline. In urban areas such as Tokyo (and Kanagawa, which includes Yokohama, the nation's second-largest city), markets skew away from single-family homes.

The March 11, 2011 ("3.11") earthquake in northern Japan created very strong demand for temporary housing and permanent replacement homes; 120,000 homes were completely damaged by the earthquake and tsunami; an additional 240,000 were partially damaged – equivalent to "yellow-tagging" in the US. With evacuations caused by Fukushima's nuclear meltdown, 344,000 people were displaced and in need of new housing.[47] JPCSMA data from 2012 reflects surging demand. The three prefectures most affected by the earthquake were Iwate, Miyagi, and Fukushima; temporary housing for evacuees was also built in surrounding prefectures (e.g., Ibaraki, Tochigi). All three prefectures show a spike,

	Housing starts	Prefabricated units	Prefabricated share of total
Fukushima	+45%	+48%	20%
Miyagi	+62%	+60%	16.1%
Iwate	+58%	+92%	14.6%

Table 12.3 **Housing starts and prefabricated market share, 2012, in areas affected by the 3.11 disaster**

Source: Japan Prefabricated Construction Suppliers and Manufacturers Association, www.purekyo. or.jp/3-1.html, accessed July 20, 2013.

but the intensity varies. There are no JPCSMA factories in Iwate; it is very remote and coastal transportation routes, both rail and road, were battered by the tsunami on 3.11. Fukushima is more centrally located and suffered less damage to its transportation network.

In order to assure speedy response, prefectural governments contract with the JPCSMA to match fabricators and local governments after disasters. National guidelines set the maximum size of temporary units at 29.8 square meters (321 square feet), with subsidies of no more than ¥2,387,000 ($28,800) per unit.[48] Temporary housing is not designed to be desirable or durable; it is intended for only two years' use, though the slow pace of rebuilding has kept many in these "barracks" for far longer this time.

Twenty days after 3.11, the Japanese government announced 72,290 temporary houses would be required: 24,000 in Fukushima, 30,000 in Miyagi, and 18,000 in Iwate.[49] The first temporary housing was completed that same day in Rikuzentakata, Iwate; construction began on March 19, only eight days after the earthquake.[50] By late August, over 47,000 housing units were installed and in use in northern Japan.[51] Construction continued in Fukushima into 2012.[52]

However, the unprecedented level of need overwhelmed production capacity; the government then conceded that subsidies could be used to rent existing housing found independently. Temporary housing quality is modest: not only are units small, but most also lack insulation, even though in Tohoku winter temperatures fall below freezing. Refugees enthusiastically pursued rental alternatives. In response, the national government then reduced the number of temporary units it would subsidize.[53]

Problematically, the industry had already responded to initial estimates: revisions in demand caused a drop in average cost per unit of about ¥500,000 (just short of $5,000), because suppliers had already ordered materials and were suddenly scrambling for a share of the smaller market.[54]

Two industry leaders took a big role in furnishing temporary housing: Daiwa House produced 11,041 temporary housing units, as well as temporary buildings for schools, warehouses, and medical clinics.[55] Sekisui House supplied

Prefecture	Original estimate	Revised estimate
Fukushima	24,000	15,200
Miyagi	30,000	23,000
Iwate	18,000	14,000

Table 12.4 **Original and adjusted targets for temporary housing, post-3.11**

Source: Satoru Tanaka (2012) "A Sustainable Public Procurement System for Large-Scale Natural Disasters: The Case of the Temporary Housing Program after the East Japan Earthquake", *Proceedings 5th International Public Procurement Conference* (IPPC 2012), p. 3544.

4,000 temporary homes; it quickly provided temporary kitchens and sanitary facilities as well.[56]

Daiwa House also performed 157,100 damage checks on their homes located anywhere ground movement exceeded M5.0, a territory that extended to Tokyo.[57] Sekisui House was in contact with its customers in the affected region to check on repair needs within three weeks of the earthquake; 177,458 of its houses experienced forces of at least M5.0 and about 2 percent of them required repair.[58] As might be expected in light of the emphasis on safety and seismic performance, no homes supplied by industry leaders were found uninhabitable by inspectors.

Bottlenecks affected replacement housing sales.[59] The difficulty in getting mortgage financing, a short construction season impacted by winter weather, and labor shortages all contributed to delays. In spite of these problems, Sekisui House saw sales in the three prefectures go up by 20 percent; the Tohoku branch of Misawa Homes reported a 250 percent increase in demand for renovations;[60] and PanaHome saw a nationwide 8.8 percent increase in sales in fiscal year 2011–12.[61]

Daiwa House opened several "Daiwa House Housing Reconstruction Consultation Centers" in May 2011, where the company promoted a low-cost single-family house called "xevo K" "specifically designed to meet the needs of the disaster-hit region, with superior earthquake resistance and a quicker construction period."[62] New owners of xevo series homes in the Tohoku region or those who relocated to the nearby Kantō region and possessed a disaster victim certificate from the government could receive a complimentary 2kW solar power generation system.[63]

Although Japan is considered a global leader in energy conservation, practices accepted in most of the developed world are rare: roughly three-quarters of existing single-family homes and about 60 percent of multi-family residences have no exterior insulation, and double-pane glazing and thermal breaks are not the norm.[64] These features are, however, commonplace in factory-built housing; in fact, many factory-built homes feature insulation in interior walls as well, since people tend to heat only the rooms that are in use. Prefabricated homes flaunt their low-e finishes, insulated glazing, and weatherstripping as well. (Because most housemakers source windows domestically, they often lacked thermal breaks, but this began to change in 2015 with new windows matching international standards.) Heating and cooling costs in prefabricated homes are one-third of those of site-built homes, a point frequently made in pamphlets.

Interest in energy-related technologies rises and falls with the cost of oil and electricity – a team of US academics were surprised to discover very little interest when visiting Japan's residential prefabricators in 1991 – but industry expertise goes back to the 1970s Oil Shock, which had a profound impact on Japan's economy.[65] Misawa, for example, introduced its first solar home in 1974.[66] It displayed a Zero-Net Energy prototype at an international exposition as early as 1990. Exotic proof-of-concept prototypes are exhibited before they are market-ready, attracting publicity, enhancing the brand by underscoring technological expertise, and suggesting trajectories for new products ahead. Asahi Kasei, cooperating with company affiliates on R+D, played an important role in the invention of the lithium ion battery. Sekisui House, by July 2006, had sold 50,000 houses with solar power generation installed; a 3kW system reduced commercial electricity use by half, to about ¥72,247 ($630) a year.[67]

The 3.11 earthquake and tsunami triggered nuclear meltdowns; over the next few months, every nuclear power plant was idled and the nation's electric power supply dropped nearly 30 percent. Electricity supply was still limited nearly five years after the earthquake. In response to shortages, the Japanese government rolled out generous feed-in tariffs for energy returned to the grid (¥42, or 53¢, per kWh for PV power), spurring demand for power-generating equipment unfamiliar to small builders. Residential fuel cells that convert natural gas to electricity also boomed: almost 25,000 Ene-Farm units were sold in 2012.[68] Sekisui House's Green First home is sold with either PV power generation or a fuel cell; in 2011, the line accounted for nearly 79 percent of all detached homes the company sold.[69] The company also promoted fuel cell technology to customers who were remodeling, even paired with PV, encouraging owners to profit from high feed-in tariffs by selling power back to the grid. As a result of aggressive sales, Sekisui House reported selling 5,356 Ene-Farm fuel cell systems in 2011 – 40 percent of all Ene-Farm sales for the year.[70] Thirty percent of their low-rise apartment buildings were also equipped with PV panels.[71] PanaHome, moving into real estate development, also uses advanced technology to brand its "smart communities" in Japan's major metropolitan areas. House-makers' expertise, not only in the technologies but also in helping consumers tap into feed-in tariffs and other subsidies, spurred market diffusion of unusual technologies like fuel cells at a critical time.

Figure 12.16
**PanaHome @
Fujisawa SST**

Newer model lines promoted disaster resiliency, with PV power feeds to emergency outlets or tanks storing hundreds of liters of non-potable water. Taken together, energy conservation and disaster resiliency were the most powerful reasons for optimism in Japan's prefabricated housing industry. Insulation and energy-efficient doors and windows may soon be required even in Japan's detached houses. Small builders fear they cannot profitably meet energy conservation requirements ahead; house-makers already are.

Finally, the factory-built housing community was creating a secondary market for homes, buying back their products, updating them, and renting or selling them to new owners. In response to a 2004 government White Paper, nine housing industry leaders formed the Quality Housing Stock Association (a.k.a. SumStock) in 2008, including Misawa Homes, Toyota Homes, Asahi Kasei, Sekisui House, PanaHome, Daiwa House, Sekisui Heim, and Mitsui Home.[72] Sekisui House rolled out its Everloop program in 2007; its renovated houses came with new windows, finishes, and equipment and a ten-year warranty. SumStock is strongly biased toward the factory-built housing industry: owners must have complete data on their home (materials used, etc.) and the new owner must also receive a maintenance plan going at least 50 years into the future. In a market where few existing homes are resold, the alternative to SumStock is a home that, no matter how well built and well maintained, becomes a liability after only a few short decades of use. This new market for renovated homes should not only expand house-makers' operations, but also create greater confidence in the value of its new homes.

Industry leaders were also moving abroad. Sekisui House opened a subsidiary in West Germany in 1973, though it floundered due to a poor understanding of the market and labor resistance; that plant closed in 1982.[73] However, Sekisui House had development projects underway in Australia, Singapore, China, and the US; it reported plans to expand to Russia as well.[74] Misawa Homes' operations in Beijing date back to the sale of 134 homes in 1986. Sekisui Heim, in a joint venture, recently completed a factory in Thailand with a capacity of 1,000 homes a year.

Japan's factory-built housing industry began with many advantages: government support, large industrial partners, unquenchable market demand, and little resistance from competing builders working on site. House-makers quickly hit a scale that allowed them to tap into international financial markets when facing challenges. Industry leaders are unusually long lived, established between 1955 and 1975. International financing and government subsidies also allowed them to pursue factory automation early on; production lines turn out a house in well under ten minutes, at a rate of between one and four houses per full-time employee annually. The time from a customer ordering a home to moving in usually takes no longer than it does to order and take delivery of an automobile with specific options – generally two or three months, though larger and more luxurious models take as long as half a year. Sekisui Heim even boasts that they can demolish an existing house and have the family back on the same lot in a new home in less than two months.

House-makers offer a reliable, though standardized, product for a price only slightly higher than site-built construction, with advanced structural safety in the face of earthquakes, better energy performance, and sophisticated equipment out of the reach of most competitors building on site. Manufactured housing comes with warranties, access to services, and new plug-in components that allow homes to be kept up to date and feeling new for many, many decades – and company longevity buttresses consumer confidence in long-term products like maintenance contracts. Homes can remain ideally suited to their owners' needs over a long period of time and in the face of many life changes. While I have found no evidence to back this up, original owners likely have lower lifetime housing expenses thanks to easy modifications and maintenance. With new resale and renovation opportunities, homeowners can now even get a return on their original investment, almost unheard of in Japan's residential market.

However, Japan's economy has been stagnant for two decades and population declines offer little room for optimism. Demand has dropped; large factories are not operating at capacity – and have not for some time. The house-makers' market share has been stable at around 15 percent of overall housing starts, but annual reports increasingly state that consumers are leaning toward smaller, lower-priced models.

Industry leaders are attempting to diversify into new domestic markets: real estate development and facilities management, or the construction of nursing homes, office buildings, stores, clinics, schools, gymnasiums, factories, or warehouses. Only 27 percent of Sekisui House's 2012 consolidated net sales were derived from selling detached houses; 41 percent came from rental and real estate management. Other industry leaders have slightly different profiles, but all are struggling to discover ways to exploit their industry know-how in new settings as the remarkably robust postwar residential market that nurtured their growth slows down.

Acknowledgments

My warmest appreciation to Riyo Namigata for her assistance in dealing with the house-makers discussed in this chapter.

Author note

Writing in late 2014, I was temporarily residing in an upscale Tokyo neighborhood. A dozen houses were outside my window, more than half clearly prefabricated products, recognizable by their simple orthogonal geometry set against unusual trapezoidal sites and by their solar panels. My apartment, built ten years ago, was clearly site built – but it was speedily renovated by Asahi Kasei before I moved in, and Asahi Kasei also managed the building, replacing the older practice of an on-site concierge. It is yet another reflection of industry shifts.

Notes

1   Ishida, Yorifusa (2003) "Japanese Cities and Planning in the Reconstruction Period: 1945–55," in Carola Hein, Jeffry M. Diefendorf, and Yorifusa Ishida, eds. *Rebuilding Urban Japan after 1945*, New York: Palgrave Macmillan, p. 18; "Arumi Hausu Projekuto

Sutorii 02: Sengo no Jyūtaku Seisaku ni Manabu ["Aluminum House Project Story #2: Learn Japanese Housing Policy"], *ecoms* 26 (February 2009), 4; Sackett, James G. (1986) *Japan's Manufactured Housing Capability: A Review of the Industry and Assessment of the Future Impact on the US Market*, St. Louis, MO: Energy Design Resource, p. 6.

2   Kaneko, Yujiro and Atsuto Niwa (1968) "Report for the Case Study [sic] on Prefabrication of Housing in Japan," United Nations Seminar on Industrialization of Housing, Copenhagen, Denmark., pp. 19 & 46.

3   Watanabe, Hiroshi (1986) "Japan: Selling Houses like Automobiles," *Architecture: The AIA Journal*, 75(10): 96.

4   Nakayama, Shigeru and Kunio Gotō. (2001) *A Social History of Science and Technology in Contemporary Japan: Volume 3: High Economic Growth Period 1960–1969*, Melbourne: Trans Pacific Press, p. 425.

5   Nakayama et al., *Social History of Science and Technology*.

6   The two even use different writing systems in Japanese to underscore the distinction: Sekisui House (積水ハウス) uses *kanji* characters, which implies indigenous Japanese character; Sekisui Heim (セキスイハイム) uses *katakana*, suggesting foreign provenance.

7   Coaldrake, William (1986) "Manufactured Housing: The New Japanese Vernacular, #3," *Japan Architect* 353 (September): 62.

8   Gann, David M. (1996) "Construction as a Manufacturing Process? Similarities and Differences between Industrialized Housing and Car Production in Japan," *Construction Management and Economics* 14(5): 444; Watanabe, "Japan: Selling Houses," 95.

9   Source: Honda, Shōichi, "Evolution of the Housing Industry" in Nakayama and Gotō, *Social History of Science and Technology*, pp. 419–429.

10 On top of the widely held lack of concern for resale value, a home will not affect social status beyond the neighborhood, since the Japanese do not tend to entertain at home.

11 Japan Prefabricated Construction Suppliers and Manufacturers Association (JPCSMA) (2012) "Prefabricated Steel-Frame Housing in Japan," *Steel Construction Today and Tomorrow* 37 (December): 5.

12 Source: *Jyutaku Keizai De-tashuu* [*Collected Economic Data on Housing*] (2014), Tokyo: MLIT, p. 185. (Original data: Ministry of Land, Infrastructure, Transport and Tourism).

13 Gojo, Wataru (2011) "The Aneha scandal: Fraud in Japan," *Forensic Engineering* 164(4): 181–182; Ministry of Land, Infrastructure, Transport and Tourism (MLIT) (2005) *White Paper on Land, Infrastructure, Transport and Tourism in Japan*, Tokyo: Gyōsei, pp. 21–22.

14 Sekisui House (2010) *FY2010 Mid-Term Management Plan*, p. 17. www.sekisuihouse.co.jp/company/data/current/newsobj-1407-datafile.pdf, accessed January 25, 2016.

15 Source: Gojo "The Aneha scandal," 186 (Original data: Ministry of Land, Infrastructure, Transport and Tourism).

16 Source: *Jyūtaku Kin'yū Shien Kikō* [Japan Housing Finance Agency] and Shuichi Matsumura, via personal correspondence. (Original data: Ministry of Land, Infrastructure, Transport and Tourism).

17 Noguchi, Masayoshi (2003) "The Effect of the Quality-Oriented Production Approach on the Delivery of Prefabricated Homes in Japan," *Journal of Housing and the Built Environment* 18(4): 357.

18 Nottage, Luke (2006) "The ABCs of Product Safety Re-Regulation in Japan: Asbestos, Buildings, Consumer Electronic Goods and Schindler's Lifts," *Griffith Law Review* 15(2): 264.

19 Sekisui House (2009) *Corporate Profile*, Osaka: Sekisui House, p. 44.

20 www.abcd.ne.jp/housing/, accessed January 25, 2016.

21 www.abc-housing.co.jp/whatabc/index.html, accessed January 25, 2016.

22 Barlow, James and Ritsuko Ozaki (2005) "Building Mass Customized Housing through Innovation in the Production System: Lessons from Japan," *Environment and Planning A* 37: 15.

23 Patchell, Jerry (2002) "Linking Production and Consumption: The Co-Evolution of International Systems in the Japanese Housing Industry," *Annals of the Association of American Geographers* 92(2): 292.

24 Brasor, Philip and Masako Tsubuku (2011) "Buying a Brand New Home: Cookie Cutter or Order Made?" *Japan Times* (October 4, 2011), www.japantimes.co.jp/community/2011/10/04/how-tos/buying-a-brand-new-home-cookie-cutter-or-order-made/#.Uevs X1O-JZ1, accessed January 25, 2016.

25 www.panahome.jp/shukuhaku_tenjijyo/, accessed January 25, 2016.

26 There is another magazine with the same name; Sekisui House prints its title in Japanese-language characters while the other uses the Roman alphabet.

27 Sekisui House (2012) *Corporate Profile*, Osaka: Sekisui House, p. 58.

28 Sekisui House (2011) *Sekisui House Sustainability Report 2011*, Osaka: Sekisui House, p. 46.

29 The book is called *Sumai no Bunka Shi* [*Culture of Houses*]. The award was the Kensetsu Daijin Hyōshō [Commendation of the Ministry of Construction].

30 Watanabe, "Japan: Selling Houses"; *Nikkei Ākitekuchua* (2007) "Jūtaku Kaisha + Kenchikuka: no Michi Hiraku. Shōhinka ha Dannen; Kenchikagawa ni ha Shikorimo" ["Opening a New Path: 'House Company + Architect.' Giving Up on Commodification; Architects also Unbending"] *Nikkei Ākitekuchua* [*Nikkei Architecture*] 858 (September 24): 63.

31 *Nikkei Ākitekuchua*, 64.

32 Sanyo was purchased by Panasonic in 2010 and in 2013 Panasonic announced it would close Sanyo; it is unclear how this will affect the Sanyo Homes line, which covered a very similar market territory to PanaHome, though at a smaller scale.

33 Toyota Home News Release, April 10, 2013.

34 www.asahi-kasei.co.jp/hebel/product/family/04.html/, accessed July 21, 2013.

35 Furuse, Jun and Masayuki Kitano (2006) "Structuring of Sekisui Heim Automated Parts Pickup System (HAPPS) to Process Indivisual [sic] Floor Plans," *Proceedings 23rd International Symposium on Automation and Robotics in Construction (ISARC 2006)*: 352.

36 *Ibid.*; Bock, Thomas and Thomas Linner (2010) "Fusion of Product and Automated Replicative Production in Construction," *Proceedings 27th International Symposium on Automation and Robotics in Construction (ISARC 2010)*: 18–19.

37 Source: US Census data; Japan Statistics Bureau, 2013.

38 www.purekyo.or.jp/3-1.html, accessed January 25, 2016.

39 Source: US Census data; Japan Statistics Bureau, 2013.

40 "Arumi Hausu Projekuto Sutorii 04: Sengo ni Shutsugen Suru Jyūtaku Sangyō, sono Keninsha • Jyūtaku Mēkā ni Manabu" ["Aluminum House Project Story #4: Learn Postwar Emergence of the Housing Industry, its Causes"], *ecoms* 28 (September 2009), 7.

41 *Japan Times* (2003) "Misawa to Change Group Structure," *Japan Times* (January 30), www.japantimes.co.jp/news/2003/01/30/business/misawa-to-change-group-structure/#.UexWBIO-JZ0, accessed July 20, 2013; Uranaka. Taiga (2004) "Daiei, Misawa to Get IRCJ Bailout," *Japan Times* (December 29), www.japantimes.co.jp/news/2004/12/29/national/daiei-misawa-to-get-ircj-bailout/#.UexVwIO-JZ0, accessed July 20, 2013; Industrial Revitalization Corporation of Japan (IRCJ) (2006) "IRJC Receives Payment in

Full for Misawa Holdings, Inc. and Group Company Debt," IRJC Press Release (March 31).

42 Source: Japan Statistics Bureau, 2013.

43 Source: Japan Statistics Bureau, 2013.

44 Gann, "Construction as a Manufacturing Process?" 446.

45 Sekisui House, *FY2010 Mid-Term Management Plan*, p. 12.

46 Barlow and Ozaki, "Building Mass Customized Housing," 17.

47 MLIT (2011) *White Paper on Land, Infrastructure, Transport and Tourism in Japan*, Tokyo: Gyōsei, p. 19.

48 Exchange rate for March 31, 2011, when most contracts were being negotiated.

49 MLIT (2010) *White Paper on Land, Infrastructure, Transport and Tourism in Japan*, Tokyo: Gyōsei; Tanaka, Satoru (2012) "A Sustainable Public Procurement System for Large-Scale Natural Disasters: The Case of the Temporary Housing Program after the East Japan Earthquake," *Proceedings 5th International Public Procurement Conference (IPPC 2012)*: 3543.

50 Tanaka, "A Sustainable Public Procurement System," 3543.

51 MLIT (2010) *White Paper*, p. 54.

52 Shinohara, Naohide, Masahiro Tokumura, Misae Kazama, and Atsushi Mizukoshi (2013) "Indoor Air Quality, Air Exchange Rates, and Radioactivity in New Built Temporary Houses Following the Great East Japan Earthquake in Minamisoma, Fukushima," *Indoor Air* 23(4): 334.

53 Tanaka, "A Sustainable Public Procurement System," 3544.

54 *Ibid.*, 3550.

55 Daiwa House (2012) *Annual Report*, Osaka: Daiwa House, p. 45.

56 Sekisui House (2011) *Sustainability Report*, p. 3.

57 Daiwa House (2012) *Annual Report*, p. 45.

58 Sekisui House (2011) *Sustainability Report*, p. 3.

59 Yamashita, Ryuichi and Nobuyoshi Nakamura (2011) "Construction Boom Hits Tohoku, but not Everyone is Happy," *Asahi Shimbun* (July 4), http://ajw.asahi.com/article/0311disaster/analysis/AJ201107042846, accessed July 20, 2013.

60 *Ibid.*

61 PanaHome (2012) *Annual Report*, Osaka: PanaHome.

62 Daiwa House (2012) *Annual Report*, p. 44.

63 *Ibid.*

64 Taniguchi, Ayako, Yoshīyuki Shimoda, Takahiro Asahi, Yukio Yamaguchi, and Minoru Mizuno (2007) "Effectiveness of Energy Conservation Measures in Residential Sector Japanese Cities," *Proceedings Tenth International Building Performance Simulation Association*: 1647.

65 Brown, G.Z. with Margot McDonald and Matt Meacham (1991) "Computer Use in Industrialized Housing Sales, Design and Manufacturing Processes," Center for Housing Innovation, University of Oregon.

66 Noguchi, Masa and Karim Hadjri (2009) "Mass Custom Design for Sustainable Housing Development," in Frank T. Piller and Mitchell M. Tseng, eds. *Handbook of Research in Mass Customization and Personalization: Applications and Cases, Vol. 2*, Singapore: World Scientific, pp. 898–899.

67 Noguchi, Masa and Jun-Tae Kim (2010) "The Impact of the Zero-Energy Mass Custom Home Mission to Japan in Industry Education Toward Commercialization," *Proceedings Renewable Energy 2010, Yokohama, Japan*.

68 www.ace.or.jp/web/works/works_0090.html, accessed January 25, 2016.

69 Sekisui House (2012) *Sekisui House Sustainability Report 2012*, Osaka: Sekisui House, p. 45.

70   *Ibid.*, p. 46.
71   Sekisui House, *FY2010 Mid-Term Management Plan*, p. 25.
72   MLIT (2004) *Kokudo Kōtū Hakusho* [*MLIT White Paper*], Tokyo: Gyōsei, pp. 125–126.
73   JPCSMA (2012) "Overseas Operations of Japanese Prefabricated Homebuilders", *Steel Construction Today and Tomorrow* 37 (December): 13; Coaldrake, William (1987) "Manufactured Housing: The New Japanese Vernacular, #4", *Japan Architect* 357 (January): 60.
74   Sekisui House, *FY2010 Mid-Term Management Plan*, p. 3.

Chapter 13

Offsite construction in Sweden

From technology-driven to integrated processes

Helena Lidelöw

The Swedish context

Industrialization in Sweden has had a steady development over the course of 250 years. Despite the small size of the country (9.5 million people), Sweden has seen domestic car production (Volvo and Saab), automation in mining (LKAB and Boliden), production of steel components (Sandvik), production of cell phones and network gear (Ericsson), and power plant technology (ABB). Internationally recognized construction companies originating from Sweden include Skanska, NCC, and PEAB.

The first attempts at prefabricated homes in Sweden were made in 1840 by the architect Fredrik Blom, who was commissioned to build a movable structure somewhere between a tent and a house to be used by high-ranking military. Knowledge was exchanged with other European countries and Canada. Between 1870 and 1900, Sweden along with the rest of Europe saw bad harvests, leading to one-third of the population emigrating to the USA. Some houses for emigrants were produced in flat elements and transported in the hold of emigrant ships. After the bad years, industrialization spurred on the Swedish economy, leading to urbanization and a widespread housing shortage in the growing cities. World War I stifled the development and in 1920 the situation was unbearable. The Swedish government then funded the development of several homebuilding companies through lending money and developing standard designs. Up until World War II, the expansion was rapid in the homebuilding industry, but the war once again hindered progress.

Sweden remained neutral in both wars, leaving the industrial infrastructure intact, and directly after the end of World War II, the first national building code was issued. At the same time, a national collection of practically and theoretically viable design details was compiled (in Sweden known as AMA), helping new construction companies to produce good-quality designs. Standardization of sizes was agreed for, for example, concrete hollow decks and windows. This standardization system remains intact today. The three measures (national building code, national collection of design details, and standardized component sizes) stabilized the Swedish construction market and set the basic rules for its function.

Between 1965 and 1975, Sweden produced a million dwellings as a result of a political initiative, bringing to an end the 50-year-long housing shortage. During these intense years (constructing housing for one-sixth of the population), the housebuilding industry transformed from being led by smaller, local master builders to the formation of large, professional contractors. These were golden years for homebuilders and prefabrication and offsite construction was realized in concrete-, steel-, and wood-frame construction. The development of new processes was rapid and the construction industry borrowed knowledge from other industries such as car production and shipbuilding. It all ended with an outcry! And that outcry came from the end users i.e., the people living in the houses. The strong focus on production had set aside the importance of living quality and now the residents demanded to be seen as individuals. Up until this point, architects in Sweden had been the driving force behind standardization and production-friendly design. Now, they (their trade organization) stated that from now on, architects would work for the end user and defend architectural quality.

As a result, Swedish construction in general saw a development focused on small-scale housing between 1980 and 2000. Environmental issues became important as the energy crisis in 1974 was the beginning of the end of oil as the primary energy source for heating homes. At first, the switch was made to electricity, but later years saw a massive development of district heating. In 1994, the government removed all subsidiaries to housing construction in Sweden and for the first time in 70 years, the housing market was governed by market forces only. Construction companies and developers now needed to learn customer focus.

As a result of the historical developments, Sweden has a good foundation in offsite construction:

- *A well-trained workforce*. The education level in general is high, even for blue-collar workers, which means that the workforce is also expensive. As a result, it is cheaper to produce goods off site, where automation is possible.
- *Knowledge of methods in offsite production*. The most common structure (50 percent) for a multi-family house in Sweden is precast hollow decks on prefabricated steel columns. For single-family homes, it is a wooden frame made of prefabricated planar elements assembled on site (90 percent).
- *Knowledge of customer needs*. Since 1994, fragmentation in market segments has occurred as a result of new market conditions. Urbanization has restarted, leading to a situation in which the housing shortage in the cities is at levels parallel to those of the 1960s.
- *Knowledge in green building*. The environmental focus of the 1980s and onward has resulted in customers and clients being knowledgeable in demanding green solutions. Wood-frame construction has moved from single-family homes to multi-family permanent housing built up to ten storeys high with a 10–15 percent market share in the multi-family housing segment.

From technology-driven to integrated processes

The development of offsite construction was technology driven in Sweden up until 1970. After failing to meet architectural and customer demands with the large-scale developments, technology was not seen as a viable route forward any longer. It took two decades for offsite construction to somewhat recover and of course this was linked to the demand in the market. When demand is high, the ideas around industrialization seem to re-emerge and construction companies start to rethink their earlier "project-to-project" strategy. The question for a construction company with a long-term commitment is how to sustain offsite construction regardless of economic fluctuations. Swedish companies have attempted a solution based not only on technology, but also on process industrialization. It provides greater flexibility in the technical solution itself, but preserves the idea of industrialization in the realization of building projects. There are some ingredients to frame such an idea: market position, operative platform, and business offer – together forming the business model.

Market position

When venturing into offsite construction, there are investments. These investments are commonly in production equipment and even factories, but also in personnel, training, and the supply chain. Most construction companies working on a sequence of building projects find it difficult to sustain heavy investments since future cash flow is unsecure. Therefore, it is essential to choose your market segment with knowledge and care. In Sweden, some stable market segments have emerged in housing, based on a century of experience:

- *First home.* The single-family homes market for low-income families seeking their first home. Sweden has only one building code i.e., there are no exceptions for modular construction or manufactured homes. But Sweden also has a history of attacking this particular market segment in other sectors; IKEA and H&M are two other companies that target people with little money in need of satisfactory goods. This also works in homebuilding. Some of the companies with the longest traditions in offsite construction are actors in this market. They succeed through offering fixed prices, well-defined delivery, low prices, and enough quality to satisfy requirements. They seldom allow much flexibility for the customer. Larger producers in this segment sell around 400 homes each year at a price of approximately 1.5 MSEK each.
- *Core home.* The second successful market segment is also in the single-family homes market and targets middle- to upper-class families building the family home (where children grow up and parents grow old). Since this group of customers is larger than the low-income segment, the number of companies active in the segment is also larger. The customer is invited into the design process and flexibility is a selling point. There is less standardization in the product, leading to fewer automation possibilities and a higher price. Quality is high and often there are possibilities to choose environmentally friendly solutions in materials and energy technology. Larger producers of single-family homes in this segment sell around 200 homes each year at a price of approximately 3 MSEK each.
- *City home.* The multi-family homes market for middle-class families wanting to live in the city. In the suburbs of larger cities such as Stockholm and Gothenburg,

there are areas where multi-family houses dominate city planning. Zoning is not used the same way in Sweden as, for example, in the USA. Multi-family homes are difficult to organize in house models as the surrounding area affects the house design to a large extent. Instead, standardization is achieved at a lower level, looking at, for example, standardized bathrooms and kitchen solutions and of course structural elements that can be both flat and volumetric. In the multi-family market, the customers are not private consumers but professional clients. Flexibility is important to them, as is long-term quality. Producers in this segment sell around 1,000 dwellings each year and the price varies depending on the project type, but a typical cost per square meter is 30 kSEK/m^2.

In all these three market segments, there are several actors. In the single-family homes segment, they are single-business companies that only work in one market niche. In the multi-family homes segment, larger construction companies take part that also have other businesses (road works, bridges, offices, etc.).

Operative platform

Mastering a technology is the basic skill in having an operative platform in construction. Examples of technologies are prefabrication of flat elements, assembly of prefabricated building parts as columns and slabs, and prefabricating and assembling volumetric elements. One of the most important decisions to make and then sustain in the long term is to determine the decoupling point for the operative platform. This is illustrated in Figure 13.1.

In the three market segments presented, the decoupling point has different locations. When targeting the first home segment, the customer is not let into the design process, rendering the construction company able to organize both design and production according to their liking (standard products). Design and production automation are viable options and investments in automation technology can be sustained if the market niche exists over some time.

Targeting the core home segment, the construction company must be able to meet the design changes from the customers by allowing flexibility both in design and production. Typically, this means less automation and a longer design process. Communication with the customer can be organized using trained salesmen, architects, and/or interior decorators. The design process is a configuration of possible options, sometimes combined with unique design within a closed building system.

The same situation as for the core home segment applies to city home segment, where flexibility must be allowed. An added complication is the fact that each project involving city homes is much larger in scale than for a core home. This means that errors can replicate during production. Therefore, the design process must be timely, precise, and with few errors to be profitable. The demand for flexibility means that most production of city homes is realized using open building systems, but some producers use a closed building system.

Swedish construction companies' operative platform can best be described using the theoretical framework of platform technology (see Figure 13.2).

Figure 13.1
**Different design
strategies
in housing.
Strategies
lower down in
the diagram
lead to
more offsite
construction.
Developed from
Lidelöw et al.
(2015)**

Decoupling or order point

Detailed design of building parts based on codes and standards

Configuration and combination of pre-designed building parts organized in an open building system

Combination and configuration of pre-designed building parts organized in a closed, proprietary building system

Selection of pre-designed variant buildings organized as standard products

Figure 13.2
**Platform
technology use
in construction,
Jansson et al.
(2014)**

0%   Level of pre-design   100%

Design work based on forecast

Design work based on customer order

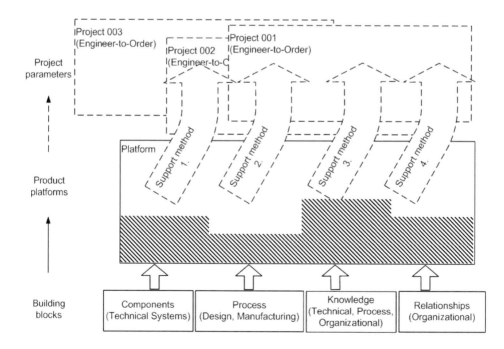

Project parameters

Project 003
(Engineer-to-Order)

Project 002
(Engineer-to-O

Project 001
(Engineer-to-Order)

Platform

Support method 1.

Support method 2.

Support method 3.

Support method 4.

Product platforms

Building blocks

| Components (Technical Systems) | Process (Design, Manufacturing) | Knowledge (Technical, Process, Organizational) | Relationships (Organizational) |

An operative platform has four constituents: components, process, relationships, and know-how. The components are captured through the technologies and equipment used by the company to produce its goods. The process part is the most interesting part when allowing flexibility. Although the physical parts that pass through the production system can be different, the process to handle them is the same. A simple example is the mounting of kitchen cabinets. Cabinets can be mounted in more or less the same way regardless of their look. Thus, it is a viable option to allow full flexibility in choosing kitchen cabinets and instead work on standardizing the method of mounting them. Why is this not the case, then? It is due to the third constituent in the platform: relationships. This entails the company's relationships with suppliers. If the customer is allowed to choose any kitchen cabinet, the number of relationships with suppliers will rise, giving rise to administrative costs and loss of time due to constant restarts in the business relationships. Consequently, building good relationships with a few, strong suppliers will lead to a larger profit and a lower price for customers.

Finally, what makes the platform a vehicle to outperform competitors is know-how. In the Swedish market, there are several companies that have the same operative platforms when looking at their structures. However, when comparing their profits over time, it is clear that some do better than others. The know-how that separates better from worse is above all the ability to avoid sub-optimization. This means that marketing/sales, design, and production must be level with each other, all working together to create the result. A common situation in offsite construction is the opposite: the marketing/sales people sell houses that production cannot really build, the design department works to create near-perfect drawings without asking production how the solutions fit them, and the production chain is left with resolving these problems – and does it! Synchronizing know-how in offsite construction is the absolute key to success.

Business offer

Offsite construction opens up new ways to create an offer to the customer. The reason is that the construction company have knowledge about the end product already before it is created. In ordinary construction, the basic offer is capacity: the production of a specific artefact delivered by a certain time at a certain price. Using offsite construction, the basic offer is a product: a predefined artefact with known characteristics delivered in a certain way by a certain time at a certain price. The difference can be monumental to the customer. Swedish examples from offsite construction include:

- paying for the house after the final audit is approved i.e., the offsite manufacturer takes the risk during design and production (so far only used for single-family homes);
- paying some part of the contract sum at first delivery and the rest at approved final audit (used for all market segments described);
- paying continuously during design and production according to a predefined plan (this model is the default in Swedish construction; there are no quantity surveyors linked to approval of the payment plan).

When successful, offsite construction creates a steady and predictable cash flow, which enables the company to risk money and delay payments in the projects. The content of the offers ranges in terms of integration and completeness:

- Delivery of structural elements only, with or without the service of assembling the elements on site. The customer will be in charge of organizing completion of the structure.
- Delivery of structural elements and their completion – a turnkey arrangement. This is by far the most common in Sweden. Attempting to keep costs at a minimum by coordinating the work of the parade of trades often ends up in more costs since only professionals can foresee the order and the extent of work needed. A reminder here is that Swedish homes are among the most service-intense in the world; single-family homes are equipped with heat recovery ventilation, wirebound and wireless electrical services, fiber-optic internet connection, district heating, sensors to regulate temperature, fresh water supply (at times recirculated to extract heat loss to save energy), fireplaces with heat recovery, and a structure built to sustain a temperature range between −25C and +25C with a constant indoor temperature of +20C ± 2C.
- Delivery of the structural elements, their completion, and the site work to produce a finished building. This requires the construction company to have the capability to also handle groundworks. A lucrative combination with this offer is to take ownership of the land in the first place and then act as a developer, closing the engagement by selling the finished apartments.

Experience shows that the more integration of different stages in the offer, the higher the profit (and the risk).

Challenges met

Over the course of the century of offsite construction development in Sweden, some key learning points have emerged as established truths in the business:

1. *If you own it, control it.* Any processes that you have ownership of should be carefully controlled, which does not mean that you should have a control function checking the finished products but rather that production is preplanned, and workers are trained properly, have the right tools, and are supervised through focusing production flow.
2. *If you do not own it, consider whether you should.* Numerous examples in Sweden have shown that once a subprocess is integrated into the company (e.g., installing electrical services), the quality increases and the cost decreases. The only drawback is that this involves an investment, which makes many companies hesitant.
3. *If you do not own it, control the interface.* The operative platform contains relationships to suppliers as well as technology. In practice, this means that the interface with the suppliers must be very well defined. It could, for example, entail asking the supplier to label the goods in a certain way or organize them

in assembly order. Even though this is more costly, it is often worthwhile since the flow increases (and when the flow increases the return of money from the customer comes faster). Given that the market niche is stable or growing, making decisions that increase the flow is economically sound.

4. *Always look at the entire process – do not suboptimize.* In larger companies, the overview of the process is often lost and decisions are made with one specific aspect or function in focus, forgetting that it is the entire flow that needs to be optimized. A very simple example is the speed at which things are completed. When listening to factory personnel, they will most often tell you that they need investments at their station to produce faster. This is basically a good reaction – but not when resources are limited. As a manager, the job is to identify the bottleneck i.e., the slowest process in the production sequence and make sure its speed increases.

5. *Pay attention to detail.* The largest risk with offsite construction is actually in its repetition, which is the very reason for wanting to do it. Errors are rapidly replicated in offsite construction, but those are easy to detect as they often lead to poor quality. The trick is to pay attention to the solutions that are extensively used and make sure that they are as optimal as possible at any given time. This task entails constantly looking for better materials suppliers, studying production sequences to discover the best method to use, and using design for assembly.

6. *Standardize what you can, leave the rest.* Many offsite construction companies are inspired by the car industry and its tools and methods. Keep in mind that the car industry has a decoupling point where the entire design of the car is made beforehand. Consequently, the production line can also be predefined; the number of variants that can occur can be large but is not endless. In construction, you always have the risk of unique designs appearing. Therefore, it is wise to standardize what customers do not want to change (the load-bearing structure, connections between elements, foundation works, etc.) and either leave the rest or attempt to limit the number of possible options. Most often, customers want to have some choice over surface finishing, materials, colours, the placement of windows, and to some extent the floor plan.

7. *Level the functions in the company.* The easiest way to make an offsite construction company go bankrupt is to run the production system out of balance. The functions in an offsite construction company are most often the marketing/sales department, the design department, the purchasing department, and the production department. When the economic climate is tough, the marketing/sales department is tempted to sell something that is beyond the capabilities of the production department. As a consequence, the design department spends too much time on design since their normal methods do not work, the purchasing department must approach new suppliers, and finally the production department cannot use their normal methods and tools. The budget made when delivering the price to the customer is based on earlier experience (coming from the normal business situation) and, since the economic climate is tough, it is tight, allowing no room for error, which most certainly will happen given the uncertainties introduced into the

system. Therefore, it is extremely important that an offsite construction company operates in a stable market niche and that the salesmen are trained to consider the cost of the whole production chain.

This seventh and final point is so important that many offsite construction companies have realized that they need a strong internal operations strategy to handle the situation. A popular operations strategy has been to run a lean implementation, since it supports visualizing work for others and focuses flow.

How lean and platform thinking interlace

The lean operations strategy was originally developed to enable the production of high-quality goods with a small amount of resources in a short amount of time (Womack and Jones, 1990). It was developed in the context of car production in Japan, but has spread today to many other industries, including construction, as in lean construction (Koskela, 1992). Offsite construction is easier to organize according to lean principles than ordinary construction. This is due to the value flow being predefined and resources known at the start of the project.

A lean operations strategy accomplishes two things in an organization: a visualization of the value flow and the continuous improvement of it based on this visualization (Modig, 2012). In concrete terms, the visualization is accomplished through working with visualizing and measuring the flow of operations and then documenting the best practice of how to perform operations. Once documented in, for example, standard operations sheets, it becomes evident when operations are running according to standard or not. Standard operations can then also easily be improved through observation and improvement work. Apart from visualizing the product flow, the information flow is also visualized through daily, short meetings where progress and experience feedback are reported. Continuous improvements are realized separately from the operations and implemented when fully tested. This is a basic distinction in all lean operations, which is mirrored in a platform.

A platform consists of documentation and know-how on the goods that are produced. For the sake of reasoning, assume that a company produces doors. The product documentation is all the drawings and specifications of the door. The process documentation is how the door is produced, essentially the same thing as a standard operations sheet. The relationships concern how different production units inside and outside the door producer are intertwined and are captured in the daily meetings. A predefined meeting structure that is repeated often is the core. These meetings also involve the closest suppliers. The know-how is all the knowledge needed to run the production of doors. With a lean implementation, know-how is constantly trained and self-corrected through the movement back and forth between standard operations and improvement work (Figure 13.3).

In Sweden, several offsite construction companies have recognized this link and organized their operations accordingly with success. Thus, an integrated process has been created where not only is the production technology of offsite construction focused, but rather the combined effect of offsite technology, how it is realized and improved, and how the entire supply chain is aligned.

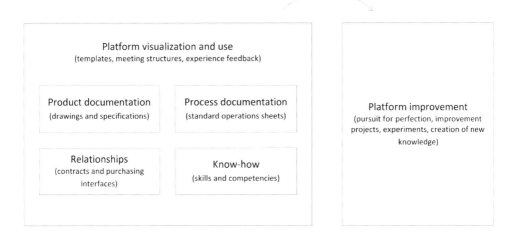

Figure 13.3
**The function
of a platform
using lean as
the operations
strategy**

References

Jansson G., Johnsson H., and Engström D. (2014) Platform Use in Systems Building. *Construction Management and Economics*, 32(1–2): 70–82.

Koskela L. (1992) *Application of the New Production Technology to Construction.* Technical Report, Center for Integrated Facility Engineering, Stanford University, CA.

Lidelöw H., Stehn L., Lessing J., and Engström D. (2015) *Industriellt husbyggande* (in Swedish). Studentlitteratur, Lund.

Modig N. (2012) *This is Lean: Resolving the Efficiency Paradox.* Rheologica, Stockholm.

Womack J.P. and Jones D.T. (1990) *The Machine that Changed the World.* Rawson Associates, Scribner, New York.

Chapter 14

A Scottish perspective on timber offsite construction

Robert Hairstans and Fausto Sanna

Introduction

This chapter exemplifies the recent advancements in Scottish offsite construction through the research work carried out at the Centre for Offsite Construction + Innovative Structures (COCIS) at Edinburgh Napier University, Institute for Sustainable Construction (ISC). COCIS has been instrumental in promoting a culture of interdisciplinary collaboration around the creation of novel building solutions especially for low-rise, residential buildings.

The Centre's holistic approach includes structural safety, thermal performance, environmental impact, acoustic behaviour and fire safety. In order to adopt such an approach, COCIS has relied upon its numerous industrial partners (designers, consultants, building manufacturers and constructors) and other research bodies within Edinburgh Napier. It can be said that the Centre's activities are aligned with a research movement at a wider scale that seeks improvement and sustainable development of the sector.

The work conducted on innovative systems aimed at increasing the level of offsite construction and improving the overall building performance, while minimising economic cost and thus ensuring social accessibility. One of the objectives of this body of work is, indeed, to develop solutions that are easily implementable and affordable for most households and therefore socially inclusive, as opposed to solutions that, due to their elevated costs, are only affordable for higher-income households.

Some pilot projects are here illustrated which were carried out at COCIS and exemplify its applied research, whereby new products were conceptualised, prototyped, tested and employed in full-scale buildings, in order to achieve higher environmental sustainability, enhanced building performance and structural safety.

As far as environmental sustainability is concerned, several aspects have been considered in the research presented: reduction of energy use for space heating, decrease in the global warming potential in terms of carbon dioxide equivalents emitted into the air, feasibility studies towards a wider use of locally sourced materials (for instance, timber from Scottish forests), recycling of waste materials from the manufacture of other products (for example, waste textiles from Scottish wool mills) and implementation of new building processes through

Scottish facilities (for instance, the monitoring and study of the environmental impact of the timber-kilning process in the Scottish Highlands). Where necessary and applicable, the environmental sustainability of the novel products under study has been considered through the application of life-cycle assessment techniques.

Finally, this chapter presents some of the findings of an investigation into the offsite sector in Scotland, which was commissioned by the Scottish Government and conducted by Edinburgh Napier University's ISC, in 2012. Numerous construction companies were interviewed by the investigators and asked to answer a standardised questionnaire. These companies operated in different areas of offsite delivery and offered steel- and mostly timber-based construction.

The legislative, natural and cultural context

Across the UK, the construction industry is characterised by several regional differences, including the level of uptake of offsite production.

As regards low-rise housing, Scotland has, since the 1970s, gradually developed offsite solutions (based on timber framing), which now account for about three-quarters of new dwellings (UKCES, 2013; Timbertrends, 2013). The remaining houses adopt more traditional techniques, such as load-bearing masonry, generally in the form of cavity walls with internal blockwork and external brickwork or block and render. In England, the proportion of timber frame to masonry is approximately reversed, with timber frame being adopted for about one fifth of new houses (Timbertrends, 2013). Finally, in Wales and Northern Ireland, the level of adoption of timber frame has increased since the 2008 recession, reaching a market share of approximately 27 per cent and 22 per cent respectively in 2012 (Timbertrends, 2013).

However, in all regions, most timber buildings are still clad in masonry, with an external leaf of rendered blockwork, or, more rarely, of exposed brickwork. Timber cladding is, indeed, not very widespread (especially in mass construction). This preference about cladding materials reveals the trends of the property market: timber buildings are easily sold if they exhibit what potential buyers perceive as a 'robust' and 'safe' masonry wall. Timber cladding is more often used in one-off projects, where designers tend to experiment more with materials and question the trends of conventional construction.

One of the reasons why the uptake of offsite construction has prevailed in Scotland might be that the local, rainy climate makes it more desirable to shift part of the production into a factory's protected environment and to erect buildings that become weather-tight sooner during the construction process.

The situation for the non-residential sector is very different. In this respect, the south-east of England shows the largest adoption of offsite methods, where steel is the predominant structural material, for such buildings as schools, hospitals, student accommodation and retail facilities (UKCES, 2013).

The regulatory framework

The residential field in the whole UK is characterised by a severe shortage of social housing: the number of dwellings available is not sufficient to meet the demand created by emerging demographic trends and their quality is often below acceptable standards. This problem is due to the inadequate housing policies of the past. As a result, numerous households are on a waiting list to obtain a dwelling from the government.

In this scenario, cost-effective, fast and sustainable construction has become a priority and public bodies are interested in the construction methods that can prove most suitable to address the housing problem.

The Scottish Government has set a target to subsidise 30,000 new affordable homes through the 2013–18 period. Of these, 80 per cent will be new build and the remaining 20 per cent rehabilitation of the existing stock (Scottish Government, 2013).

In the UK's devolved administrations, regional policies define the strategies to meet the requirements of the Climate Change Act 2008, which applies to the whole country (Committee on Climate Change, 2015). This Act, in turn, is strongly influenced by the Kyoto Protocol, to which the UK adhered in 1995.

The Scottish Government (2011) has set a target to achieve a 42 per cent reduction in carbon emissions by 2020 compared to 1990, through the Climate Change (Scotland) Act 2009 (Committee on Climate Change, 2015). Since a quarter of the carbon emissions in the UK are attributable to energy consumption, for space heating and, to a lesser extent, for water heating, these targets have severe repercussions for the built environment. In Scotland, the improvement of dwellings' energy performance will be delivered through the Home Energy Efficiency Programmes, which started with pilot projects to improve houses in fuel-poor areas, by making space heating more economical (Scottish Government, 2013). This policy deals with both thermal retrofitting of the existing stock and enhancing the performance of new build.

The urge to construct large numbers of dwellings and the need to meet the increasingly stringent energy performance requirements has led stakeholders to seek to identify the construction techniques that are most adequate to meet these goals. Since the early 2000s, the UK and the Scottish governments have, on different occasions, taken the initiative to promote modern methods of construction (MMC), including offsite techniques that adopt this ethos.

The raw material: local timber resources

In the UK, conifers represent the vast majority of current silvicultural practice when compared to broadleaves. In 2013, for instance, broadleaves only counted for 5 per cent of total removals from woodland (Forestry Commission, 2014). Coniferous forests are concentrated in Scotland and, to a lesser extent, Wales.

The Scottish climate is, in comparison with other countries with extensive silvicultural activity, a warmer region. The relatively warm weather leads to faster growth of the trees and this, in turn, causes their annual rings to be wider. The width of the rings is directly correlated to the mechanical properties of the material and to its adequacy for structural applications. In softwoods, fast growth and wide rings cause the woody material to have low density and to be more difficult to work by hand and by machine (Davies, 2011). For these reasons, the average quality of Scottish conifers for structural purposes is generally lower than that of conifers grown in Scandinavia or Canada, at a much slower rate (Ross, 2011).

Currently, home-grown timber in Scotland is not mainstream for constructional or structural applications. It is generally employed for products of lower value (e.g. pallets, fences, packaging). The UK-wide statistics follow a very similar trend: in 2013, for instance, 34 per cent of sawn softwood produced by larger sawmills was used for fencing, 32 per cent for packaging and pallets, 29 per cent for the construction sector and 5 per cent for the other markets (Forestry Commission, 2014).

The UK, in 2012, was the third largest net importer (i.e. imports less exports) of forest products. Three-quarters of the sawn softwoods that are imported into the UK are from European countries (mostly from Sweden, Latvia and Finland). On the other hand, about half of sawn hardwoods are imported from Europe (Italy, France and Estonia) and the remaining half from other continents (especially the US and Cameroon) (Forestry Commission, 2014).

The use of locally sourced timber plays a significant role in improving sustainability. If Scottish wood is produced through good silvicultural practices and is properly utilised in the construction sector, the import of raw material from other countries can be drastically reduced, with several advantages. In the first instance, the economic and environmental cost due to transportation drops. Secondly, supplying the material becomes safer and independent of the fluctuations of the international markets and their prices. Home-grown wood can then also be used for offsite MMC.

In addition, from an economic and social point of view, home-grown wood resources contribute to the Scottish economy, thanks to the jobs in forest management, wood processing, wood haulage and associated industries (Forestry Commission Scotland, 2014).

From a structural point of view, where the natural characteristics of the woody material are not satisfactory, engineered wood-based materials can now be utilised, which overcome the natural limitations of raw timber.

It becomes therefore very important to assess the feasibility of using locally sourced timber for structural components. This entails experimental programmes where structural members and assemblies (beams, wall panels, roof panels, etc.) made from this material are fabricated and tested according to the relevant standards. Edinburgh Napier University's COCIS has carried out extensive research in this area and some examples are offered in the present chapter. The Centre's investigation has included the re-engineering techniques that allow the use of lower-grade materials, thus making the most of locally available resources. Although manufacturers of these products are in hard competition with their international counterparts, there is scope for import substitution and for adding value to local timber.

The cultural environment for growth and innovation

In Scotland, innovation in the construction sector is often driven by large companies that can invest a quota of their turnover in research and development to create new products, experiment with new materials or develop more efficient methods of erection. However, innovation can also occur through other channels, and, in particular, through collaborative projects involving different stakeholders of the construction industry that, for their size and profit, can be defined as small enterprises: designers (architects and structural engineers), manufacturers, construction companies and housing associations. These co-operate with universities and the committees of innovation showcases. Such collaborative projects allow individual participants to benefit from the expertise and the human and material resources that they do not have in-house.

Innovation showcases are other effective opportunities for introducing novel building solutions and to physically realise and exhibit innovative construction projects. In the 2010–12 period alone, three major innovation showcases were organised in Scotland: in 2010, Scotland's Housing Expo in Inverness and in 2012, both the Housing Innovation Showcase in Dunfermline (Fife) and the BRE Innovation Park in Ravenscraig. In the case study section of this chapter, some of the collaborative work carried out by Edinburgh Napier University is illustrated, which has also been exhibited in one innovation showcase.

In October 2014, an ambitious initiative in the construction sector was launched: the inauguration of the Construction Scotland Innovation Centre (CSIC). This is one of eight new Innovation Centres established to deliver transformational change across various key industry sectors in the region. It is funded by the Scottish Funding Council (SFC), Scottish Enterprise (SE), Highlands and Islands Enterprise (HIE) and 11 Scottish University partners (Scottish Enterprise, 2014). It promotes transformation and innovation in the construction industry by establishing partnerships between industry academia and the public sector and encouraging business models that can create new opportunities.

CSIC also assists companies in developing new products or solutions – offering support from inception to commercialisation – developing manufacturing systems or assembly methods and penetrating the local and international markets. The administration of CSIC is carried out by Edinburgh Napier University.

The status quo of Scottish timber offsite construction

The majority of Scottish companies delivering offsite construction are based either in the Edinburgh or in the Glasgow industrial areas, otherwise regarded as the 'Central Belt'. Some of them are located in northern Scotland, near Inverness (Smith *et al.*, 2013).

Available building products and processes

In order to describe the Scottish offer of offsite-manufactured components, a categorisation has been proposed (see Table 14.1).

The first distinction made is between two-dimensional and three-dimensional elements. The former can be panels to construct walls, floors or roofs. The latter refer to offsite, volumetric construction, where whole pods are fabricated in the factory and then delivered to the construction site: the majority of the

Figure 14.1
**Geographical
distribution of
the companies
interviewed**

Table 14.1
**Categorisation
of the level
of offsite
construction
offered for
2-D elements
(walls, floors
and roofs) and
3-D elements**

CATEGORIES			
2-D elements			**3-D elements**
Walls	**Floors**	**Roofs**	
0 Uninsulated open panels: with first skin on only one side (e.g. OSB on one side of timber panels).	Uninsulated floor panels with decking only on one side and exposed joists/beams.	Uninsulated open panels: with first skin on only one side (e.g. OSB on one side of timber panels).	Uninsulated modules whose surfaces have first skin on only one side.
1 Insulated open or closed panels without finished linings (e.g. SIPs).	Insulated floor panels without finishes.	Insulated open or closed panels without finished linings.	Insulated modules without finished linings.
2 Insulated closed panels finished on one side (either internally or externally).	Insulated floor panels finished on one side (either upper or lower side).	Insulated closed panels finished on one side (either internally or externally).	Insulated modules with finished lining on one side (either internally or externally).
3 Insulated closed panels fully finished internally and externally, with integration of services (i.e. with electrical and mechanical services, windows and doors).	Insulated floor panels fully finished on the upper and lower sides, with integration of services (i.e. with electrical and mechanical services).	Insulated closed panels fully finished internally and externally, with integration of services (i.e. with electrical and mechanical services, windows).	Modules fully finished on all sides, with integrated services (i.e. with electrical and mechanical services, windows and doors).

SUBCATEGORIES

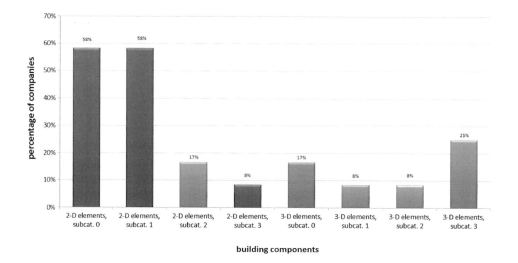

Figure 14.2
Percentage
of Scottish
companies
producing
various
components
when they
started
operating in the
offsite sector

offsite offering in Scotland is 2-D panelised systems; however, there are also some volumetric offerings.

Four subcategories have been consistently identified for both 2-D and 3-D elements, depending on their level of completeness when they leave the factory and are transported to the construction site. Subcategory 0 groups panels or pods without insulation and with their first skin on one side only, e.g. an orientated-strand board (OSB) sheet. Subcategory 1 designates insulated panels or pods without finished linings. Subcategory 2 indicates elements that are finished on either the inside or the outside. Finally, subcategory 3 group panels and pods that are fully finished both internally and externally.

In Scotland, panellised components generally leave the factory gate only with the structural members and with sheathing on one side. With the uptake of offsite solutions, however, the insulating material is now added in the factory more often than it used to be (i.e. subcategories 1–3).

The most widespread technique for low-rise dwellings in Scotland is platform timber frame (in its two variations of open and closed panels) and, secondarily, structural insulated panels (SIPs).

A large number of the firms interviewed by Edinburgh Napier University (Smith *et al.*, 2013) started producing offsite components in the 2001–10 decade. Most of them only used to produce 2-D elements, belonging to subcategories 0 and 1, when they started operating in the offsite sector of the market. One quarter of the companies interviewed produced volumetric modules of subcategory 3 at the time. These findings are very similar to those obtained by Pan *et al.* (2005), when they interviewed the 100 largest builders in the UK.

Economic value

The total annual turnover (for the offsite sector) of the companies contacted by Smith *et al.* (2013) was estimated at slightly more than £100 million in 2012. Due to the economic recession, the annual turnover in 2008 went down by 25 per cent. The companies expected to grow in the next few years and to reach an overall value of about £130 million. Despite the recession, the firms involved in the survey only lost about 150 full-time employees out of the 1,591 they had in 2008, before the economic crisis.

The number of employees who were directly employed on site (in 2012) was very small compared to the staff employed off site: 7 per cent versus 93 per cent.

More than 50 per cent of the companies were involved in the manufacturing of products other than offsite building components. In particular, 42 per cent of the companies produced doors.

With respect to the categorisation introduced above, the breakdown of the products manufactured off site was analysed: 42 per cent of the turnover coming from offsite manufacturing was related to the production of open, 2-D elements (i.e. subcategory 0).

Productivity, drivers and barriers

According to Edinburgh Napier University's 2012 survey, most of the companies seeking to improve their production process attach low importance to reducing batch size, but consider other measures more important, such as avoiding unnecessary transport of material, changing plant layout to reduce movement and minimising the production of defective parts and waste.

The companies indicated that, for both the design and fabrication stages, they needed external support to reduce waste, for management to improve transparency and for procurement to reduce complexity.

Figure 14.3
**Areas in which
Scottish
companies
can offer
customised
offsite products**

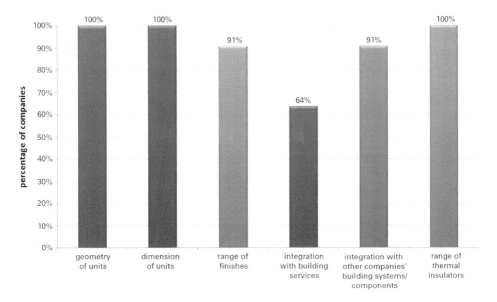

The companies were asked if they were able to produce customised products for their clients and to what extent they manufactured these. On average, 60 per cent of the offsite products offered were bespoke, whereas 40 per cent were standardised. All of the companies could offer customised products in terms of geometry of the units, their dimension and choice of thermal insulation. Most of them (91 per cent) could customise the finishes of their products.

The potential level of customisation is extremely important for offsite solutions, as it differentiates today's pre-assembled construction from prefabrication of the past, which was characterised by little flexibility and generally led to poor architectural results.

For Scottish companies, on average, the most important advantage of offsite construction resides in the higher level of quality assurance and predictability. Improved levels of profitability are also considered another important advantage over traditional construction. The issue of sustainability is not considered a major advantage. According to a survey conducted by Homes for Scotland (2015), instead, sustainability is deemed one of the largest advantages of offsite construction among home-builders.

The barriers to offsite construction that building companies perceive to be predominant in Scotland are the fluctuations in the economy and in the construction market, the shortage of capital to be invested, the scarcity of government incentives and the lack of demand within the market (Smith et al., 2013). The answers obtained are similar to those received by Pan et al. (2005) within their survey: the top 100 UK builders indicated the higher capital cost of offsite solutions as one of the most relevant barriers to their adoption. Homes for Scotland (2015) identified this economic factor as one of the major obstacles to the uptake of offsite construction: 70 per cent of its survey respondents (organisations among the home-building industry) declared that the cost of offsite construction is prohibitive of its use. This 2015 study also identified two other barriers: the lack of information from the supply chain and the fact that construction companies prefer to rely on the knowledge they already possess rather than engaging in innovation.

The most significant drivers for offsite construction are considered by the Scottish respondents to be government policies, the housing shortage and environmental credentials, whereas less importance is attached to advanced systems and production methods. Pan et al. (2005) found slightly different results during their survey: the companies that they interviewed indicated the opportunity to address the skill shortage as one of the most important drivers for offsite construction (on this topic, see also pp. 234–6).

Current and future market sectors

The 2012 Edinburgh Napier University survey found that constructors (as opposed to manufacturers of components) operate mostly in housing (both public and private), which is the main sector for many companies. Hotels and tourist accommodation are also an important share of their workload.

In 2012, the market value for offsite manufacturing was mostly coming from Scotland. After that, a smaller percentage came from the other regions of the UK.

The importance of the international market was negligible and exports tended to be low and mostly with France. The regions predominantly targeted for potential growth (supplying and licensing) were Scotland itself, England and Wales. These Scottish-based findings on the international market for offsite construction are very similar to the UK-wide data from UKCES (2013) and the Department for Business, Innovation and Skills (2013) (see the next section).

Supply chain and business models

In the British construction industry, small and medium-sized enterprises (SMEs) are very numerous and account for about 95 per cent of the sector (UKCES, 2013). Large-scale projects are generally realised by large construction companies, acting as main contractors, and several small businesses, as subcontractors. However, it is the large companies that carry out the majority of the work by value (Breuer, 2012). SMEs are generally not involved in offsite activities (see the next section).

From a financial and economic point of view, the UK offsite sector is facing several challenges related to the fact that there is insufficient understanding of the business models and *ad-hoc* arrangements that are needed for offsite solutions.

First, higher demand needs to be created among the public. Second, for the existing demand, accessibility to investments, mortgages and insurance is limited, since financial institutions still do not view offsite methods as much established, tested and therefore reliable as onsite methods (UKCES, 2013). When compared to other industries, construction companies are less inclined to apply for bank finance and, if they do apply, their application is more likely to be turned down (Lomax *et al.*, 2015). On top of this, construction enterprises are also less aware of the support available than their counterparts in other economic segments.

Furthermore, employers in construction (especially SMEs) tend to experience late payment from their customers more often than other employers. This is a major obstacle, worsened by the 'cascading' nature of the trade credit provision in the industry: if contractors in the lower tiers have difficulties obtaining trade credit, this will have repercussions throughout the supply chain (Ive and Murray, 2013).

Another limitation of the supply chain in the UK's construction sector is its high fragmentation and the low level of internal collaboration, which makes not only domestic production, but also access to foreign markets, more difficult (Department for Business, Innovation and Skills, 2013). Fragmentation extends to the customer base, in that most of the construction workload comes from one-off commissions; this prevents customers from successfully approaching the industry in a strategic manner (this would only be possible for repeat customers with greater experience and better knowledge of the supply chain). In addition, the UK supply chain for offsite systems in particular is still considered relatively immature (Miles and Whitehouse, 2013).

Offsite construction has a different cash-flow model when compared to more conventional building methods; offsite methods incur higher immediate costs, which require different financial arrangements. However, this drawback is partially mitigated by the overall construction process being faster.

Dedicated training in offsite manufacturing should create more opportunities for export sales (UKCES, 2013), following, for instance, the example set by Germany and Austria with timber-based offsite solutions (i.e. roof, floor or wall panels made of cross-laminated timber), especially for social housing and industrial construction, where time-efficient solutions are highly valued. The need to improve exports is, however, a common issue across the whole construction industry; the Department for Business, Innovation and Skills (2013) has noted that 'construction businesses may not be fully aware of potential benefits of exporting and lack the necessary knowledge of management skills to successfully exploit overseas markets'.

Goulding and Arif (2012) have pointed out that more manufacturing facilities are needed, both to produce the amount of offsite components required and to create economic competition and business growth.

Knowledge base, occupational skills and training provision

The UK Government (2013) has recorded a substantial fall in the completion of apprenticeships in construction over the 2010–13 period, while completions in other sectors have continued to grow. However, the number of personnel holding university qualifications is increasing even in the construction industry.

The Scottish Government (2013) has launched some programmes to support MMC, including offsite construction, through skills development, to meet the current and future needs of employers. These programmes include the provision of training events to Scottish SMEs and the delivery of apprenticeship starts (see also the final section).

In the years before the financial crisis commenced in 2008, it was often suggested that the skills shortage (especially of joiners, electricians and bricklayers) would act as a driver for the adoption of offsite construction (BRE, 2002). Cole and Stevens (2006, cited in UKCES, 2013), for instance, reported that some contractors started utilising panelised wall systems to compensate for the shortage of skilled bricklayers. However, according to Barker (2006), the shortage of skills was the most significant obstacle to the adoption of offsite methods.

Since the beginning of the recession, the situation has changed and there is much debate among industrialists and academics about the implications that widening offsite construction can have on skills demand (UKCES, 2013). According to one school of thought, offsite methods are able to reduce the overall skills demand made by the building process, thanks to increased efficiency and automation. The other school, instead, argues that the skills demand is displaced rather than solved, on the grounds that the adoption of offsite construction requires fewer workers on site but, at the same time, poses a problem of a lack of skills and trained operatives in the factory, for the manufacturing activities (Buildoffsite, 2012). In other words, although offsite construction has the potential to alleviate the general skills shortage, its own skills challenges need to be addressed in the first instance, with the creation of modern apprenticeships and better-defined skills pathways.

Some experts also believe that, while some trades (carpenters, electricians, plasterers, etc.) will be needed less for onsite activities with the shift to offsite solutions for new build (where they will be replaced by less skilled labour), they will still be needed in the industry for the maintenance of existing buildings (UKCES, 2013). Therefore, the de-skilling effect of the spread of offsite construction would only be partial.

It has also been pointed out that widening offsite construction entails more demands in the knowledge base, as is always the case when, within an industry, there is a shift towards a method of working that relies more extensively on technology (UKCES, 2013). In the case of offsite fabrication, the issues relating to the knowledge base are about the importance of accuracy and tolerances and awareness of other job roles.

All of the personnel involved in a building project, indeed, need to have an awareness and understanding of the various phases of the project itself and especially of the requirements of the subsequent stages of the process. Designers need to be trained and to become familiar with the manufacturing and assembly process – with its complexities and constraints – in order to produce final designs that are compatible with it (Goulding and Arif, 2013). In a similar way, the staff involved in the manufacturing phase need to know the site assembly process in terms of logistic issues such as transportation and handling of what has been fabricated in the factory.

Certain skills for conventional works on site will remain unvaried: for instance, those related to the preparation of the site, including drainage and foundations.

As regards gender diversification among operatives, offsite construction tends to attract more women than traditional construction, because it offers better working conditions, such as shifts and a safer, cleaner environment.

The skills that are envisaged to be needed more over the next decades by higher-level occupations are both 'softer skills' (e.g. team working and problem solving) and core skills such as project management, marketing, quality control and computing (e.g. BIM, CAD and automated tools) (UKCES, 2013). This is due to the fact that, with the expansion of offsite techniques, sites increasingly become areas of assembly and require different professionals to collaborate more extensively towards an efficient integration of manufacturing and construction. In particular, the project management skills for these types of integrated solutions are about coordinating the supply chain, taking care of the timing and sequencing of offsite and onsite activities and managing innovative ways of working, such as the 'just-in-time' approach to the manufacturing process. This approach avoids holding surplus stock of building components and thus allows improved efficiency, savings and waste reduction.

The survey conducted by UKCES (2013) suggests that one of the main barriers to skills integration lies in the fact that small construction firms within the 'wet trades' (i.e. traditional builders) are often reluctant to widen their knowledge base and to adopt offsite methods. The latter, indeed, seem to be attracting large companies only.

Among higher-level professions, architects will need to develop the capacity to coordinate more collaborative projects and to integrate products for a manufacturing process into their designs. Architects are also often resistant to the adoption of offsite solutions, as these require them to commit to a final product at an earlier stage in the design process than onsite solutions do (i.e. early 'design freeze time'). The latter, instead, offer a greater level of flexibility throughout the design process.

In addition, there are more general issues that affect all industries. Demographic trends clearly show an ageing population. As a consequence, important skills can be lost due to retirement and attracting younger labour to construction is proving problematic (UKCES, 2013). The difficulties in the recruitment of new staff are immediately followed by those experienced in their retention. Since offsite methods require more trades to work in factories, it is expected that more young people could be attracted to jobs in the construction industry, as they would not have to work in the more challenging onsite environment.

The adoption of offsite methods can reduce accidents since they generally require less work at height and fewer tradespeople to be on site at the same time, with consequent lower risk (UKCES, 2012).

As far as the skill gaps are concerned, the Scottish firms interviewed by Edinburgh Napier University in 2012 considered that a certified bespoke training package would be the most suitable qualification needed to address the gaps relating to production assemblers and erectors.

Edinburgh Napier University's research into the skills and training for offsite construction has been subsequently taken forward through a project funded by the UK Commission for Employment and Skills (UKCES) and the associated creation of an Offsite Hub within CSIC, as described in detail in the final section.

Case study: Future Affordable – home-grown resources for sustainable housing

Project overview

The case study presented in this section is an example of the research work on offsite construction carried out by Edinburgh Napier University and its partners over the last years.

Future Affordable was a collaborative project in the residential sector. It led to the construction of three terraced houses at the Housing Innovation Showcase in Fife in 2012. The houses employed two innovative systems: a pre-assembled service pod (e.CORE), devised by David Blaikie Architects, and a new type of closed panel (K2), conceived by Kraft Architecture.

The e.CORE module revolves around the development of a solid-wood technique, nail-laminated timber, to meet the requirements of the Scottish housing market and to create the relevant supply chain in this region.

The other building solution, the K2 wall system, is about the optimisation of an existing construction method: closed-panel timber frame, with its complex structural and thermal implications.

Each phase of the project was conducted at a different scale: from the assessment of the novel components in isolation to the assessment of their performance within the whole building, so as to ensure that overall efficiency and system compatibility was met. This multi-phase and systematic approach to the creation and validation of innovative building solutions was fundamental to guarantee the robustness of the research outputs generated.

This case study exemplifies the offsite projects that are undertaken in Scotland and whose success rests on the creation of synergy between various players within society and the construction industry, including small-sized businesses and professional practices. Such partnerships allow their members to achieve results that they could not have obtained by working individually.

Future Affordable also illustrates an approach to innovation – in terms of products and processes – that encompasses several environmental issues: reduction of energy loss through the building fabric, utilisation of local resources and import substitution, exploitation of lower-grade construction materials and recycling.

From an economic point of view, the project also shows how development in offsite construction can be driven sustainably, in terms of utilisation of the existing, easily available assets (experimental laboratories, manufacturing facilities, technical equipment, etc.).

Another important element of the case study is its social dimension, with the involvement of charitable organisations that are strongly connected with Scotland's local communities and support their welfare in key areas, such as employment, training and housing.

The house type to be constructed and its layout was determined by Kingdom Housing Association. The two-storey terraced houses have a kitchen and living room on the ground floor and two spacious bedrooms on the first floor. There is a bathroom on each floor, which is fabricated with nail-laminated timber panels. This pre-assembled service pod is the evolution of a bathroom module designed and constructed in a previous experimental project: Lios Gorm House at the Scotland's Housing Expo 2010. In this dwelling, a service pod was installed that had been prefabricated off site.

The aims of the Future Affordable project were:

- to use home-grown, lower-grade timber;
- to use recycled materials where possible;
- to design a high-performing building envelope that would reduce heat loss and allow for energy savings for space heating;
- to devise innovative construction techniques;
- to achieve sustainability in the economic, social and environmental spheres.

Within Future Affordable, COCIS contributed to the realisation of the project at several levels: it facilitated the integration of the supply chain, carried out structural tests on the nail-laminated solid-timber components and timber-frame panels and conducted analytical work to guarantee system compatibility.

Figure 14.4
The three houses built at the Housing Innovation Showcase 2012 in Fife within the Future Affordable project

Figure 14.5
Ground-floor and first-floor plans of one Future Affordable home (Courtesy of David Blaikie Architects)

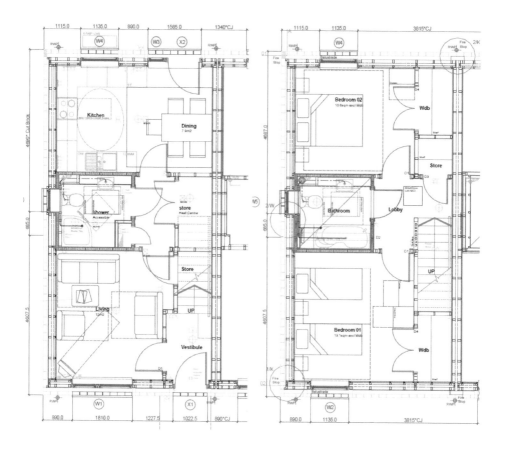

Construction aspects

The e.CORE service module

TECHNOLOGICAL BACKGROUND

Solid timber is generally fabricated from softwood planks which can be connected by different means: these are, most commonly, nails, dowels or glue.

Nail-laminated timber (NLT) consists of posts of sawn timber laid side by side, continuously nailed together to create solid structural elements (around 600mm wide). With this versatile laminating technique, panelised systems can be realised for walls, roofs, floors, decks and elevator and stair shafts (reThink Wood, 2015).

NLT is currently becoming more popular, but it is not a completely new system. It is, indeed, similar to a construction method adopted in North America in the early twentieth century (Canadian Wood Council, 2014), especially for agricultural or industrial purposes, such as the erection of warehouses.

Either aluminium or steel nails can be used to connect the lamellas. However, this material specification has repercussions for the sequence of the manufacturing process; if aluminium nails are utilised, the timber panels can be cut to shape even after the nailing has been performed, without damaging the machinery. If steel nails are used, instead, the panels are generally cut to their final size before the nailing is carried out.

In NLT, plywood or OSB sheathing can be added to the lamellas, so as to improve the structural performance of the system. If the sheathing is added across adjacent NLT panels, continuous joints will be minimised and, as a consequence, diaphragm action improved. In order to enhance the response in case of fire, the thickness of the panels can include a sacrificial charring layer; this will allow the system to achieve the desired fire resistance for a set period of time (Canadian Wood Council, 2014).

NLT, like other solid-timber panelised systems such as Brettstapel, can utilise low-grade timber that would otherwise be unsuitable for use in construction, to form load-bearing solid-timber wall, floor and roof panels. Brettstapel, also known as dowel-laminated timber, utilises timber dowels rather than nails. The dowels have a lower moisture content than the planks that are used, and over time the dowels expand to reach moisture equilibrium, thus 'locking' the lamellas together and creating a structural load-bearing system. Once the planks have been connected together, indeed, the influence of defects in each individual plank (such as knots) is strongly reduced. In addition, human selection ensures that knots and defects found in posts are never placed next to one another (Henderson et al., 2012).

The building products created using these techniques are normally manufactured out of untreated timber. They can be finished to a wide variety of specifications, which take into account individual aesthetic, structural, financial and acoustic considerations. The inside of wall panels, or the intrados of roof/floor panels, can achieve sufficient visual quality to be left exposed and create a warm ambience inside a building.

These construction methods are widely used throughout central Europe today, especially in Austria and Germany, and are now spreading in Switzerland and Norway as well (Henderson *et al.*, 2012). The market for NLT is expanding, as designers consider it a viable alternative to cross-laminated timber (CLT, a glued solid-timber panel system) for low- and medium-rise construction, where lower structural capacity is required.

In addition, NLT can be preferred to CLT from an environmental point of view, since it does not require any synthetic structural glue, with benefits in terms of healthier indoor air and reduced carbon emissions from the manufacturing process.

MATERIALS AND COMPONENTS

The ground-floor unit of the e.CORE has a bathroom with accessible sanitaryware and a small service control compartment with electrical distribution board, a smart meter, the control gears for the central heating, the whole-house mechanical ventilation with heat recovery and the micro-renewables devices. The first-floor unit of the e.CORE has a larger bathroom.

It was decided to use timber for the structure of the service pod, so that its integration into the remainder of the building would be eased. Therefore, the more widespread option of a steel-structured pod was avoided. It was decided to use massive timber as opposed to timber frame, in order to reduce the thickness of the wall panels. Within the massive-timber category, three possibilities were considered: cross lamination, nail lamination and dowel lamination. CLT was excluded because it requires high capital investment for the necessary technical equipment. Dowel-laminated timber was an attractive option, in that it is an all-timber technique, but, in comparison with NLT, it requires operatives with higher skills (to fix the dowels) and additional machinery and its manufacturing process is more time-consuming. For these reasons, the project team decided to employ NLT, which also allowed using lower-grade materials for a structural application with added value.

To simplify the supply chain, standard-dimension planks were employed. The material was Scottish Sitka spruce, of a relatively low structural grade. Since steel nails were used (as opposed to aluminium ones), the planks had to be cut to length for the openings before they were nailed together (see the previous section).

Nail lamination was used for both the floor and the wall panels. After the fabrication of the individual panels, these were assembled into the three-dimensional lower and upper units, transported to site and craned into position (Sanna *et al.*, 2012). After the installation on site, the finishing layers were added to the e.CORE modules.

All of the offsite operations were easily conducted by low-skilled trainee workers from a charitable social enterprise, Living Solutions.

The e.CORE pod adds stability to the whole building by acting as a semi-rigid core tied to the external shear wall; this makes it possible to have wide openings in the front and rear walls of the terraced houses.

In addition, using massive-timber panels allows adding several nails to connect the OSB layer with its support. If timber frame is used, instead, the support for the OSB (provided by the studs) is discontinuous and not as much nailing is possible.

For the reasons mentioned above, by employing this solid-timber technique, the load-bearing structure was optimised in comparison with the more traditional and widespread timber-frame system.

ground-floor unit

1. Soil vent pipe
2. Whole-house mechanical ventilation with heat recovery
3. Locating and fixing battons
4. Electrical distribution board
5. Smart meter
6. HMVR control, CH timber and control gear
7. Renewables technology control
8. Integrated heating installation
9. WC, wash hand basin and 900x900 shower in compliance with Housing for Varying Needs
10. Service distribution duct

Figure 14.6
Cut-away view of the ground-floor unit of the e.CORE service pod (Courtesy of David Blaikie Architects)

Figure 14.7
Cut-away view of the first-floor unit of the e.CORE service pod (Courtesy of David Blaikie Architects)

first-floor unit

1. Soil vent pipe
2. Whole-house mechanical ventilation with heat recovery system
3. Service distribution duct
4. Whole-house ventilation duct work
5. Bathroom fittings in compliance with Housing for Varying Needs
6. Integrated heating installation

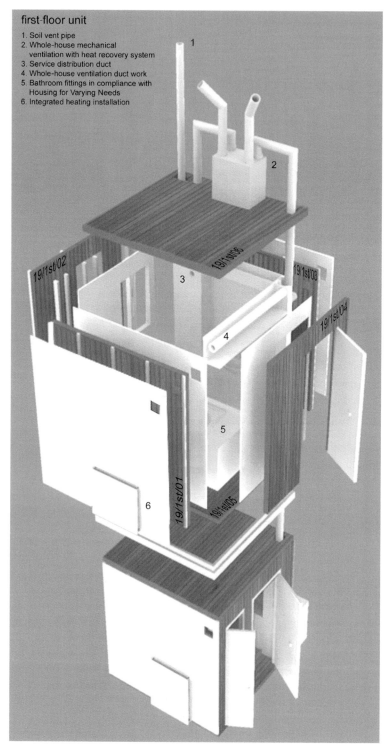

Figure 14.8
**Fabrication of
one panel of the
e.CORE service
pod: the timber
planks are
being stacked
together and
then nailed with
a pneumatic
gun**

Figure 14.9
**The panels are
ready to be
assembled into
pods (Courtesy
of David Blaikie
Architects)**

Figure 14.10
Construction of the timber floor, after the installation of the bottom units of the e.CORE service pod (Courtesy of David Blaikie Architects)

Figure 14.11
Completion of the first floor of the houses: the upper units of the e.CORE service pod are being craned into position (Courtesy of David Blaikie Architects)

ASSOCIATED RESEARCH

Before the construction of the e.CORE modules, Edinburgh Napier University carried out a series of structural tests on panels of NLT with the same specifications, to assess various properties, such as racking and bending performance. These

Figure 14 .12
Various types of structural tests were carried out on the NLT panels, in order to assess their performance when used for the walls and floors of the e.CORE service pod

experiments allowed an understanding of the structural response of the panels when used either as wall or floor components to be determined.

After the tests, the racking behaviour of the NLT panels was compared with that of standard timber-frame panels; the stiffness is very similar, whereas the strength is higher for NLT (Sanna *et al.*, 2012).

The bending tests (for floors) demonstrated that the stacked-plank panels have very good bending stiffness; it is therefore possible to reduce the thickness of the sheathing layer.

The K2 closed-panel system

TECHNOLOGICAL BACKGROUND

The K2 wall panel system was designed by Kraft Architecture, an architectural practice based in Glasgow and led by architect Bruce Newlands, with the collaboration of Edinburgh Napier University's COCIS. K2 is a closed-panel timber-frame system that minimises cold bridging through the structural studs, which are, thermally speaking, the weakest points within typical wall panels, due to the thermal transmittance of the wood being higher than that of the insulant. While generally each stud is just one piece of timber that occupies the whole gap between opposite sheathing layers, here each stud consists of two parallel elements (one on the internal and one on the external side of the wall). This dual configuration of the studs allows for a layer of insulant to be interposed between the two parallel timber components; in this way, the thermal transmittance in the cross-section through the studs is noticeably improved by providing a thermal break.

MATERIALS AND COMPONENTS

The K2 wall panels, as they were originally conceived, were fabricated from locally sourced timber. Such a choice required carrying out a programme of structural tests to demonstrate the feasibility of using this locally sourced material for this advanced stud-wall configuration. This programme of work was undertaken via the Wood Project Innovation Gateway, an initiative supported by the European Regional Development Fund. Its aim was to prove the feasibility of the K2 home-grown panel based on laboratory tests and design codes. In particular, the experiments focused on the racking performance of the walls – that is, the structural response to horizontal forces applied to the walls (such as wind loads). These tests also allowed an assessment of the importance of factors such as the presence of openings, wall length and the material chosen for sheathing (orientated strand boards, or, as alternatives, wood-fibre boards or plasterboard).

ASSOCIATED RESEARCH

The wall panels for the tests were manufactured using 45 × 95 mm outer stud and 45 × 45 mm inner stud. The racking performance of the K2 panels was assessed in accordance with the relevant British and European Standard codes of practice. This involved utilising a United Kingdom Accreditation Service (UKAS) test rig to appraise the wall panels, applying the horizontal loads to them, and then observing and measuring the structural response as prescribed by the standards. The results achieved showed that the K2 system is valid for racking design where the critical aspect lies in the robustness of the base fixing rather than the quality of the timber used for the wall frame.

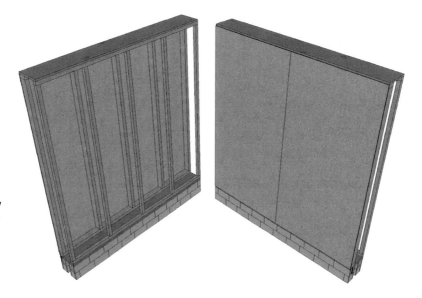

Figure 14.13
Schematic view of the K2 panel, with its dual-stud system (the insulating material is omitted for clarity)

Figure 14.14 **Offsite fabrication of a K2 wall panel**

Figure 14.15 **Installation of the K2 panels on site (Courtesy of David Blaikie Architects)**

Figure 14.16
The three
terraced
houses
approaching
completion

Looking ahead: promoting the growth of the offsite sector

There are currently regional hubs of offsite expertise in the UK, and Scotland has been recognised for its specialism in timber offsite systems, with a particular focus on housing. Since building off site represents a change in the construction culture aiming at continuous improvement and increased productivity, this change and innovation process needs to be underpinned with research programmes and adequate delivery of training.

The UKCES funded a collaborative project between industry (CCG(OSM) and Stewart Milne Timber Systems) and academia (Edinburgh Napier and Heriot-Watt Universities) in 2015. Within the remit of this project was the creation of an Offsite Hub, which is currently being taken forward by CSIC (see p. 228).

The establishment of the Hub stems from the intention to fully exploit the potential of the offsite sector in Scotland, in terms of the specialist knowledge, expertise, technical know-how, infrastructure and resources that reside in the region's private companies and higher-education institutions.

As seen in the section on the regulatory framework (pp. 225–6), the central government's policies are promoting offsite solutions to meet its ambitious environmental targets and to satisfy the high demand for housing. There is therefore an opportunity for Scotland to maintain the momentum and promote a wider adoption of offsite construction.

Projects such as the Hub have a strategic role, since a major barrier to innovation lies in the fact that currently 'collaboration between industry, academia and research organisations is patchy' and this 'limits effective knowledge transfer' (HM Government, 2013).

The Hub will act as a centre of expertise and will define skills needs and promote collaboration between professions in the design–construction process with a view to maintaining high standards in the industry. The Hub will produce interactive learning material to share in the construction sector, in order to upskill the workforce and provide training on the management and delivery of offsite solutions.

The Hub will operate through three different levels of membership: 'Core', 'Advanced' and 'Community'. Core membership groups together partners from Scottish advanced-manufacturing companies that provide offsite MMC solutions such as enhanced closed panels or volumetric units. Advanced will bring together the supply chain (up and down) and Community will interact with the wider community such as the government agencies, not-for-profits, trade organisations and the public at large.

The Hub aims at creating a robust framework for collaboration, allowing its partners to operate collectively and yet maintain their individualisms and unique selling points. This entails a new model for operation, which places innovation-sharing and collaboration at the heart of its primary activity. The Hub, therefore, will be a consortium run by, and for the benefit of, its members. Edinburgh Napier University's COCIS will, in the first phase, liaise with the Core partners and review their product portfolio to identify, by means of a questionnaire, their specific needs. These findings will subsequently inform the Hub's strategy plan.

While the Hub will initially consist of pre-identified lead industry partners, at a later stage it will evolve to encapsulate other players, particularly as they enter the market or enhance their product offering.

One of the goals of the Hub is to scale the current offsite provision from a regional level to a UK-wide level and to identify segments of the international market that could be targeted. This will be achieved by developing manufacturing processes, creating pathways for knowledge exchange, influencing standards and devising a strategic plan at an industry and company level.

At a national level, the priority is to secure a strong market share, with an emphasis on import substitution (see pp. 226–7) with the creation of further offsite products and services. Support from the public sector will be instrumental in integrating and facilitating a well-networked supply chain and in improving business development performance.

The development of the market for offsite construction and the laying of strong foundations domestically is envisaged to instil ambition into the Scottish companies involved and act as a springboard for further growth abroad. In particular, there is an intention to capitalise internationally on the provision capacity of low-carbon, affordable homes, taking advantage of the global interest towards this construction field in which Scotland has a particular strength.

Another strand of work to be undertaken will consist of the formalisation of an outreach plan, which will include the implementation of a branding, sales and promotional strategy for the Scottish offsite sector, including the facilitation of a net of suitable partnerships at home and abroad.

Joint projects on product or process innovation may, in some instances, require the partners to share intellectual property and resources, to increase impact levels.

Finally, the creation of the Hub is seen as a pilot for CSIC's future approach to other common sectors or themes and a way forward for collaboration in the sector between established major players and SMEs.

Acknowledgments

The authors would like to thank Edinburgh Napier University's partners, with whom they have collaborated in the project described in this chapter: David Blaikie Architects and Kraft Architecture.

The authors also acknowledge the collaboration of the Housing Innovation Showcase, Springfield Properties PLC, MAKAR Construction, CCG (Scotland) Ltd and Living Solutions Ltd.

The study on the e.CORE module and the K2 wall panel system presented were supported by both European Regional Development Funds (ERDF) and funding from the Engineering and Physical Sciences Research Council (EPSRC): *Structural Optimisation of Timber Offsite Modern Methods of Construction.*

Finally, the authors thank Prof. Sean Smith and Russell Macdonald of Edinburgh Napier University, who were coordinator and investigator respectively in the research project entitled *Strategic Review of the Offsite Construction Sector in Scotland,* funded by the Scottish Government in 2012.

References

Barker, K. (2006). *Modern Methods of Construction for the Provision of Housing: Technical Report Covering the Barriers to the Greater Use of Modern Methods of Construction and the Mechanism to Overcome Them.* Barker 33 Cross-Industry Group.
BRE. (2002). *Non-Traditional Housing in the UK.* London: Building Research Institute.
Breuer, Z. (2012). *Sector Skills Assessment: Construction, Building Services, Engineering and Planning. Evidence Report 65.* London: UK Commission for Employment and Skills.
Buildoffsite. (2012). *Buildoffsite Review 2012.* London: Buildoffsite.
Canadian Wood Council. (2014). *Mountain Equipment Co-op Head Office.* Ottawa: Canadian Wood Council.
Committee on Climate Change. (2015, March 1). The Climate Change Act and UK regulations. From *Committee on Climate Change*: www.theccc.org.uk/tackling-climate-change/the-legal-landscape/global-action-on-climate-change/ (accessed 8 December 2016).
Davies, I. (2011). Wood as a designer's material. In P. Wilson (Ed.), *Designing with Timber* (pp. 33–8). Belfast: Adleader.
Department for Business, Innovation and Skills. (2013). *UK Construction: An Economic Analysis of the Sector.* London: UK Construction.
Forestry Commission. (2014). *Forestry Statistics 2014.* Edinburgh: Forestry Commission.
Forestry Commission Scotland. (2014). The Scottish timber industry and Scotland's Timber resources. From *Forestry Commission Scotland*: http://scotland.forestry.gov.uk/supporting/forest-industries (accessed 8 December 2016).
Goulding, J. and Arif, M. (2013). *Offsite Production and Manufacturing.* Rotterdam: International Council for Research and Innovation in Building and Construction.

Henderson, J., Foster, S. and Bridgestock, M. (2012). What is Brettstapel? From *Brettstapel Construction*: www.brettstapel.org/Brettstapel/What_is_it.html (accessed 8 December 2016).

HM Government. (2013). *Construction 2025*. London: HM Government.

Homes for Scotland. (2015). *Research into Mainstreaming Offsite Modern Methods of Construction (MMC) in House Building*. Edinburgh: Homes for Scotland.

Housing Innovation Showcase 2012. (2012). Monitoring and evaluation programme. From *Housing Innovation Showcase 2012*: www.kingdomhousing.org.uk/development/home/housing-innovation-showcase (accessed 21 December 2016).

Ive, G. and Murray, A. (2013). *Trade Credit in the UK Construction Industry: An Empirical Analysis of Construction Contractor Financial Positioning and Performance*. London: Department for Business, Innovation and Skills.

Lomax, S., Wiseman, J. and Parry, E. (2015). *Small Business Survey: SME Employers*. London: Department for Business, Innovation and Skills.

Miles, J. and Whitehouse, N. (2013). *Offsite Housing Review*. London: Construction Industry Council.

Pan, W., Gibb, A. and Dainty, A. (2005). *Offsite Modern Methods of Construction in Housebuilding*. Loughborough: Loughborough University.

reThink Wood. (2015). Nail-laminated timber. From *reThink Wood*: www.rethinkwood.com/tall-wood-mass-timber/products/nail-laminated-timber-nlt (accessed 8 December 2016).

Ross, P. (2011). The practicalities of designing with hardwoods. In P. Wilson (Ed.), *Designing with Timber* (p. 39). Belfast: Adleader.

Sanna, F., Hairstans, R., Leitch, K., Crawford, D., Menendez, J. and Turnbull, D. (2012). Structural optimisation of timber offsite modern methods of construction. In P. Quenneville (Ed.), *World Conference on Timber Engineering 2012 (WCTE 2012)* (pp. 369–77). Auckland: WCTE 2012 Committee.

Scottish Enterprise. (2014). Construction Scotland Innovation Centre. From *Scottish Enterprise*: www.scottish-enterprise.com/microsites/construction-scotland/innovation-centre (accessed 10 November 2016).

Scottish Government. (2011). *Low Carbon Scotland: Meeting the Emission Reductions Targets 2010–2022*. Edinburgh: Scottish Government.

Scottish Government. (2013). *Scotland's Sustainable Housing Strategy*. Edinburgh: Scottish Government.

Smith, S., Hairstans, R., Macdonald, R. and Sanna, F. (2013). *Strategic Review of the Offsite Construction Sector in Scotland*. Edinburgh: Scottish Government.

Timbertrends. (2013). *Market Report 2012*. Alloa: Structural Timber Association.

UKCES. (2012). *Sector Skills Insight: Construction*. London: UK Commission for Employment and Skills.

UKCES. (2013). *Technology and Skills in the Construction Industry. Evidence Report 74*. London: UK Commission for Employment and Skills.

Glossary of terms

This glossary was developed through the amalgamation of the following: terms used in the contributing chapters of this book, *Prefab Architecture* by Ryan. E. Smith (Wiley, 2010), *Glossary of Terms* by Alistair Gibb and Martyn Pendlebury (Buildoffsite, 2006), *Glossary of Off-Site Construction Terms* by the National Institute of Building Sciences Off-Site Construction Council (National Institute of Building Sciences Off-Site Construction Council, 2015), *Building Offsite* by Robert Hairstans (Architecture Design Scotland, 2015).

Aesthetics – a set of principles concerned with the nature and appreciation of beauty, especially in art, media, and design. Offsite construction has historically been accused of producing poor aesthetic design. However, there are many examples that refute this accusation. Offsite construction is only as good as the demands placed upon it by designers. As such, it is a production method and not a particular style.

Assembled to order (**ATO**) – ATO products have set designs and established standards. Many of the attributes of made to stock (MTS) are found in ATO, but customization is introduced. The principles of assembly line production and mass customization are often associated with ATO, where customers request variation within a set system of form and relationship of elements to one another. Outside of the building industry, computer companies and shoe companies are now offering customizable options for their standardized products. Examples of ATO fabrication in architecture include International Standard Building Units (shipping containers), mobile homes, and multi-family/dormitory/hospitality housing modules that do not change from project to project. *See Made to stock (MTS)*.

Assembly – an act of fitting elements together on site. In manufacturing, assembly refers to the final point of assembly, and in construction, this is the job site. *See Element*.

Authorship – origin, especially with reference to an author, creator, producer, etc., of a work. Offsite construction fundamentally questions the traditional role of the architect as creative artistic author. Architects designing for prefabrication are required to balance the traditional design approach to function and beauty with designing a process for building production. *See Modularity*.

Automation – the use of largely automatic equipment in a system of manufacturing or other production process. In offsite construction, the use of automation within the factory environment is increasing, and this is predicted to continue into the foreseeable future.

Brick tiles or thin bricks – commonly used on offsite-manufactured external walls to replicate the appearance of conventional brickwork. Brick tiles are generally ¾-inch (20mm) in width, compared with the standard 2¼-inch (100mm) brick. The tiles are fixed with glue to the metal or plastic frame of an external wall panel.

Building Information Modeling (BIM) – the utilization of computer model data for the effective design, creation, and maintenance of building assets and results in a collaborative way of working that is visualized via three-dimensional computer models. BIM software is based on parametric modelling, which involves the use of dimensional parameters defined by the user or the available data set. BIM also relies upon information-rich data that is linked to 3D solids and X,Y,Z coordinates, differentiating it from pure geometry modelers. BIM is not one type of software, but realized in the interoperable interactions of many commercially available programs.

Building systems – (1) Any pre-engineered method of building that has a pre-defined scope and configuration limits. Building systems can be modular, panel, stick built, or hybrid. (2) Structures assembled from manufactured components designed to provide specific building configurations (e.g., large steel arch structures, large-span tension fabric structures, panelized buildings, and pre-engineered buildings). (3) Fundamental physical categories of buildings including structure, enclosure, services, and interior systems.

Closed construction – a building, component, assembly, subassembly, or system manufactured in such a manner that all portions cannot be readily inspected at the installation site without disassembly or destruction thereof. It also implies factory-added enhancements such as insulation, prewiring, preplumbing, and finishes in a panel or module.

Codes – *see Regulatory.*

Compliance assurance agency (aka **third-party inspection agency**) – an architect or professional engineer, or an organization, specially qualified by reason of facilities, personnel, experience, and demonstrated reliability, to investigate, test, and evaluate modular buildings; to list such buildings complying with standards; to provide adequate follow-up services at the point of manufacture to ensure that production units are in full compliance; and to provide a label as evidence of compliance on each manufactured section or module. *See Regulatory.*

Component – uniquely identifiable input, part, piece, assembly or subassembly, or system or subsystem, that (1) is required to complete or finish an activity, item, or job, (2) performs a distinctive and necessary function in the operation of a system, or (3) is intended to be included as a part of a finished, packaged, and labeled item. Components are usually removable in one piece and are considered indivisible for a particular purpose or use.

Composite – a generic term covering a wide variety of construction techniques, particularly where two different materials are used in combination to fulfill a specific function. For example, composite floor slabs can comprise in situ concrete with profiled metal decking, which acts as structural reinforcement. These slabs are supported on hot-rolled steel beams. The beams are also often composite themselves, using shear connectors (normally welded headed studs) to achieve structural interaction with the slab. This form of construction is extremely structurally efficient with good spanning capability. Composite construction can also use precast concrete slabs with a composite structural screed. Composite construction is also known as hybrid construction. *See Hybrid.*

Computer-aided design (CAD) – a generic term that describes a computer-aided design tool that acts as a platform for the end user to produce a customized conceptual design based on the standard components that reflect their requirements.

Computer-aided manufacture (CAM) – controlling the manufacturing machines utilizing computer software is regarded as computer-aided manufacture. If this is integrated with computer-aided design, it is regarded as CAD/CAM.

Computer numeric control (CNC) – a CNC machine is a production machine that is controlled electronically via computer technologies to reduce production time and increase quality and efficiency. A CNC machine therefore uses digital information to control the movements of tools and parts for processes such as cutting. *See Automation.*

Concurrent scheduling – the scheduling of two or more scopes of work constructed simultaneously (i.e., in volumetric construction, the foundation and modules are constructed at the same time, allowing for concurrent scheduling).

Configuration – interrelated functional and physical characteristics of a product defined in product configuration information.

Cross-laminated timber (CLT) – a prefabricated solid engineered wood panel. CLT is made from three or more layers of solid sawn lumber or structural composite lumber (SCL) that are orthogonally bonded together with structural adhesives to form a solid, straight, rectangular-shaped panel. Stacking the layers crosswise increases the structural and dimensional stability of the product. CLT is intended for use in load-bearing wall, floor, and roof applications in residential and non-residential buildings. The panels are available in a range of sizes and can be customized to fit specific needs.

Deconstruction – the process of taking a building or structure, or portion thereof, apart with the intent of repurposing, reusing, recycling, or salvaging as many of the materials, products, components, assemblies, or modules as possible. *See Design for disassembly* (DFD).

Design for disassembly (DFD) – a design modality that allows easier access to the materials, parts, and products of a building when it is renovated and/or disassembled. It provides flexibility in renovation, disassembly, or conversion. It is intended to maximize value and minimize environmental impact through reusing, recycling, repairing, and remanufacturing the whole or part of a building. (e.g., Cellophane House™ by KieranTimberlake).

Design for manufacture and assembly (**DFMA**) – designing for the modality of manufacturing and assembly. Sometimes this is separated into two modalities: design for manufacture and design for assembly. Design for manufacture (DFM) simplifies the factory parts in a subassembly and design for assembly (DFA) reduces the number of subassemblies in a final assembly at the job site. These strategies are intended to reduce the number of operations (and potential errors) in manufacture and assembly, increase quality, reduce waste, and reduce speed. *See Part, Subassembly, and Assembly.*

Design for reuse – a design modality that allows the reuse of a building or element again after its initial installation of its original location.

Digital fabrication – a process that joins design with production through the use of 3D modeling software or computer-aided design (CAD) and additive and subtractive manufacturing processes. 3D printing falls under additive, while machining falls under subtractive.

Dressed product – a generic term applying to factory-pre-assembled products (usually building services) that would otherwise be assembled on site. A typical example is a hand basin fitted with taps and waste.

Economies of scale – the cost advantage that arises with increased output of a product. Economies of scale arise because of the inverse relationship between the quantity produced and per-unit fixed costs; i.e., the greater the quantity of a good produced, the lower the per-unit fixed cost because these costs are spread out over a larger number of goods. *See Mass production.*

Economies of scope – an economic theory stating that the average total cost of production decreases as a result of increasing the number of different goods produced. *See Mass customization.*

Element – part of a building or structure that could be considered for standardization and offsite production such as foundations, structural frame, envelope, services, internals, and modular units. It sometimes refers to subassembly, component, panel, or module.

Embodied energy – the energy consumed by all of the processes associated with the production of a building, from the mining and processing of natural resources to manufacturing, transport, and product delivery. *See Life cycle analysis.*

Engineered to order (**ETO**) – this includes designed to order, adapted to order, and engineered to stock. These products represent the most complex and demanding products available. This is the largest category of building creativity and development in architecture. It also represents the greatest challenge for manufacturers and fabricators trying to determine how to deliver entirely customized products at competitive pricing. ETO products generally have the longest lead times and the highest price points. Examples of ETO products for building include precast unique sectional elements, facades, and other per-specification construction. This is different from traditional bespoke design and construction in that the factory is still leveraged for its just-in-time delivery, optimization of labor, and use of lean manufacturing techniques.

Envelope – the external walls and roof that form the perimeter or enclosure of a building. Walling may include lightweight curtain walling in aluminum, steel, or glass, or heavyweight components in concrete, brick, or stone. Roofing includes flat or pitched roofs. The extent of offsite manufacture will vary between systems for curtain walls:

- stick system – components all assembled on site;
- unitized – components pre-assembled off site into story-height, standardized-unit-width (1 m or 4') panels;
- panelized – components pre-assembled off site into story-height, bay-width panels.

Equifinality – the principle that in open systems a given end state can be reached by many potential means.

Erection – the action of erecting a structure, building, or other assembly on site. *See Setting.*

Factory-engineered concrete (FEC) – this applies to precast concrete elements of a structure. This includes wall and floor elements, ceilings, staircases, columns, and beams. FEC elements can also include building service containment routes, window and door openings, and possibly thermal insulation.

Field factory – a factory facility set up adjacent to the construction site, usually to reduce the need for long-distance transportation of pre-assembled products, and particularly relevant for large-scale, often civil engineering or infrastructure projects such as airports or bridges. *See Multi-trade prefabrication.*

Flat pack – prefabricated elements or systems that are transported to the site as 2D elements, rather than in 3D volumetric forms. These can be used where volumetric options are not feasible. Flat pack refers to the method of transport as well, panels stacked horizontally on a trailer bed providing a more efficient means of transport than vertically stacked panels and volumetric (transporting air). *See Panel.*

Flat slab – while not part of the offsite spectrum, flat slabs are included in the Concrete Centre's definition of modern methods of construction (MMC). Flat slabs are built quicker than traditional methods due to modern formwork being simplified and minimized and a combination of early striking and flying formwork systems. Use of prefabricated services can be maximized because of the uninterrupted service zones beneath the floor slab and there are no restrictions on the positioning of horizontal services and partitions.

Floor cassette – a factory-manufactured panel comprising a series of floor joists joined together with trimmers or end joists to form a load-bearing element of floor construction. Floor cassettes are generally used for residential or low- to medium-rise buildings and usually made of steel or timber. Floor cassettes can be open or closed, with more or less enhancements. *See Open construction and Closed construction.*

Fordism – a term widely used to describe (1) the system of mass production that was pioneered in the early twentieth century by the Ford Motor Company or (2) the typical postwar mode of economic growth and its associated political and social order in advanced capitalism. *See Mass production.*

Foundation (fast track) – precast concrete systems can be used to construct foundations rapidly. The elements are usually to a bespoke design and cast in a factory environment. These systems improve productivity, especially in adverse weather conditions, and reduce the amount of excavation required – particularly advantageous when dealing with contaminated ground. Offsite foundation techniques also include steel mini piles and helical screw piles.

Frame and framing systems – this typically refers to the post-and-beam super-structure of a building and may be constructed from heavy timber, engineered wood, hot-rolled steel, or precast sections. The term may also be used to describe the light supporting structure (dimensional lumber or light-gauge metal) for a pod or other volumetric unit. Below are definitions for a number of terms related to frames and framing:

- **Light-gauge steel frame (LGSF); light steel frame (LSF)** – structural panels assembled from cold-formed galvanized steel sections. They are normally factory assembled but field factories can be utilized. Light steel framing is typically used for the primary structure of housing and low- to medium-rise buildings of two to four stories. For taller buildings, it can be complemented by the use of hot-rolled members at key locations.

- **Open (cell) panel timber frame** – structural timber panels forming the inner load-bearing leaf of the cavity wall which are manufactured in factory conditions, brought to the site, and fixed together to form a rigid load-bearing superstructure. These consist of timber studs and beams, stiffened on one side with wood-based panels, such as oriented strand board, or plasterboard. The lining of the second side of the building component, and the application of insulation and other features, usually happens on site. Open cell timber frame is currently the conventional form of timber frame in the UK and is often just referred to as timber frame.

- **Advanced panel timber frame** – this generic term covers the latest developments in conventional panelized timber frame. Advanced panel timber frame is a factory-manufactured timber-stud constructed frame with sheathing in the conventional timber frame manner. Manufacturers are now beginning to fit rigid insulation between the studs and prefinished windows and external doors in the panel prior to dispatch to site.

- **Frame mounted** – a term used to describe units mounted on a frame or other supporting structure, used either for transportation, final support, or both.

- **Precast concrete frame** – a structural frame using precast concrete columns and beams, and/or panels. These may be factory finished internally or externally and may remain exposed in the final building. The extent of onsite work may vary significantly between projects. The members may be single columns or beams with factory-made connections, or the members may be pre-assembled into larger sections, either off site or at low level adjacent to the works. Precast concrete may be used together with in situ concrete or structural steel as part of a hybrid frame.

- **Steel-frame building systems** – building systems that use steel as the primary structural material. In domestic-scale construction, they are generally formed from light steel framing. For larger buildings, hot-rolled sections are used in pre-engineered buildings. Typically, such frames need site-applied finishes although fire protection may be applied in the factory and in certain circumstances exposed columns may appear in the final building. Elements may be single columns or beams with factory-made connections, or the members may be pre-assembled into larger sections, either off site or at low level adjacent to the works. Structural steel may be used together with in situ or precast concrete as part of a hybrid frame.
- **Mass-timber frame** – structural members that are used to build a super-structure frame. A mass-timber frame consists of solid heavy timber members, glue-laminated timber, laminated-veneer lumber, parallel-strand lumber, etc. Mass-timber frame systems are often in hybrid with mass-timber panels and concrete systems. This system is usually used for mid-rise and commercial construction projects.

Head wall assemblies – pre-engineered and fabricated hospital head walls that are prefitted with services and finished for rapid installation on site.

Hollow-core floor – prestressed, precast concrete slab units that derive their name from the voids or cores that run through the units. The cores can function as service ducts and significantly reduce the weight of the slabs, maximizing structural efficiency.

Hot-rolled steel – used in the form of structural beams, channels, angles, and plate, the elements are fabricated in the factory with attachments and connections for ease of site erection. Additionally, offsite processes provide facilities for services and add fire protection.

HUD Code – a manufactured home (formerly known as a mobile home) is built to the Manufactured Home Construction and Safety Standards (HUD Code) and displays a red certification label on the exterior of each transportable section. Manufactured homes are built in the controlled environment of a manufacturing plant and are transported in one or more sections on a permanent chassis.

Hybrid – a term describing something that is a combination of more than one discrete system or material. For example, it may be a combination of modular and panel systems where the high-value areas (kitchen and bathroom) are typically formed from pods and the rest of the structure is formed from some form of framing system. This term, in the context of offsite construction, should not be confused with its use to describe the combination of structural steel and concrete in the frame of a building or structure.

Industrialized building – any part of a building or other structure that is in whole or in substantial part fabricated in an offsite manufacturing facility for installation or assembly at the building site.

Industry, service/product – capital markets are defined as being either service or product oriented. Service industries require a high level of customer (client) input while product industries maximize the output per client input. Offsite construction suggests moving the design of buildings from a service enterprise to a product business.

Insulating concrete form (**ICF**) – ICFs are basically forms for poured concrete walls that stay in place as a permanent part of the wall assembly. The forms, made of foam insulation, are either preformed interlocking blocks or separate panels connected with plastic ties. The left-in-place forms not only provide a continuous insulation and sound barrier, but also a backing for drywall on the inside, and stucco, lap siding, or brick on the outside.

Integrated plumbing system (**IPS**) – wash hand basins, urinals, lavatories, etc. assembled off site into "units" with range of backboards, taps, etc. Most units are designed to be removed and replaced with new units once they have reached the end of their serviceable life.

Integrated product delivery – an integrated product is a multi-technological complex part of a building that can be configured and customized to a specific construction project. It is furthermore developed in a separate product development process based on the principles in integrated product development. In its actually produced and specifically customized state and when delivered to a customer, this building assembly becomes an integrated product delivery (IPD) that – at a kind of supra level – also can include marketing, shipment and servicing.

Integrated project delivery – a project delivery approach that integrates people, systems, business structures, and practices into a process that collaboratively harnesses the talents and insights of all participants to optimize project results, increase value to the owner, reduce waste, and maximize efficiency through all phases of design, fabrication, and construction.

Interchangeability – to be effective, a standard component should be able to be interchanged for another. This presupposes detailed understanding and rigorous control of the interfaces and connections between components. Above all, the interfaces should be predictable. This issue becomes even more important when these components are pre-assembled remotely from the project site.

Interface – place of connection, or interrelationship, of offsite elements.

International Standard Building Unit (**ISBU**) – the ISO intermodal shipping container revolutionized the international shipping trade nearly 50 years ago. Today, 90 percent of all non-bulk cargo is transported by ship, rail, or truck via the intermodal container. With the proliferation of shipping containers around the globe, an excess of containers in some regions is inevitable. This international trade deficit has made unused shipping containers potentially useable in architectural applications. Also known as ISBUs, or International Standard Building Units, shipping containers are ideal for prefabrication architecture because they can be loaded on to different modes of transport with their unique stackable chassis. Because the containers are constructed to transport a wide variety of goods safely in bulk quantity, their engineering makes them suitable for almost any built environment condition.

Jack leg building – a volumetric building with steel legs that can be adjusted to suit uneven ground. Lifted into place by crane, the units can be stacked on top of each other and are typically used for temporary site accommodation.

Just in time – a lean strategy that corresponds to zero time between program events that are sequential and rely upon each other. By implementing just-in-time principles, the overall critical path (the sequence of events that are most critical to program completion) can be reduced, resulting in an earlier completion/handover date.

Kit-of-parts – a set of standardized components used to produce buildings. The concept is adopted from Industrial Revolution-era mass production and repetition. An architectural example might be the Crystal Palace. Offsite construction vernacular uses "kitting" to refer to pre-assembled, prelabeled, and shipped packages (precut wood packages of studs, joists, and trusses) of components rather than enhanced panels or modules.

Label – identification applied on a product by the manufacturer that contains the name of the manufacturer, the function and performance characteristics of the product or material, and the name and identification of an approved agency and that indicates that the representative sample of the product or material has been tested and evaluated by an approved agency (International Building Code).

Lead time – the time between the initiation and completion of a production process. It refers to the duration between ordering and delivery that is often projected in order to predict an overall construction schedule and then tracked during the actual construction process.

Lean construction – a project-oriented framework where objects or systems are being gradually enhanced by tradesmen or craftsmen who are not necessarily organized in a flowing manner. It is therefore more difficult to implement lean theory and achieve the corresponding long-term goal of perfection given that lean theory is applied to a series of "temporary" production systems that are linked to other temporary and permanent production systems for materials, equipment, labor, etc.

Lean production – the aim for perfection through continuous improvement is the foundation of lean production, a concept that stemmed from the production system of the Japanese car manufacturer Toyota. The principles of lean are teamwork, robust communication, and efficient use of resources and elimination of waste.

Life cycle analysis (LCA) – the systematic approach of looking at a product's complete life cycle, from raw materials to final disposal of the product – in this case, a building. It offers a "cradle-to-grave" look at a product or process, considering environmental aspects and potential impacts.

Lifting points – *see Setting.*

Made to assemble or **make to assemble (MTA)** – a manufacturing production strategy where a company stocks the basic components of a product based on demand forecasts, but does not assemble them until the customer places an order. This allows for order customization. MTA production is basically a hybrid of two other major types of manufacturing production strategies: made to stock (MTS) and made to order (MTO).

Made to order or **make to order (MTO)** – MTO products are pulled forward through their supply process to arrive on site just in time. These products do not sit on shelves as in MTS or have a set geometry as in ATO but have determined the design and engineering options within a product. MTO products are not made until the last responsible moment but do require more lead time than ATO products due to their increased variability from product to product sold. Examples include custom windows, doors, and other elements that have a myriad of options and are custom-made for a project within a product line. Many modernist prefab systems and customizable modular housing solutions on the market today represent MTO.

Made to stock or **make to stock** (**MTS**) – MTS products are best handled through inventory replenishment strategies. In order to keep inventory replenished, manufacturers have used standardization, or reduced complexity and increased repetition. Supplier-managed inventory has proven successful for some companies and projects, where suppliers take on the job of determining requirements, and maintaining and distributing materials. Examples of MTS products include warehoused building goods such as lumber, wood, steel, and aluminum sections, ceiling tiles, and panel material such as gypsum board or plywood.

Manufacturing – the creation and assembly of components and finished products for sale. Three common types of manufacturing production are made to stock (MTS), made to order (MTO), and made to assemble (MTA). Manufacturing and fabrication are differentiated in other industries, with manufacturing meaning the process by which raw material is converted into a supply chain product that can then be applied to advanced fabrication processes. In offsite construction, the two terms are conflated with fabrication sometimes implying more intricate craft work.

Mass customization – the benefits of mass production are creatively combined with systems that offer greater choice for the individual customer, improved control of the total construction process, and flexibility of assembly options.

Mass production – the production of a large number of identical or very similar components in order to realize the benefits of economies of scale. This term was used commonly in prefabrication discussions in the 1950s and 1960s but is rarely used now with respect to offsite construction.

Mass-timber construction (**MTC**) or **solid-timber construction** (**STC**) – different types of mass-timber planar or frame elements used for walls, floors, roofs, partitions, and core elements of a building. Construction with solid-timber elements optimizes the inherent structural behavior of wood, creating a more homogeneous structural product. Mass timber includes glued and non-glued products. Glued MTC includes glue-laminated timber (GLT), structural composite lumber (SCL) including laminated-veneer lumber (LVL) and parallel-strand lumber (PSL), and laminated-strand lumber (LSL), and cross-laminated timber (CLT). Non-glued mass timber includes dowel-laminated timber (DLT), nail-laminated timber (NLT), cross-nail-laminated timber (CNLT), and interlocking cross-laminated timber (ICLT).

Mate-line stitching – the process of finishing the construction between two modules or panels at the building site. Typically, this is the final step in the setting process that includes structural connection and bridging exterior and interior finishes.

Materials flow analysis – *see Life cycle analysis.*

Mechanical rack – a prefabricated rack that holds data and power writing, plumbing, fire suppression, and other services. Pre-assembled racks are often fabricated near site utilizing multi-trade prefabrication in the construction of hospitals and other complex structures. *See Multi-trade prefabrication.*

Megastructure – a very large manmade object, though the limits of precisely how large this is vary considerably. Megastructures provide a support for prefabricated elements to be housed, but are rarely prefabricated themselves.

Metal building system – a complete integrated set of mutually dependent metal components and assemblies that form a building, including primary and secondary framing, covering, and accessories, and are manufactured to permit inspection on site prior to assembly on site.

Micro-housing – any residential structure, foundation built or on wheels, with full utilities (electric/water/sewer) and living facilities (kitchen/bedroom/bathroom/commode) designed for full-time occupancy that accommodates occupants at less than 300 square feet (28 square meters) per person. It usually refers to multi-level urban living developments that utilize an efficiency or a single-room apartment configuration.

Mobile housing – *see HUD Code.*

Mock-up – in manufacturing and design, a mock-up, or mockup, is a scale or full-size model of a design or device, used for teaching, demonstration, design evaluation, promotion, and other purposes. A mock-up is a prototype if it provides at least part of the functionality of a system and enables testing of a design.

Modern methods of construction (**MMC**) – the term adopted by the UK Housing Corporation and the DCLG (Department for Communities and Local Government) as a collective description for both offsite-based construction technologies and innovative onsite technologies that provide efficient product management of more products, to a higher standard, in less time. It can be classified in various ways and may involve key services such as plumbing; key items such as foundations; inner shell, walls, etc.; external walls; or any combination of these elements. It can also be classified by material (i.e., timber modern methods of construction).

Modular construction, **modular system**, **modular**, **volumetric system**, **modularization**, **module** – volumetric building modules where the units form the structure of the building as well as enclosing useable space. The terms are also sometimes used to describe room modules, which do not incorporate the macro-building superstructure. *(See Megastructure.)* They are particularly popular for hotels and student residences due to the economies of scale available from many similarly sized modules and the particular benefit of reduced site construction time. Modular also refers to non-structural service pods, and a level of modular coordination. *See Pod and Permanent modular construction.*

Modular building label/insignia/seal – *see Label.*

Modularity – credited to A.F. Bemis, an early twentieth-century industrialist, in his seminal book published in 1936, *The Evolving House.* Modularity combines the standardized dimensions and components of a larger more complex system that can be interchangeable. It was adopted in the 1970s to describe IBM System/360, a platform of flexible interchangeable hardware options. It is used in the manufacturing sector and now in offsite construction as well in the following definitions:

- **Component-sharing modularity** – the same fundamental components with variability of appearance within each discrete product (i.e., changing cladding options initially from project to project).
- **Component-swapping modularity** – the same configuration of appearance with ability to swap out component function (i.e., changing cladding options post-occupancy).
- **Cut-to-fit modularity** – varying length, width, or height of a product by cutting to size based on a fixed module (i.e., standardized cladding that can be increased or reduced in size in production).
- **Mix modularity** – variation is achieved by mixing products (i.e., cladding in which multiple layers can be added or taken away in fabrication).
- **Bus modularity** – a base structure that supports a number of attachments, sometimes called platform design (i.e., a base frame to which numerous cladding materials and systems can be attached).
- **Sectional modularity** – parts are all different but share a common connection method (i.e., cladding panels may vary, but the connection to the frame is always the same).

Modulor – an anthropometric scale of proportions devised by the Swiss-born French architect Le Corbusier. It was developed as a visual bridge between two incompatible scales, the imperial and the metric system. It is based on the height of a man with his arm raised.

Montage building – the term "montage" is commonly used in the arts (e.g., graphical montage). It means an assemblage of elements into a cohesive whole. In offsite construction, it is prefabricated building elements that are assembled at the construction site in a process of montage. The word is commonly used in Scandinavian prefabrication, where the focus is on the efficiency of the onsite assembly process, just as much as it is on the factory work. In the US, Bensonwood Homes refers to montage building as a three-part process of 3D virtual modeling, controlled factory production, and rapid assembly on site.

Multi-purpose riser – multiple-service vertical distribution module, constructed from primed or galvanized mild steel and incorporating appropriate building services that may or may not be insulated. These modules can be connected off site, but are often transported in 24'-6" (7.5m) lengths to avoid transportation problems. Modules can carry combined mechanical and electrical services but most manufacturers specialize in one or the other. The majority of the electrical risers are manufactured using a mesh or ladder system to allow easy distribution at floor levels in various directions. These systems are often custom in design and while the base structure may offer a level of standardization, the dimensions and carrying capacity will vary between projects.

Multi-trade prefabrication – a mode of construction in which the general contractor sets up a factory or warehouse near the job site in order to pre-fabricate specific elements using multiple trades subcontracted for the project. Elements often prefabricated in multi-trade include bathroom pods, mechanical racks, multi-purpose risers, and enclosure panels.

Near-site – a geographic location term that refers to the building site in relatively close proximity. *See Multi-trade prefabrication.*

Non-volumetric pre-assembly – items that are pre-assembled, but non-volumetric in that they do not enclose usable space. *See Panel.*

Offsite construction – planning, design, fabrication, and assembly of building elements at a location other than their final installed location to support the rapid and efficient construction of a permanent structure. Such building elements may be prefabricated at a different location and transported to the site or prefabricated on the construction site and then transported to their final location. Offsite construction is characterized by an integrated planning and supply chain optimization strategy. Offsite manufacturing (OSM), offsite production (OSP), and offsite fabrication (OSF) are used when referring primarily to the factory work proper.

On site – the location of a project where the building or structure resides permanently, or in some cases temporarily.

Open building – this relies on a theory that the user is central in the process of design and construction, and that design and construction are open, adaptable, changeable, and flexible. Open building was first defined by John Habraken and includes supports and infill. *See Megastructure.*

Open construction – a prefabricated element that is manufactured in such a manner that it is open for inspection when installed on site. Open construction usually does not include value-added enhancements such as insulation, prewiring, preplumbing, and finishes in a panel or module.

Operation Breakthrough – a program initiated by George Romney, US HUD Secretary, from 1969 to 1973 to encourage large national corporations to enter the housing industry by provision of a federally assembled mass market. It focused on R&D of new systems and technologies in housing. Designs and prototypes were fabricated but volume-scale operation was halted by Nixon's administration cutting housing funding. Much of the current offsite and prefabrication vernacular in housing used today was developed during this time.

Panel – a generic term describing a planar unit, typically manufactured off site, which may or may not have a structural as well as an enclosure function. Related terms are listed here:

- **Panel building system** – comprising walls, floors, and roofs in the form of flat pre-engineered panels that are erected on site to form the box-like elements of the structure that then require various levels of finishing. This term applies to all different material types.

- **Precast flat panel system** – floor and wall units are produced off site in a factory and erected on site, ideal for all repetitive cellular projects. Panels can include services, windows, doors, and finishes. Building envelope panels with factory-fitted insulation and decorative cladding can also be used as load-bearing elements.
- **Advanced panel timber frame** – this generic term covers the latest developments in conventional panelized timber frame. Advanced panel timber frame is a factory-manufactured timber-stud constructed frame with sheathing in the conventional timber-frame manner. Manufacturers are now beginning to fit rigid insulation between the studs and prefinished windows and external doors in the panel prior to dispatch to site.
- **Structural insulated panels** (**SIPs**) – this form of construction is used in panel building systems, typically in the residential sector. Structural sandwich panels typically comprise a core of foam with plywood, oriented strand board (OSB) or cement-bonded particleboard skins, bonded together to form a one-piece structural, load-bearing panel. The cores of SIPs can be made from a number of materials, including molded expanded polystyrene (EPS), extruded polystyrene (XPS), and urethane foam. When engineered and assembled properly, a structure built with these panels needs no frame or skeleton to support it.
- **Panelized** – for social housing, this is a Housing Corporation MMC category where flat panel units are produced in a factory and assembled on site to produce a 3D structure. The most common approach is to use open panels, or frames, which consist of a skeletal structure only, with services, insulation, external cladding, and internal finishing occurring on site. More complex panels (or closed panels) involve factory-based fabrication and may include lining materials and insulation. These may also include services, windows, doors, internal wall finishes, and external claddings. The term is also used more generally outside social housing.

Parametrics – see Building Information Modelling (BIM).

Part – a piece or segment of something such as an object, activity, or period of time, which, when combined with other pieces, makes up the whole. In offsite construction, a part refers to a material piece or component. In production theory, the goal is to limit the number of parts in a subassembly and the number of subassemblies in the final point of assembly. See Subassembly and Assembly.

Passive House – the term "Passive House" ("Passivhaus" in German) refers to a rigorous, voluntary standard for energy efficiency in a building, reducing its ecological footprint. It results in ultra-low-energy buildings that require little energy for space heating or cooling.

Permanent modular construction (**PMC**) – an innovative, sustainable construction delivery method utilizing offsite, lean manufacturing techniques to prefabricate single- or multi-story whole-building solutions in deliverable module sections. PMC buildings are manufactured in a safe, controlled setting and can be constructed of wood, steel, or concrete. PMC modules can be integrated into site-built projects or stand alone as a turn-key solution, and can be delivered with MEP, fixtures, and interior finishes in less time, with less waste, and with higher quality control compared to projects utilizing only traditional site construction. PMC is also referred to as volumetric construction, particularly in the UK.

Permitting – *see Regulatory.*

Pick point – *see Setting.*

Platform (as in **operative platform**) – the procedural operations in the factory to achieve the optimal efficiencies in production. It includes the components (technical systems), processes (design and manufacturing), relations (organizational structure), and know-how.

Pod – prefabricated volumetric pod, fully factory finished and internally complete with building services but probably not completed externally, except for roof-mounted plant rooms, which may include external cladding. Types of pods include bathrooms, shower rooms, office washrooms, plant rooms, and kitchens. Applications for pods include commercial offices, public buildings, hotels, airports, sport stadiums, hospitals, universities and schools. Pod framing or structure may be light steel frame (LSF) or rolled hollow-section (RHS) steel, timber frame, precast concrete or GRP (mainly for smaller pods). Floors are typically suspended timber or concrete, tiled or finished as appropriate. Ceilings and wall coverings are typically plasterboard, except for GRP/precast concrete where that is the pod build material, tiled or finished as appropriate. Occasionally, pods may be delivered as flat-pack assemblies.

Portable building and portable accommodation – *see Relocatable buildings.*

Pre-assembly – *see Prefabrication.*

Precast concrete – a construction product produced by casting concrete in a reusable mold "form" which is then cured in a controlled environment, transported to the construction site, and lifted into place. Precast includes structural and enclosure building elements.

Pre-engineered – standardization of product allows the development of pre-engineering, which is a term very loosely used in offsite manufacturing circles. Often, it means no more than the production of the drawings before the product is made by adapting or modifying drawings from a previous application of the system. The correct use of the term is where a product is fully engineered and can be described in a technical manual or catalogue; where it is fully detailed and programmed for manufacture; and where it is fully cost estimated and the price is available. For example, the manufacture of room modules begins with a 3D CAD (computer-aided design) model, which details each component and ascribes a unique part number. This detailed model provides the bill of materials for each module and is then converted into CAM (computer-aided manufacture) files. The CAM files contain all of the data for the module, broken down into the subassemblies of walls, floor cassettes, roof cassettes, etc. The CAM files also contain all of the machine codes that control the various stations on the automated assembly line. It is this linkage between the product and production equipment that provides the repeatable dimensional accuracy of a manufactured product when compared with other, more traditional methods of construction. The term is also used to distinguish between custom, prototype building (traditional), and factory manufacture, which by its very nature requires predesign and testing prior to being incorporated into the works on site.

Prefabrication – a general term for the manufacture of entire buildings or parts of buildings off site prior to their assembly on site. Prefabricated buildings include both portable buildings and the various types of permanent building systems. Offsite construction is now the more commonly used term for permanent buildings procured in this manner.

Productivity – a measure of the efficiency of a person, machine, factory, system, etc., in converting inputs into useful outputs.

Project delivery – a project delivery method is a system used by an agency or owner for organizing and financing design, construction, operations, and maintenance services for a structure or facility by entering into legal agreements with one or more entities or parties. *See Integrated project delivery.*

Proprietary system – the intellectual ownership of a technique, process, structure, etc. for the purpose of commercialization and licensing.

Prototype – the original or model on which something is based or formed. In offsite construction, this often refers to test fabrications in order to refine a product offering. *See Mock-up.*

Regulatory – to control or direct by a rule, principle, method, etc. For example, in the US, building and construction is regulated by government entities to ensure the health and safety of a building's occupants. The authority having jurisdiction (AHJ) is the regulatory agency responsible for establishing and upholding the standards by which buildings are constructed in their domain (i.e., cities, counties, municipalities). *See Compliance assurance agency.*

Relocatable building – a partially or completely assembled building that complies with applicable codes and state regulations, and is constructed in a building manufacturing facility using a modular construction process. Relocatable modular buildings are designed to be reused or repurposed multiple times and transported to different sites. They are semi-permanent and have a relatively short life span of 20–30 years. Many are rented out to users (i.e., construction site trailers and classroom pods).

Riser – *see Multi-purpose riser.*

Roof cassette – a factory-manufactured panel similar to a floor cassette. For pitched roofs in residential applications, they will usually be timber- or steel-based SIPs spanning from eaves to ridge. They are supplied insulated and require no additional truss-style support, making them ideal for providing additional roof space in housing applications. They are also used in commercial situations.

Service pod – *see Pod.*

Setting – the act of hoisting a component, element, module, etc. and placing it in its defined location in the building. When hoisting the element, either pick-points (i.e., hooks or eyelets preset in the element for specific lifting) or wrap-around belt straps (i.e., for modular construction) are used to distribute loads for onsite assembly. *See Assembly.*

Shipping container – *see International Standard Building Unit (ISBU).*

Single-trade prefabrication – the reduction of operations in prefabrication to as few trades as possible to reduce the complexity of multi-trade scheduling and overlaps. This may include multiple trades, but be contracted under a single agreement and warranty (e.g., a bathroom pod where plumbing, electrical, and finishes converge) *See Multi-trade prefabrication.*

Skids – transportable frames for carrying standardized pre-assembled products, mainly building services – for example, pump skids, boiler skids, etc.

Skilled – performing an act or job well and with competence. *See Workforce.*

Standardization – the extensive use of components, methods, or processes in which there is regularity, repetition, and a background of successful practice. This may include standard building products, standard forms of contract, standard details, design or specifications, and standard processes, procedures, or techniques. It can also mean generic, national, client, supplier, or project standardization.

Subassembly – a major building element that is manufactured off site but does not form the primary structure of the building. Foundation systems and cassette panels are typical examples.

Supply chain – the sequence of processes involved in the production and distribution of a commodity. Although the supply chain is important for construction generally, supply chain management becomes critical to the timely and effective delivery of offsite elements.

System – applied to offsite construction, a system is any pre-engineered method of building that has a predefined scope and configuration limits. Building systems can use a number of different materials, or combinations of materials, and can be modular, panel, stick built, or hybrid:

- **System building** – internationally, this term is typically used to describe open or closed building systems that invariably incorporate a significant amount of standardization, either in components and/or dimensions.
- **Open panel system** – the construction of the structural frame for the building using panels assembled in the factory. Open panel systems of various materials are delivered to the site purely as a structural element with services, insulation, and cladding and internal finishes installed in situ.
- **Closed panel system** – similar to an open panel system in that the structural elements of the building are delivered to the site in flat panels. However, closed panel systems typically include more factory-based fabrication such as lining materials and insulation and may even include cladding, internal finishes, services, doors, and windows.
- **Steel-frame building system** – stick-built systems that use steel as the primary structural material. It is common to hear the term "light steel frame (LSF)" which, in this context, refers to thin-gauge steel sections supplied as components or panelized elements.
- **Stick-built system** – this consists of pre-engineered frame elements in steel, pultrusions, and timber or precast concrete that are typically bolted

together on site to erect a skeletal structure that is then enclosed and finished on site.

Taylorism – a production efficiency methodology that breaks every action, job, or task into small and simple segments that can be easily analyzed and taught. Introduced in the early twentieth century, Taylorism aims to achieve maximum job fragmentation to minimize skill requirements and job learning time; separates execution of work from work planning; separates direct labor from indirect labor; replaces rule-of-thumb productivity estimates with precise measurements; introduces time and motion study for optimum job performance, cost accounting, and tool and work station design; and makes possible the payment-by-result method of wage determination.

Techne, **technics** – terms established by Lewis Mumford in *Technics and Civilization* (1934), which describe the relationship between technical systems and social systems within society and civilization.

Tilt-up panel – tilt-up, tilt-slab, or tilt-wall is a type of building and a construction technique using concrete. With the tilt-up method, concrete elements (i.e., walls, columns, structural supports, etc.) are formed horizontally on a concrete slab – usually the building floor, but sometimes a temporary concrete casting surface near the building footprint. After the concrete has cured, the elements are "tilted" to a vertical position with a crane and braced into position until the remaining building structural components (roofs, intermediate floors, and walls) are secured.

Tolerance – tolerances exist to accommodate the normal manufacturing and installation inaccuracies that occur in construction as a result of moisture, thermal differential movements, material discrepancies, and human error during assembly. During detailing, designers need to work with fabricators and contractors to determine the tolerances for a given project. Each detail has its own accommodation for forgiveness in dimension discrepancy, and if two materials are coming together, each must respect the other in its accuracies. Larger elements require greater tolerances, especially if they cannot be altered.

Transport – to take or carry (goods) from one place to another by means of a vehicle, aircraft, or ship. Offsite construction requires careful consideration to design and fabricate elements that fit within the transportation envelope.

Trussed rafters – typically used for pitched roofs on residential developments, trussed rafters, fabricated off site from small section members, have been in use for many years. Materials include timber and light-gauge steel.

Unitized curtain wall – *see Envelope.*

Variability – the ability to mass customize a product, where in contrast, a non-variable product does not change from its stock design. *See Mass customization.*

Virtual design and construction – *see Building Information Modelling (BIM).*

Void (interstitial) space – an intermediate space located between floors to allow for the mechanical, electrical, and/or plumbing systems of the building.

Volumetric – *see Modular.*

Wet service core – *see Pod.*

Workforce – the people engaged in or available for work, either in a country or area or in a particular company or industry. Offsite construction requires skills training of a unique set of labor operations different than that required by onsite construction. *See Skilled.*

Wrap-around belt strap – *see Setting.*

Index